No Single Story

Amplifying the Voices of Asian American and Native Hawaiian, Pacific Islander Early Educators

Debbie LeeKeenan, Iris Chin Ponte, Caryn Park, Sandy Baba

National Association for the Education of Young Children
Washington, DC

naeyc®

National Association for the Education of Young Children

1401 H Street NW, Suite 600
Washington, DC 20005
202-232-8777 • 800-424-2460
NAEYC.org

NAEYC Books

Senior Director, Publishing and Content Development
Susan Friedman

Director, Books
Dana Battaglia

Senior Editor
Holly Bohart

Editor II
Rossella Procopio

Senior Creative Design Manager
Charity Coleman

Creative Design Specialist
Makayla Johnson

Publishing Business Operations Manager
Francine Abdelmeguid

No Single Story: Amplifying the Voices of Asian American, Northern Hawaiian and Pacific Islander Early Educators.

Library of Congress Control Number: 2026940913
ISBN: 978-1-952331-52-7
Item: 1180

We stand on the shoulders of our ancestors and dedicate this book to future generations of AANHPI children, families, and educators.
- Debbie, Iris, Caryn, Sandy

To my grandchildren, Tabatha, Maya, and Reya, you are my inspiration and hope for the future.
- Debbie

To my children, William and Charlie, always be proud of who you are and where you came from.
- Iris

To Carter and Louis, may your generation's stories be our ancestor's dream come true.
- Caryn

To the warriors who walked this journey with me, to my family who held me steady, and to the hearts I hope to reach—thank you for giving these words a home.
- Sandy

Acknowledgements

We would like to thank each of our contributing authors for joining us on this book journey and being part of our community of Asian American and Native Hawaiian, Pacific Islander (AANHPI) writers. Sharing your story with your heart, mind, and soul, you have modeled vulnerability and collaboration, creating a space of trust, belonging, collaboration, and lifelong learning. For us, these memories of working together will be as precious to us as the final published product. We hope our conversations will continue in future collaborations.

To the children and community members who generously shared their perspectives and experiences of AANHPI identity, it is an honor for us to be able to include your voices in this book. We feel a deep gratitude towards Dana Battaglia and her National Association for the Education of Young Children (NAEYC) publishing team for their support, guidance, expertise, and trust in bringing this book to fruition. We could not have done it without you.

We thank Michelle Kang, the first Asian American CEO of NAEYC, for her leadership in this critical moment in our history and providing a space for this work to be nurtured. Alissa Mwenelupembe's book, *Stories of Resistance: Learning from Black Women in Early Care and Education*, provided inspiration for this book project. We would like to thank her for paving the way and for inviting us to bring our book to NAEYC. Thank you to the many attendees at our NAEYC conference presentations over the last two years for reminding us why it is so important to amplify the voices of Black, Indigenous, and People of Color (BIPOC) educators, create spaces for them to share their stories, and have the necessary conversations to build coalitions across our differences and work in solidarity together.

We thank our colleagues and collaborators, Filiz Efe McKinney of Brave Sprout Productions, John Nimmo, Louise Derman-Sparks, NAEYC's AANHPI Interest Forum, and Henry Frost Children's Program for their ongoing support and feedback.

Our appreciation goes out to the many friends, colleagues, mentors, students, and community members along our journey who have informed our understanding of our identities, pondered with us many big questions about what it means to move in the world as AANHPI, and helped us to imagine the future we want to create for our children.

Finally, thank you to our dear families for their love, patience, and unwavering support.

Contents

About the Authors and Contributors

Authors

Debbie LeeKeenan is codirector of Anti-Bias Leaders ECE (www.antibiasleadersece.com), a lecturer, and author. She has been in the field for over 50 years, a former preschool, special education, and public school teacher. She was director of the Eliot-Pearson Children's School at Tufts University and a member of the early childhood faculty at Tufts University, Lesley University, and the University of Massachusetts in Amherst. Debbie is the producer of two award-winning anti-bias education films. Her work has been published in numerous journals and books, including *Young Children*, *Exchange*, and *Theory Into Practice*, *From Survive to Thrive: A Director's Guide for Leading an Early Childhood Program*, and *Leading Anti-Bias Early Childhood Programs: A Guide to Change, for Change*. Debbie is Chinese American, the child of immigrant working-class parents, and part of a mixed-race family.

Iris Chin Ponte, PhD, is the director and a classroom teacher at the Henry Frost Children's Program in Belmont, Massachusetts. She is an adjunct faculty member in the Graduate School of Education at Lesley University. Recognized as an Exchange Emerging Leader in 2015, Iris is a former Fulbright Scholar with expertise in cross-cultural issues in education in the United States, United Kingdom, Taiwan, China, Japan, and Newfoundland. She has published in the topics of children and technology, behavior management, children's play, outdoor environmental design, early education program leadership and birth parent reunions, and heritage trips for adoptees in China. Dr. Ponte has received professional recognition from the Children's Defense Fund, CBS, and the American Educational Research Association. Dr. Ponte was also awarded the Thomas J. Watson IBM Fellowship.

Caryn Park, PhD is nearing her 30th year as an educator and has taught in early childhood and higher education classrooms, mentored and coached preservice and in-service educators, and served as an anti-bias/anti-racist education consultant and workshop facilitator for schools and parents. Her primary areas of interest include qualitative research and teacher inquiry, supporting immigrant and multilingual learners, teacher identity and pedagogical development, and social emotional learning for students and educators. Her interest in social emotional learning and mental health in particular has most recently led her to pursue licensure in marriage and family therapy. Caryn is an immigrant from South Korea, a mom of two young adult children, and lives in the beautiful Pacific Northwest.

Sandy Baba, PhD, is a researcher and practitioner specializing in early care education and family service development. Her work includes leadership of statewide and national quality rating and improvement initiatives and the development of a culturally responsive family engagement framework for low-income Asian American immigrant families, recognized by the US Department of Education. Dr. Baba's current work is artificial intelligence (AI) focused, examining the responsible application of artificial intelligence in human services and workforce development. Her scholarly and applied pursuits emphasize human-centered coaching and mentoring approaches that support social service practitioners, with particular attention to mental health support, reflective practice, and professional resilience. In 2008, she founded the NAEYC AANHPI Interest Forum with colleagues to advance the global early childhood workforce. She currently serves as vice president of the board of directors for the Council for Professional Recognition.

Contributors

Kamalei Brandon, MAT, is a Kanaka Maoli/Native Hawaiian mother and educator. She is the Pilimakua Department Director at Hummingbird Indigenous Family Services in Seattle, Washington, and an Indigenous teacher, doula, and home visitor.

Xyzlora Brownell, MSW, has over 25 years in early childhood education and is the Infant Early Childhood Mental Health Manager at the Department of Children, Youth, and Families in Washington State.

Jamie Cho, PhD, is a consultant, teacher educator, and scholar in the field of early childhood education. She is the Governing Board Vice President-Elect of the National Association for the Education of Young Children (NAEYC).

Sang eun Choi (Irene) holds an AA in Social and Behavioral Sciences and a BA in Fashion Design. She is a dedicated teacher/coteacher at Kai Ming Head Start in San Francisco, California, where she is passionate about creating secure and welcoming classrooms in which children can express themselves and learn happily.

Sarah Elahi, MA, is a curriculum writer and researcher. She researches, writes about and teaches culturally sustaining pedagogy, and is the founder of a consultancy, Raising Resistance.

Sarah Fong holds a BA in Early Childhood Education and currently serves as Site Manager at Kai Ming Headstart, San Francisco, California. Sarah's art background influences her approach to her work as an educator by combining creativity and care to inspire curiosity, resilience, and a love of learning in young minds.

Ninderjit Gill, MEd, is a full-time tenured faculty at North Seattle College and is an early childhood educator and advocate whose work centers on racial equity, language justice, and anti-bias education that has been shaped by her ethnic identity and lived experiences.

Shin Ae Han, PhD, is an Assistant Professor at the University of Hawaiʻi at Mānoa who studies early childhood education through the lenses of culture and place, with a focus on culturally grounded teaching across diverse contexts.

Sophia Han, PhD, is a Professor of Early Childhood Education and teacher education at the University of South Florida. She engages in collaborative and advocacy-focused scholarship to support teachers, children, and families.

Bick Hang holds an MA in Human Development with specialization in Bicultural Development in Young Children and Early Childhood Education. Bick serves as an early learning curriculum and instructional coach for a team of 35 teachers for the Seattle Preschool Program.

Clare Juico, BAS, is a family child care provider, project manager for EarlyEdU, and a co-organizer of Filipino Story Time—Seattle. Born in the Philippines and based in Seattle, Washington, she is a proud North Seattle College and Eastern Washington University alumna.

Jinhee Kim, PhD, is a Professor of Elementary and Early Childhood Education at Kennesaw State University. Her research focuses on immigrant children and poverty (homelessness) within the curriculum and teacher education.

Manju Kumari holds an MA in Economics from India and an AA in Child Development in the United States. Manju is Director of Akshara Learning Center in San Jose, California. Her work has involved supporting survivors of domestic violence through Maitri, a non-profit organization that provides safety and resources to victims.

Alethea Kuʻulei Serna, PhD, is a Professor in the School of Teacher Education at the University of Hawaiʻi at Mānoa. She is currently collaborating to help establish an early childhood education policy and leadership center in Hawaiʻi.

Lisa Luke Lee, BA, is a retired Program Officer, Quality Enhancement & Professional Development, at First 5 San Francisco Preschool for All.

Kira LeeKeenan, PhD, is an Associate Professor of Secondary Education at Cal State University at Fullerton, with an emphasis on English, language, and literacy education. Her areas of expertise are in anti-oppressive teaching and learning, humanizing writing pedagogy, and critical literacy.

Theresa F. Lock, PhD, is the Director at the Hawai'i Early Childhood Educator Excellence and Equity Project at the University of Hawai'i at Manoa. Her focus is on driving early childhood education workforce innovation, equity, and systems change through research, policy, and collaborative initiatives across Hawai'i and beyond.

Sim Loh, BA, is a Public Policy Specialist at First Up: Champions for Early Education, where she and her team drive systems and policy change by amplifying the lived experiences of educators and families—especially those too often unheard—ensuring legislators and policymakers shape decisions rooted in real stories, real needs, and lasting impact.

Sohyun Meacham, PhD, is Professor of Literacy Education and Associate Dean for Graduate Studies and Research in the College of Education at the University of Northern Iowa. Her scholarship explores dialogic pedagogy, suda, and culturally sustaining practices in teacher education and leadership.

Misa Okayama holds a BA in Child and Adolescent Development, with a concentration in the Young Child and Family, from San Francisco State University and is an Early Childhood Professional at Nihonmachi Little Friends.

Bandi Lim Park, MEd, is a Regional Manager at Kai Ming Head Start in San Francisco who values equity and respect in the classroom, regardless of ethnicity or language, and believes in inclusive classrooms where communities from many cultures learn together.

Josephine Pulido, BA, is an early childhood educator with a distinguished career progression that began in elementary school settings. Her career journey solidified her belief in the paramount importance of the foundational years.

Donna Elizabeth Kaleiokalani Reid-Hayes, MEd, EdD, is a recently retired kindergarten teacher from Punahou School. She continues to work within the early childhood community on professional development workshops and publications. She researches how the interweaving of Hawaiian culture-based education and Reggio Emilia-inspired pedagogy transformed her practice and her evolving sense of Indigeneity.

Rosemarie Rideout holds a BA in Early Childhood Development and Learning and is a dual citizen of the United States and Philippines. She is currently the Lead Teacher in a Pre-K for All classroom in a parochial school in Flint, Michigan.

Nicol Russell, EdD, is the Chief Academic Officer at Teacher Strategies in Phoenix, Arizona. Her greatest ambition in life is to leave a legacy of love in action. Her professional interests are grounded in the ethics of knowledge—how we know what we know, and how we use that knowledge responsibly in systems that affect people (children and adults).

Sala Sataraka, EMPA, is the Professional Learning Associate Director at School's Out Washington. She is a Samoan mother and educator with nearly 20 years in early learning, higher education, and expanded learning.

Charis-Ann F. Sole, MS, MEd, is a P-3 Program Specialist at Hawai'i P-20 on O'ahu island. She holds master's degrees in Child Development (Erikson Institute) and Early Childhood Education (University of Hawai'i). She is especially interested in the intersections between early childhood and mo'okū'auhau (family lineage/genealogy).

Jordan A. Taitingfong, MEd, is an educator passionate about inclusive early childhood and joyful, accessible learning. Her work focuses on disability and race, centering lived experience, addressing disparities, and uplifting identity and belonging.

Yuji Uchida holds a BA in Sociology from San Francisco State University and has been an educator at Nihonmachi Little Friends for the past 23 years, where he weaves the silent grace of budo (武道) into the laughter and wonder of early childhood education.

Edna Jean Vargas holds an MA in Psychology and uses a combined specialization in Psychology and Early Childhood Education to guide children's learning journeys and advocate for both families and educators. Her leadership is characterized by a strong emphasis on kindness and respect.

Su-Jeong Wee, PhD, is an Associate Professor of Child and Family Studies at California State University, Los Angeles. Her scholarship focuses on social justice and equity, children's literature, and teacher education.

Jackie Thu Hu'o'ng Wong, MSW, is a refugee-born AANHPI leader and is the first woman of color to lead First 5 California, driving equity, early childhood innovation, and transformative statewide systems change with purpose and integrity.

Jerry Yang, PhD, is the Executive Director of Kai Ming Head Start and ECE STEP in San Francisco, California, bringing experience as a teacher, assistant professor, and administrator. He advocates for humanity and cultural integration in early childhood education.

Yanling Zhao (Angel), BA, is a Preschool Lead Teacher at Kai Ming Head Start who prioritizes bilingual education, believing that helping children from multilingual families learn English while maintaining their home language contributes to their overall development across multiple domains.

Foreword

As the daughter of Korean immigrants who came to the United States 55 years ago, I have learned that identity is woven into everything we do. It shows up in the languages we carry, the family stories we tell, the cultural values we hold, the work we do, and the ways we have learned to navigate our communities.

Like many children of Asian immigrants, I am shaped by a home where adults were highly involved and where academics and extracurricular activities were treated as both opportunity and obligation. My parents gave me the gifts of learning to play classical piano music, loving to read books, and volunteering in our church. They also taught me to work hard at everything I do. Growing up, I still remember how quickly my parents would point to the television or show me a newspaper article whenever an Asian face appeared. One of the clearest memories is seeing Connie Chung on the *CBS Evening News*—one of the first Asian women to hold that seat—and feeling my family's pride, even before I fully understood why it mattered. As I got older, I understood more clearly both the privilege and responsibility of being an Asian woman in communities and workplaces. With visibility comes possibilities, and sometimes successes, but it can also bring stereotypes and assumptions about how we speak, lead, and carry ourselves.

The model minority stereotype, for example, has followed me into professional spaces, where I sometimes feel the need to overcorrect against the assumption that I will be deferential or quiet. That tension between humility and voice as well as between being visible and being understood still sits with me in my work and leadership today. In a meeting, at a podium, or in moments when decisions are being made, I have to choose not just *whether* to speak, but *how*—with clarity rather than perfection, in a way that takes up space without apology, and with input that stays anchored in purpose. Purpose, for me, is simple: using my voice and position in service of children, families, and those who do not yet have the opportunity to speak up for themselves.

The stories in this book resonate with me on personal and professional levels because they talk about that lived reality with honesty and possibility. The book has given the authors the freedom and opportunity to share their lived journeys as Asian American and Native Hawaiian, Pacific Islander (AANHPI) educators and to tell the truth about our paths, including how we navigate bias and belonging; carry family and community expectations; and find the courage to lead in ways that are rooted in care, culture, and responsibility.

In early childhood environments, we ask children and families to bring their whole selves. Yet many educators of different cultural backgrounds have been expected to leave parts of themselves at the door—masking accents, minimizing cultural knowledge, staying quiet in the face of bias, or being misread through stereotypes like the model minority. AANHPI educators and communities have long sustained early learning through intergenerational caregiving, community care, cultural continuity, and deep commitments to education as a pathway to collective well-being.

This book arrives at an important moment when the field is grappling with workforce challenges, the urgent need for inclusion and belonging, and a growing recognition that our professional knowledge must include lived experiences and community-rooted wisdom. It is a beautiful tapestry of personal narratives and professional reflections that illuminate what it can mean to be AANHPI in early childhood education. Each author tells their own story of how their identities have shaped their learning, teaching, leadership, and relationships. The personal stories describe both strengths and challenges and offer reflections on implications and recommendations for the field.

There is an incredible depth and breadth of AANHPI experiences. The contributors include Korean, Samoan, Native Hawaiian, Chinese, Filipino, Vietnamese, Pakistani American, and Southeast Asian Indian educators, among others. They are early childhood professionals who are teacher educators, coaches, professors, classroom teachers, home visitors, administrators, advocates, and working parents—people whose daily work bridges theory and practice and whose leadership is shaped by community responsibility and love. With their stories, they share reflections on disability, immigration, intergenerational tensions, home languages and bilingual education, and culturally grounded pedagogy.

For NAEYC, this book strengthens and extends core commitments to advancing a high-quality, equitable, and diverse early childhood profession. NAEYC has long affirmed that development and learning happen in the contexts of culture, relationships, and community, and that educators must cultivate reflective practice, respectful partnerships with families, and learning environments where every child belongs. The stories in this book help make those commitments concrete. They show what culturally responsive and sustaining practice can look like when it is lived, not only theorized.

NAEYC's work is also built on the belief that professional learning is most powerful when it supports inquiry, dialogue, and growth over time. The book's structure supports that kind of learning. Chapters can stand alone, yet collectively they show that we all share similar experiences, values, and dreams. Each section is introduced with themes and reflection questions. I'm excited about the discussions that this book will encourage in classrooms and trainings, as well as on airplanes and in rooms where we are elevating teacher preparations and the best possible child outcomes.

Storytelling is not simply a literary choice in this text—it is an equity practice. In early childhood settings, the stories that often dominate the narrative are based on whose knowledge is recognized, whose families are understood, and whose children feel at home. When AANHPI educators share their stories, they expand what the profession counts as expertise and what it means to lead. When colleagues read these stories with humility and care, they build the relational trust needed for stronger teams, more authentic family engagement, and learning environments that honor children's identities. In this way, the book contributes to a broader culture shift that NAEYC supports, moving from performative inclusion to deep belonging and shared power.

The focus on advocacy and leadership in the last part of the book is especially important for the profession right now. NAEYC's impact has always depended on educators who organize, advocate, and lead for compensation and working conditions that match the importance of the work, for policies that strengthen families, and for systems that respect the expertise of early childhood professionals. It can begin in classrooms and home visiting programs, in college courses and community spaces, in mentoring relationships, and in any scenario where the decision to speak is made even when silence would be easier.

I am incredibly humbled by the commitment and courage of the authors who are sharing their stories and shining a light on the contributions of AANHPI individuals in the field of early childhood education. While I am the first Asian professional to lead NAEYC, I am grateful that I stand on the foundation of all those who have championed our collective mission. I hope these stories will push our field, including NAEYC and all of us who carry its mission forward, to ensure that AANHPI educators are not only included but supported, protected, and able to thrive. May this book deepen our practice and strengthen our solidarity across communities and move us closer to early childhood systems where every child, family, and educator is seen and where our many stories are recognized as a source of wisdom and a call to collective action.

Michelle Kang
Chief Executive Officer
The National Association for the Education of Young Children

About This Book

This book is a gathering of stories and voices. Each chapter presents a different story and voice, yet, as our book title indicates, no single story can represent the entirety of our experiences, and each story gains resonance and power in concert with the others. As editors, we experienced the full power of the stories when viewing them as a collection and hope you may also have the opportunity to feel their full collective impact.

We believe this book will be useful as readings for book clubs, college courses, and professional development activities. For individual readers, we hope this book inspires and reminds you that you belong to a larger community of diverse educators, and that your story matters.

Parts of the Book

This book is organized into four parts. Each part begins with an introduction that provides context and reasoning for the stories chosen for each section. Additionally, quotes from additional members of the AANHPI community appear at the beginning of each part as a feature titled **So Many More Voices . . .** These quotes serve to emphasize that there is "No Single Story" and that the stories continue beyond the pages of this collection. While the audience is mainly early childhood education professionals, we expect the book will resonate with a wider audience. The additional quotes also add more breadth to the book as we hear from other AANHPI professionals, youth, and/or families and the intersectionality of our identities.

Part One: Where to Start is the introduction and framework for the book. We explore the complexities of what it means to be Asian American, Native Hawaiian, or Pacific Islander. The second, third, and fourth parts include the authors' personal stories grouped into three categories: Part Two: *Knowing Who You Are*, Part Three: *Connections to Our Practice*, and Part Four: *Advocacy and Leading for Change*. Each author's chapter highlights how their Asian American and Native Hawaiian, Pacific Islander identities have impacted their personal and professional lives, creating strengths and challenges, as well as implications and recommendations for the field. An introduction to each of the four parts includes common themes and reflection questions to guide your reading.

Part Two: Knowing Who You Are includes stories from Korean, Samoan, Chamorro, Native Hawaiian, Chinese, Filipino, and Vietnamese educators on how their identities impacted who they are. **Jordan A. Taitingfong**, Early Learning Specialist at the University of Washington, writes from the perspective of a Chamorro disabled woman on *Learning from Our Relations: Blood, Bone and Built*, sharing what she has learned from her families, ancestors, and built relationships, as well as what resistance and liberation can look like in early childhood education. **Caryn Park** discusses her unfolding identity journey in *Learning Myself through the Eyes of Others*. In their chapter, **Kira LeeKeenan and Debbie LeeKeenan**, teacher educators, daughter and mother, reflect how three generations of teachers in their own family were impacted by their Chinese American identities in *Searching for Who You are: Three Generations of Teachers*. **Donna Elizabeth Kaleiokalani Reid-Hayes** takes us on her Hawaiian journey in *Weaving a Lei of Kuleana, Empathy, and Commitment*. **Sala Sataraka** shares her experiences finding her identity as a Pacific Islander in *My Journey: Koko Samoa and Community*. **Jamie Cho** is a Chinese American college professor who chronicles her experiences through the metaphor of eyes in *Envisioning Just Futures Through my Phoenix Eyes*. **Alethea Ku'ulei Serna**, a Kanaka Native Hawaiian, shares her journey on becoming an ECE professor using Hawaiian flow lines to tell her story, *Ko'u 'Inoa, 'O Wau Kēia: My Name, This Is Who I am, The Shaping of My Kanaka 'Ōiwi Identity*. **Rosemarie Rideout** is an immigrant from the Philippines who shares her experiences growing up and stepping into the field in *The Land of Promise*. **Bick Hang**, a Vietnamese refugee and early childhood coach for teachers, shares lessons from her experience, *Access to Education: A Refugee Immigrant's Journeys*. **Lisa Luke Lee**, a Hawaiian-born American Chinese leader, examines the layered complexity of intergenerational expectations in *Being Asian in America: Connecting Stories Through Generation and Time*.

Part Three: Connections to Our Practice highlights stories about how the authors connect their identity to their practice. This section opens with **Jerry Yang** and six dedicated early childhood educators from KaiMing Head Start sharing their personal stories and connections in the classroom in *The Journey of Belonging: Resilience and Perseverance Among Asian Educators*. **Kamalei Brandon** helps us understand strategies to reclaim Indigenous Culture in *Indigenous Home Visiting: A Sustainable Approach to Culture and Language Reclamation for NH/PI Families Away from Our 'Āina*. **Charis-Ann F. Sole** explores how early learning settings and spaces might be reimagined, recreated, and organized to support Pacific Islander children in *Tūtū and Their Mo'opuna: Reimagining ECE Through Intergenerational Relationships, Culturally Grounded Pedagogy, and Power Sharing*. **Xyzlora Brownell** gives us insight to growing up biethnic in *Dual Language Learners in Early Childhood*. **Manju Kumari** shares her experience immigrating from India in *Grief, Growth, and a New Life in Education*. **Misa Okayama** and **Yuji Uchida** tell us about their experiences as Japanese educators in a bilingual school in California in their chapter, *Fitting In and Standing Out*. **Sarah Elahi,** a Pakistani American educator writes how the complexity of South Asian history impacts curriculum in *Beyond the Single Story: Writing Curriculum as a Freedom Practice*. **Clare Juico** writes about finding her roots in *Filipino Storytime: Reclaiming My Identity by Building Community*. **Sohyun Meacham, Jinhee Kim, Su-Jeong Wee, Sophia Han,** four Korean American professors, use *Suda*, "Korean chit-chat," as a conceptual tool in *Suda on Korean American Teacher Educators Lived Experiences*, providing a powerful example of culturally responsive research.

Part 4: Advocacy and Leading for Change includes stories of different paths to leadership. **Nicol Russell** is the daughter of a Kanaka 'Ōiwi wahine and an Alabama-born and raised Black man and Chief Academic Officer at Teaching Strategies sharing how being both insider and outsider led her to *Bringing My Whole Self to the Classroom: A Native Hawaiian Perspective on Identity in Early Childhood Education*. **Shin Ae Han** is a Korean immigrant professor who shares her journey in *Empowering Early Childhood Educators: My Journey as a Korean Migrant Teacher Educator in the Pacific* and uplifts the stories of 10 American Samoan early childhood teachers who are students in her college course at the University of Hawai'i. **Iris Chin Ponte**'s experiences in the classroom impact her advocacy for more AANHPI teachers in *Diversity Will Sustain the Education Profession: Reflections of a Biethnic Preschool Teacher*. **Sandy Baba**, a working parent, Asian American immigrant, leader, and advocate who grew up during Hong Kong's British colonial era, reveals her journey of cultural adaptation in *From Homeless Shelters to Congress: My Unexpected Journey in Early Childhood Advocacy*. **Ninderjit Gill**, a Southeast Asian Indian leader who identifies as both Asian American and Indo-Canadian, analyzes the critical relationship between power dynamics and language in *The Roller Coaster of Identity: Belonging, Loss, Reclamation*. **Sim Loh**, a Malaysian Chinese American immigrant, recounts the transformative impact of a teacher's belief in her potential while adapting to her new home, ultimately leading to her current role championing parent empowerment and policy reform in *A Journey to Be Seen and Heard*. **Jackie Thu Hu'o'ng Wong**, who fled Vietnam as a refugee, explores how the resilience forged during her childhood home displacement became the foundation of her leadership approach in *A Legacy Project: My Ancestors' Wildest Dreams*. **Theresa F. Lock**, a Hawaiian-born American Chinese leader, using the metaphor of a KOA tree, provides a reflective meditation on humility as a guiding principle throughout her career as a leader, administrator, and advocate in *Like the Koa Tree: Leading with Purpose and Resilience.*

References and Professional Development Resources

These resources can be found online at NAEYC.org/no-single-story

Guiding Questions

Below are general questions and prompts to guide your reading; the introductions to each part provide more specific reflection questions for the chapters contained within them:

- What do you connect to in each story personally and professionally?
- What new insights or different perspectives have you gained on the children, families, and adults you work with?
- What is the value of storytelling? How can you bring more storytelling into your organization?
- What ideas and action steps do you take away from the readings that can be applied to your classroom, program, organization?
- Whose stories are missing? How can we uplift more stories?
- How do the chapters you read speak to each other? What was the impact of these "conversations" for you as a reader?

PART 1

Where to Start

The chapters in Part 1 give context and provide a framework for the contributions in Parts 2 through 4. This is the place to start. In chapter 1, we, the book editors and authors, discuss our journey to bring together many diverse voices, highlighting the core ideas that provide the foundation for the book. In chapter 2, we engage with the Native Hawaiian and Pacific Islander authors in an open discussion about the complexity of the AANHPI identity from their positionality. All of the contributors were active partners on this journey. The work has proven to be more than writing and reflecting; it has created community and strength.

Reflection Questions

As you read the chapters in Part 1, we encourage you to reflect on the following questions:

- How do you incorporate anti-bias education in your work?
- How has your local and regional and world history impacted your life?
- What stories in your community are often overlooked or marginalized?
- What are the similarities and differences in the perspectives of the contributors' comments in chapter 2? What can you glean from this?

So Many More Voices . . .

As AANHPI, I come from rich heritages. We are born from love and resilience. As a queer disabled woman with other identities such as wife, daughter, and friend, I find joy in being visible together and embracing the plurality. Though intra-community disparities and intersectional discrimination continue, we prevail.

Urvasi Graham
Infant and Early Childhood Mental Health Consultant
Holding Hope

CHAPTER 1

Marginalized and Privileged, Labels and Identity

Our Book Journey

No Single Story: Amplifying the Voices of Asian American and Native Hawaiian, Pacific Islander Early Educators brings together a diverse group of AANHPI across the diaspora to share stories about how our intersecting identities and lived experiences have impacted and influenced our roles in early education and care.

The idea for our writing project was conceived in 2023, following the COVID-19 pandemic, with the backdrop of Black Lives Matter and Stop Asian Hate movements. It was inspired by the power of storytelling chronicled poignantly in two recent books: *Stories of Resistance: Learning from Black Women in Early Care and Education* (2023) by Alissa Mwenelupembe, a collection of 12 powerful essays written by Black women in early care and education sharing their personal and professional journeys, and *Disability Visibility: First-Person Stories from the Twenty-First Century* (2020), edited by the late Alice Wong, beloved disability justice activist, which highlights the joys and challenges of the modern disability experience.

As book editors seeking to elevate and amplify the stories of AANHPI educators, we invited authors from across the United States to participate in the AANHPI Voices project through networking and open posting. Obviously, one book cannot represent all the lived experiences or lessons from the field. *We each represent our own story*. We hope the book taken as a whole will provide insight into a cross-section of the experiences of AANHPI early education and care professionals, help dispel misconceptions and stereotypes, highlight the complexities of our identities, and provide insights that may positively impact the field of early childhood education.

The collection of essays in this book demonstrates the remarkable diversity of AANHPI educators, representing different ethnicities, identities, and roles in education, including family child care providers, classroom teachers, coaches, leaders, directors, teacher educators, community-based organization members serving children and families, public policy advocates, and mental health professionals.

No single experience defines what it means to be AANHPI in the United States today. We consist of people from more than 50 ethnic groups with over 100 languages and dialects, all with different cultures, religions, and our own sets of historic and contemporary international conflicts. Our communities include newly arrived immigrants, people who have been on American soil for multiple generations, and people of Indigenous heritage. Depending on immigration status, class, and other factors, there are vast differences even among those from the same country of origin. In fact, the income gaps between some Asian American groups are among the largest of any race and ethnic category in the nation (Ruiz et al. 2023). We have been both marginalized and privileged, within our AANHPI communities and outside them. Our lived experiences are in part shaped by where we were born, how connected we are to our family's ethnic origins, our intersectional identities, and how others see us and engage with us in our daily lives. Yet these complexities are rarely explored and discussed. The stories shared in this book defend against erasure, claiming space within a profession that has often overlooked them, and provide counter-narratives against dominant discourses. The collection as a whole is more powerful than any single story in the book.

Writing in community has been an important part of this book. We believe that sharing stories with others who share identities, traditions, or even past traumas can build community and joy, and wanted to create a space that would provide connection, support, affinity, and colleagueship in the writing process. For some of our contributing authors, this was their first time publishing, while others have written several books. Between 2024 and 2025, we met with our authors in person at National Association for the Education of Young Children (NAEYC) conferences, in virtual meetings in large groups, small groups, section meetings, and one-on-one meetings. Our process involved each of the book editors leading a section of writers and offering monthly meetings, which provided opportunities to share ideas, ask questions, gather information, and offer feedback to each other about the content as well as the writing process. Some of us were strangers to each other in the beginning. However, throughout this journey, many of us have found new allies, colleagues, and co-conspirators with like-minded values and commitments. For people who have been marginalized, the process of writing together can be empowering, as well as a form of collective resistance, and many of us experienced this through both our process and in seeing our product take shape.

We are not a monolithic group

Asian American

Asian Indian
Bangladeshi
Bhutanese
Burmese
Cambodian
Chinese
Filipino
Hmong
Indonesian
Japanese
Korean
Laotian
Malaysian
Mongolian
Nepalese
Okinawan
Pakistani
Sri Lankan
Taiwanese
Thai
Two or More Asian
Vietnamese
Other Asian

Native Hawaiian and Pacific Islander

Fijian
Marshallese
Chamorro
Tongan
Samoan
Other Native Hawaiian
Carolinian
Chuukese
Kosraean
Niuean
Palauan
Pohnpeian
Papua New Guinean
Tokelauan
Yapese
Other Pacific Islander

Annie E. Casey Foundation 2023

The Framework for This Book

We wanted to offer readers a framework that can illuminate some of the connections across the diverse narratives contained within this collection without losing sight of the particulars that define the families, communities, and historical trajectories that have shaped them. The core of our framework consists of the four goals of anti-bias education: identity, diversity, justice, and action (Derman-Sparks, Edwards, & Goins 2020). It is closely aligned with the NAEYC (2019) position statement advancing equity.

The Four Core Goals of Anti-Bias Education

Goal 1: Identity

- Teachers will nurture each child's construction of knowledgeable and confident personal and social identities.
- Children will demonstrate self-awareness, confidence, family pride, and positive social identities.

Goal 2: Diversity

- Teachers will promote each child's comfortable, empathic interaction with people from diverse backgrounds.
- Children will express comfort and joy with human diversity, use accurate language for human differences, and form deep, caring connections across all dimensions of human diversity.

Goal 3: Justice

- Teachers will foster each child's capacity to critically identify bias and will nurture each child's empathy for the hurt bias causes.
- Children will increasingly recognize unfairness (injustice), have language to describe unfairness, and understand that unfairness hurts.

Goal 4: Activism

- Teachers will cultivate each child's ability and confidence to stand up for oneself and for others in the face of bias.
- Children will demonstrate a sense of empowerment and the skills to act, with others or alone, against prejudice and/or discriminatory actions.

(Derman-Sparks et al. 2020)

Anti-bias education puts equity and diversity at the core of everything we do as early education and care professionals. It is the lens with which we view our roles and responsibilities: how we administer our programs, the materials we use with our students and clients, the curriculum we develop, the pedagogy we use, how we interact with families, children, and each other. More than curriculum and strategies, an anti-bias stance offers both children and adults tools to actively resist bias and systemic oppression in our society; it is a commitment to social justice.

Building on this core framework, we introduce some key concepts and themes that emerged as we engaged in conversations with our contributing authors about the experiences and stories they sought to share, and even more so as we read their compelling chapters one by one. While not every chapter will touch on every concept or theme below, we hope that readers will be able to see some of the through lines that connect the diverse narratives that come together in this collection.

Each theme we describe below is connected to Goals 1 & 2 (Identity and Diversity), or Goals 3 & 4 (Justice and Activism). In practice, the goals overlap and complement each other. For example, in supporting one child's heritage language development, an educator might be helping a child's healthy identity development, teaching another child to appreciate linguistic diversity, resisting the harmful effects of cultural assimilation, and strengthening intergenerational connections within a family and community.

Goals 1 and 2: Reflecting on the Meaning and Significance of AANHPI Identity

We invited our authors to reflect on their identity journeys and to consider how their AANHPI identity shows up in the work they do as early childhood educators, policymakers, and leaders. Our assumptions were that 1) Our AANHPI identities do inform our professional identities and practices in profound ways, and 2) Learning to understand and appreciate our own identities deeply is an important step toward learning to understand and appreciate those who are different from us.

Identity can be defined as "how individuals know and name themselves and how they are recognized and regarded by others" (Danielewicz 2001, 3). We hold multiple identities, including social identity (discussed on Intro to p. 19), cultural identity, personal identity, and professional identity. Identities are constructed and negotiated with and through our interactions with others and continuously shift across time and context. Appiah (2019) writes that identities motivate us, give us "reasons for doing things" (p. 9), and also give us "rules about how you should behave, given your identity" (p. 10). Many of the authors illustrate how their identities connect them to their ancestors and their communities, give meaning and significance to their work, and orient their practice. The significance of their own identities has led them to be deeply committed to supporting young children in developing pride in who they are and appreciation for those who are different from themselves.

Threats to Identity: Stereotypes and Erasure

Two stereotypes have persistently followed some AANHPIs and influenced our sense of belonging in this nation: the model minority and the perpetual foreigner. The model minority stereotype suggests that AANHPI individuals are a successful and well-adjusted minority group that can achieve high levels of education, income, and low crime rates. We know that this is a harmful myth that obscures diverse experiences and challenges. It is not the full story for any of us. The model minority myth treats AANHPI as a single block of people, though our experiences are diverse, complex, and multifaceted. It also ignores the challenges that our communities face, such as the generational impacts on mental health due to traumas such as colonization, persecution, and war (Annie E. Casey Foundation 2023).

Another stereotype is that we are perpetual foreigners. Lalami (2020), a naturalized US citizen originally from Morocco, has described her experience as an immigrant Muslim woman as that of a *conditional citizen*, that is, an American "who cannot enjoy the full rights, liberties, and protections of citizenship because of arbitrary markers of identity" (p. 27). She writes that "immigrants walk around with a scar left behind by their crossing into a new country, an invisible mark of the exile that became their condition when they were uprooted" (p. 85). For those perceived as perpetual foreigners, whose loyalties and trustworthiness were always subject to interrogation, the model minority stereotype may have seemed appealing, as it carried the promise, though unfulfilled, of ending the condition of exile and gaining full acceptance into American society. Instead, the model minority myth, which is said to have originated in the 1960s in William Petersen's article in the *New York Times Magazine*, has been used as a weapon of exclusion that protects and upholds white supremacy. Kim (2023) explains:

> By staging the "rehabilitation" of Japanese Americans after the camps and facilitating their assimilation into American society, the U.S. government was not only able to demonstrate anti-racism on the cheap but also depict Japanese Americans' progress as a rebuke to the Black struggle. If the Japanese can make it here, surely anyone can. This is the context in which the "model minority myth" first emerged in public discourse. (p. 125)

The model minority myth lumps all AANHPI people together; hurts Black, Indigenous, and Latine people by pitting groups against each other; and undermines efforts to dismantle structural racism. Its primary focus on economic achievement (Eng & Han 2018) also ignores the reality that there is still extreme poverty in various AANHPI communities. Despite its implied promise of inclusion, full social and cultural belonging has continued to be elusive, with a recent survey by The Asian American Foundation (2025) finding that 25 percent of Americans surveyed have "no relationship with an Asian American" (p. 3), "are concerned that Chinese Americans are a threat to U.S. society" (p. 16) especially around national security, and more than half of Americans "don't fully agree that the Japanese American incarceration was wrong" (p. 18).

In addition to stereotypes, the erasure caused by lumping all AANHPI groups and aggregating data has also caused real harm, particularly for Native Hawaiian and Pacific Islander communities. Chapter 2 of this book documents the conversation that our Native Hawaiian and Pacific Islander authors had in which they discussed this issue in depth. Aggregated data makes it appear all AANHPI groups are doing better than they really are, both economically and educationally. For example, the child poverty rate for Samoan American children is 25 percent, compared to only 5 percent for Taiwanese American children (Annie E. Casey Foundation [2023] 2025), obscuring how some groups such as Samoan Americans experience high rates of poverty, poor physical and mental health outcomes, and other disparities. Desegregating data enables policymakers and service providers to provide effective targeted interventions and policies and more culturally and linguistically appropriate services.

Goal 3: The Importance of Understanding Our Histories

Although we may be from many different places of origin, our identities and present status have been shaped by historical events that are part of the racial and colonial history of the United States, whether we are aware of this or not. It is beyond the scope of this book to actually provide this history; however, we try to make the point that our histories have important implications for how we might better understand who we are and our present circumstances. Readers will find that key historical events in the United States and the world have shaped the life trajectories of our authors and their families.

Grappling with the ways we are differently positioned, as privileged and oppressed in the racial and settler colonial history of the United States, can help us to better understand ourselves and the families and communities we serve. It can expand the boundaries of our "imagined communities" (Anderson 2016)—who we feel connected to and who we include in our sphere of care—to be more inclusive and to engage more deeply with the broader movements for racial and social justice that are taking place today.

Goal 4: Leveraging Collective Strength and Intersectional Activism

Perseverance for AANHPI people often comes from harnessing collective strengths and using an intersectional approach to advocacy. Strong communal identity and family bonds are significant protective factors that build resilience in the face of challenges such as racial discrimination. Many AANHPI organizations recognize the benefits of multiracial coalitions and work with Black, Latine, and Indigenous communities to address shared experiences of structural inequities. This solidarity allows for a more powerful, collective push for transformative justice. Intersectionality is a helpful concept to inform this work, particularly for those with multiple marginalized identities, such as LGBTQIA+ people. Actively centering the experiences of those at the most vulnerable intersections—such as refugee women, undocumented immigrants with disabilities, and transgender youth—can strengthen the entire community.

Using Privilege to Enact Change

For AANHPI individuals who may experience some degree of privilege based on socioeconomic factors or perceived "proximity to whiteness," navigating this dynamic means strategically using that position to name and to help dismantle the systems that create marginalization. Platforms can be used to advocate for those within the community who have less power. This can involve calling out microaggressions, amplifying the voices of marginalized AANHPI groups, and supporting community-based organizations.

Ultimately, the navigation of privilege and marginalization within the AANHPI community is not a simple process but a continuous journey of self-reflection, education, and collective action. By acknowledging internal diversity, rejecting harmful myths, and advocating for all, the community can move forward with strength and resilience.

We hope this collection of AANHPI stories provides mirrors and windows to the education field in hope of pursuing more fair, just, and inclusive communities. We also hope this book will resonate with many people beyond the AANHPI community as we all navigate the questions of identity and belonging. This book is a provocation to uplift stories that are often invisible in our communities, including those we were not able to include that need to be amplified. Finally, we hope this book is an opportunity to break down barriers between and outside the AANHPI communities. If you are an AANHPI early childhood professional, we hope you will see aspects of yourself in these pages, and if you are not AANHPI, we hope to build a bridge of understanding, open a dialogue, improve both policy and practice, and advance diversity and equity.

So Many More Voices . . .

Shaped by a postcolonial upbringing and as the mother of a biracial child, my intersecting identities push me to unlearn colonial and ableist narratives I was taught. I am regularly confronted by both privilege and othering, depending on the spaces I navigate. This ongoing work deeply shapes how I parent, advocate, and intentionally create spaces rooted in belonging, dignity, and positive senses of self.

Devanshi Unadkat
Assistant Professor, San Diego State University,
San Diego, California

CHAPTER 2

It's Complicated

A Conversation with Our Native Hawaiian and Pacific Islander Authors

KAMALEI BRANDON, DONNA ELIZABETH KALEIOKALANI REID-HAYES, NICOL RUSSELL, SALA SATARAKA, ALETHEA KU'ULEI SERNA, CHARIS-ANN F. SOLE, AND JORDAN A. TAITINGFONG

AANHPI early educators represent a group of diverse populations whose voices are underrepresented in our field. For this reason, we decided it was important to come together in this book to share our experiences and stories. While powerful to come together to elevate our voices, the union also presents some challenges that we did not want to overlook. For this chapter, the editors engaged in conversation with several of our Native Hawaiian and Pacific Islander contributing authors, posing specific questions. Each author shared some of their thoughts on the complexity of the AANHPI identity and their experience on what it meant to take part in this project. We acknowledge and share their ideas with honesty and gratitude.

More Than an Acronym

What does the AANHPI identity mean to you?

Donna Elizabeth Kaleiokalani Reid Hayes: I am of Native Hawaiian and Caucasian descent. I was born in Hilo on Hawai'i Island and was raised mostly in Honolulu on O'ahu. I think it's very important to understand who you are. In understanding and valuing your own identity, you can value other people for who they are and what they bring to the table, to the classroom, or to the group. I think that the more we look inside ourselves, the better able we are to be kinder and gentler to the people around us.

Alethea Ku'ulei Serna: Growing up in Hawai'i, I'm multiethnic. It's important for us to identify with all of our identities. My mom made sure we knew what all our ethnicities were, where they came from, and why they're important. I am kānaka 'ōiwi (Indigenous person of Hawai'i; Native Hawaiian), and I am part Caucasian, part Filipino as well. Another connection to identity is how much you practice it and live it, and how much it's actualized and realized in your own life. Being native Hawaiian, the matriarchs in our family were native Hawaiian, and my great-grandmother was pure, so on both sides of our family, even if my parents were mixed, the culture, hula, language, and values were dominant. It also informed my responsibility to our community and for future generations for people like us.

Sala Sataraka: For me, the AANHPI acronym is relatively new. I grew up just identifying as Samoan and didn't have to explain that. When I moved to Seattle in the early 2000s for college, my identity expanded more as Polynesian. Then I got older and expanded even more to Pacific Islander. There is value in the expansiveness of our cultural identity. I also have found it difficult to be lumped into this acronym. During the AANHPI month, I'd see more Asians and East Asians being highly represented, and I felt left out. It's really hard to find books, materials, and podcasts that are hosted by and for Native Hawaiian and Pacific Islanders. It's very complicated. There is so much beauty and diversity within the NHPI community and so much cultural richness to be able to pull from it. But I do feel like I've been playing catch-up because I was raised mostly in the stereotypes and now I'm trying to lean into precolonial education and learn more about my people and our culture so that I can pass that down to my daughter. So, I have lots of thoughts, lots of mixed feelings about the identity itself, but a lot of pride and love for the people, too.

Jordan A. Taitingfong: I'm conflicted about this acronym in itself. There's the term and then there's the human side. I'm less conflicted about humans. Practically, as an educator, it was always really apparent to me that AAPI being used as one descriptor or data group for students was harmful to Pacific Islanders. Without disaggregating data under that umbrella, we can end up ignoring unique issues within Asian American and Pacific Islander communities. We can potentially ignore the way Whiteness functions differently related to all the identities held under that umbrella, especially for those with darker skin. Still, there are many experiences that Pacific Islanders and Asian Americans have in common and lessons we can learn from each other, and building solidarity across identities and differences is critical to growing and supporting our communities, especially under white supremacy.

As a Pacific Islander, I've had a number of conversations on the addition of NH. I can absolutely see why disaggregating Native Hawaiian data is important for the same reason it's important to disaggregate PI data from AA data. But that's also true for all the identities held within PI and AA. And as a Chamorro, I wonder about the reinforcement of hierarchies within Pacific communities and siloing Indigenous struggles. It reinforces settler colonial ideas of race by calling out one Pacific community while ignoring the colonial status of communities like Guam, CNMI, and American Samoa. Many identities that fall under the AANHPI umbrella are often pitted against each other, and there is also a lot of lateral violence and discrimination against Micronesians (including from Native Hawaiians and Chamorros), and it feels like a missed opportunity to build solidarity. I'm still thinking all this through, and I'm sure I still will be when it gets changed again.

Watching people getting ripped off the street and kidnapped by ICE right now has made it endlessly clear that the way the government identifies us is not liberatory or there to protect us. It's meant to sort and control us. At the end of the day, I care less about the terms the government has created to identify us and more about what they mean for us as people and how we can coordinate power and care within and across our identities. I want us to be free, and here I think that solidarity building, recognizing the temporariness of our categories, is something Asian Americans and Pacific Islanders understand. Solidarity across these identities under this umbrella is important.

Nicol Russell: Context matters. When I am in Hawai'i, so much of our cultures are truly influencing one another—Asian American, Native Hawaiian, Pacific Islander. All of that exists there and has been a solid part of the formation of my identity in that place. When I am in Arizona, my current home, I feel more removed from this AANHPI umbrella identity. Umbrella identities are unfair. It doesn't give acknowledgement to each of those identities. And inside of those identities are all the varied ethnicities of groups—it's not a fair representation of peoples. It isn't just about *this* umbrella, because if you stick me under another umbrella, I feel the same. I am one-half Kanako or Hawaiian, and one-half Black, and if you put me under the Black umbrella, it also doesn't capture who I am, how I was raised, or how I see the world. Labeling takes away from all our individual experiences that have led us to who we are right now in this moment.

Donna Elizabeth Kaleiokalani Reid Hayes: We have all grown up to take on labels in different ways. I am not Hawaiian-looking so I always thought I wasn't Hawaiian enough to say it. It took a lot of learning to let go of that. It's who I am, and it's ok for me to claim it. You have to embrace your identity and say who you are. For me, it's how I grow that sense of identity and Indigeneity for my own children and my grandchildren. The labels get in the way. Being able to practice those values. How to make things contemporary for my children to identify as a Native Hawaiian. Letting people feel free to claim their own identities and their own stories.

Alethea Ku'ulei Serna: For me, AANHPI is another placeholder for Hawaiians to represent, and it's important to me. Because I feel like the continent needs us, with the diaspora of Hawaiians, now we're less. We have less identified Native Hawaiians in Hawai'i than we have outside of Hawai'i, and that is critical to me. But then we are voyagers. Take space. If I need to do that with all of these letters, I will take space so other Native Hawaiians can feel no matter where you're from, no matter where you're born, you got the koko, it's in your blood. You have ancestry in your blood. You're part of who we are; it is as simple as that.

Charis-Ann F. Sole: I think of the AANHPI identity as a bucket to hold us—but it is not all of us; it's just the surface. It does not capture the complexity that we all come with; people can be multiple things at once. My dad was from California, but my mom is Native Hawaiian. My dad has been here for over 40 years. My mom's people have been here since antiquity. People came and continue to move to Hawai'i for different reasons—we can be refugees, immigrants; some of us by choice, some by necessity, some by default. And then there is that mixture, that intermingling, too. My mom is Native Hawaiian Chinese from five or six generations ago. But I don't necessarily see myself as Chinese because we weren't raised in the culture, outside of token things like lion dance at Chinese New Year and eating noodles and other specific foods during the New Year. But that doesn't mean I'm not genetically Chinese—it's just a bit more complicated.

Kamalei Brandon: I feel very blessed to have had the opportunity to be a part of this AANHPI book, but, in the beginning and throughout, I questioned should I do it. I have seen this umbrella identity do more harm than good. For example, during "AANHPI Month," we are often left out. When examples are given, it is often just Asian American. I don't like when people just slap on "NHPI" but do not actually attend to it in an equitable or even equal way, furthering the invisibility of my NHPI community. When I was a kindergarten teacher in the Seattle area, we were a cross-ethnic team—that included Asian, Native Hawaiian, and White teachers. May was one of my favorite months to teach in my classroom, because I felt like we were able to balance AA and NHPI perspectives with authentic curricular experiences.

Kamalei Brandon: I would like to see the data disaggregated within the AA and NHPI identity so that the NH and PI data is not just lumped with Asian Americans. Historically, the AA and NHPI population is understudied, underrepresented, and underfunded in research. Aggregating the AA and NHPI groups into a single race/ethnicity masks the diversity between ethnic groups and limits the ability to support their unique health needs. For example, in my current job at Hummingbird Indigenous Family Services, I work with a lot of data about maternal mortality. The rates are 30 to 40 percent when they put us together. However, when you separate it out, Asian Americans are 22.4 maternal deaths per 100,000 live births, while for NHP It is 117 deaths per 100,000 births. That is a huge difference. (https://ncuih.org/maternal-health/).

Telling Your Story

Why did you decide to be part of this project? What has it meant to you to share your story and thoughts in this book?

Sala Sataraka: There is a lack of representation of Pacific Islanders in our work. It has been stereotyped and Disneyfied. Having an opportunity to share my story in authentic ways has been liberating. Doing a panel presentation at the NAEYC 2024 annual conference in Anaheim was really fun. It just poured out of me. We need to be in community and be in the space, and I appreciate the opportunities where we can connect with one another and be vulnerable. When we practice that, we can be the models we need.

Jordan A. Taitingfong: I decided to write for this project because I believe more in solidarity than labels. The acronym is a tension point, and tension points are always sites of possibility. True solidarity under the AANHPI umbrella recognizes that we are not all the same and emphasizes differences, so we can work across them. Collective resistance is critical for our survival and growth. I'm excited to see the other authors writing so I can learn from their histories and realities, how to be a better educator and human, and how to support their communities and mine.

I'm grateful for a space to write about the importance of identity and to include both disabled and Pacific Islander identities. My life has been so enriched by learning from both communities, and there are so many points of connection (like a focus on collectivism) that really support early childhood educators and build positive identities for young disabled Pacific Islander children and their peers. My life has been enriched by being able to connect my own identity to this work (which we do every day, consciously or not), by really letting me reflect and organize my thoughts on why it's so important to support identity development.

Nicol Russell: I wanted to be part of this project because I have a very prominent role in a very influential organization, and I work for one of the largest companies whose focus is on curriculum and assessment and family engagement. It's important that people recognize, in that kind of large entity at its highest level, there are folks who are thinking about this particular topic of AANHPI visibility. I'm thinking about how my stories could help people think about what this means to their communities and families.

Alethea Ku'ulei Serna: Writing a narrative, sharing my story, it was challenging for me because I am used to academic writing, but I really loved it. Showcasing our voices and the power of storytelling. I wanted to write in a narrative form and be able to put that forward. The things that your kūpuna (elders) wanted for you, and their intentionality.

Donna Reid-Hayes: I wanted to participate in a writing project that encourages sharing stories of lives lived and the growth that occurs when self-reflection and internal research are part of an educator's practice. My research was done through stories—and a method, ʻoiwi moʻolelo research, which would speak to my Hawaiian-ness. Stories are data. We bridge that gap—to get past the quantitative data and interview myself—stories from childhood and teaching and stories of conversations with my kūpuna. I began to discover and understand my kuleana to my kūpuna and my heritage. Giving yourself permission to share your story is important. All of us have a story that we are living out.

Kamalei Brandon: This book project is one of the few times where I've seen the AA and NHPI label work for good. In the beginning, I was concerned I would be the only Native Hawaiian author, but the editors have been intentional about including multiple NH and PI voices, which has been empowering. Mahalo (thank you) for this opportunity!

Looking to the Future

What do you hope the readers of this book will take away?

Jordan A. Taitingfong: I hope readers will see new *and* familiar inroads to connecting with families, other educators, and themselves. I hope they'll be reminded that positive identity is important and powerful, and children deserve the opportunity to explore and be celebrated.

Nicol Russell: Everyone has a story, it is just your story. There is not one way to tell a story. One time on a conference panel, I started by showing a tattoo on my arm—a constant reminder, a connection to my past, present, future. A colleague said, "I could never do that. You just did it, they liked it and it worked." I replied that I'm hoping to give that gift to others—you don't have to hold back who you are. You are the story. You are the most important piece of data that these others are going to connect to.

Sala Sataraka: I hope the book gives them permission to be vulnerable. We talk about our personal and social identities so others will be more comfortable sharing their stories. Typing words out can be so hard. Is there a blockage because I am meant to speak this and not write this? I connect with the oral side of this so much more than the writing part.

Donna Reid-Hayes: I hope that readers walk away with pride and dignity, with encouragement to look within and discover who they are and what drives them.

Alethea Ku'ulei Serna: Intersectionality of who we are is through stories and knowledge. There are a lot of parts to us. I am Native Hawaiian and was raised a Christian. You don't have to choose one or another. You have to stand in that space in the middle of it all. It's like a Venn diagram.

Charis-Ann Sole: I hope people will expand their ideas about diversity. It's not just Black, White, Latine, or Asian. We are much more complex and have many more ethnicities. I hope the reader will think about the children and families they serve with a wider lens and deeper insights. I also want people to know that we are here. The "NH" of the AANHPI. We are here and we are not going anywhere.

Kamalei Brandon: In my chapter, I connected my story to Indigeneity perspectives, specifically Indigenous language and culture reclamation and sustainability. Just like my Kānaka Maoli community taught me, I'm a big believer that we cannot have culture without language nor language without culture. I feel like this is especially true for our Indigenous languages, like our NHPI languages, which must be sustained amidst the dominant culture. We need both language and culture in order to survive as a community.

Sala Sataraka: I hope people will be more aware of who is still not visible and how to make space for those voices who are missing.

PART 2

Knowing Who You Are

The contributions in Part 2 provide a window into each author's identity journey and how their intersecting identities have impacted who they are both personally and professionally. Through these stories, we understand that our identity development is influenced by our context; where and how long we have lived in the United States and in other countries; what have been our educational experiences; who our family is; the extent of our connections to our ethnic language, culture, and history; and how we are perceived and treated by our neighborhoods and schools.

Our Asian American and Native Hawaiian, Pacific Islander (AANHPI) ethnic identity is one of our many social identities. Social identity refers to significant group categories that are centered and defined by culture, disability, ethnicity, economic class, family structure, gender, language, race, religion, and more. Social identities begin at birth and are shaped by family and caregivers. A common theme throughout these essays is that social identities can shift during one's lifetime, and one can downplay or emphasize certain social identities depending on circumstances. Social identities matter. They carry various statuses, assumptions, and biases that affect how people are perceived and treated. They can powerfully enhance or undermine an individual's access to opportunities or resources (Derman-Sparks, LeeKeenan, & Nimmo 2015). The intersection of our identities is also significant in our development.

Early childhood programs are crucial to supporting social identity development by ensuring visibility of all identities. While all of the chapters speak to the marginalization and privileges we have experienced in various ways, they also speak to the resilience, perseverance, and joy of finding belonging.

Reflection Questions

As you read the chapters in Part 2, we encourage you to reflect on the following questions:

- What have you learned about the complexities of the AANHPI identity?
- What is something about the cultural backgrounds of the chapter authors that was new to you? How might learning more deeply about your colleagues and their stories help inform your work as an educator?
- How do your own identities, experiences, and context shape how you talk about identity with children?
- Whose identities and voices are represented and visible in your classroom? Who is missing? How can we include the missing voices?
- How do Indigenous ideas of learning, culture, collectivity, and disability help you challenge ableist classroom norms (like independence and readiness)?

So Many More Voices . . .

It wasn't until I became an educator myself that I began to understand the value of my own identity and what it meant to me. As an educator, I spent the time learning about each child's identity, their family, how they pronounced their child's name, and who they truly were. I began to realize the impact of living my dual identity and having to hide such a big part of who I was for so long.

Binal Patel
Executive Director of Neighborhood Viillages
Boston, Massachusetts

CHAPTER 3

Learning from Our Relations

Blood, Bone and Built, Centering Disability, Identity, and Liberation in Early Childhood

JORDAN A. TAITINGFONG

After decades on this earth, I still want to be known. I think this is a shared part of being human. We all want to be known, loved, and cared for while being fully ourselves. That journey begins with understanding and accepting who we are. Community can love and care for you as you come into yourself the same way they can teach you about yourself. All the pieces tied to our identity, our ancestry, lead to who we are today. Without knowing where I come from and why I am, it can be difficult to truly understand myself. What a gift to help children explore all the possibilities of who they are, who their people have been, and who they could be. I am who I am because of all my relations, the relationships I've built, the people with whom I share blood and lineage, and the bones of my ancestors and the land. When I can stand firmly rooted in who we've been, I can be unshakeable in who I am.

In this chapter, I explore how my identity exploration, including disability and ableism, colonialism, and Indigenous knowledge, shaped my understanding of education, interdependence, and resistance. Through personal experience and research, I share how Indigenous and disabled ways of knowing challenge harmful dominant narratives and offer new possibilities for disabled Black and Brown children through education, belonging, and liberation.

The Power of Knowing Who We Are

As a Brown, disabled[1], mixed Chamorro woman, exploring my own identity has deepened my understanding of why it's vital for children to explore theirs. This personal journey made me a better educator. Educators help shape how children see the world and themselves, so we must engage in our own identity work to support children in exploring and taking pride in their identities.

Throughout my career (as an early childhood educator, consultant, coach, and preservice instructor), I've seen that teachers who do identity work are better prepared to foster pride and belonging. Educators who understand their cultural backgrounds and biases create more inclusive, affirming, and liberatory classrooms (Banks 2016; Landson-Billings 1995). This work requires time, reflection, and practice to approach with comfort and fluency.

1 Note on language: Throughout this chapter, I use identity-first language (e.g., "disabled children") to reflect how I understand disability as an essential part of identity. This aligns with the values of disability justice and the focus on identity throughout this piece. I use this language for myself and in general unless I know someone prefers person-first language. I also intentionally do not capitalize "white" when referring to race. I capitalize "Black," "Indigenous," and other terms to acknowledge shared histories and resistance.

Without exploring our identities, we can unintentionally replicate harmful systems. We bring our racial, linguistic, cultural, gendered, and disabled or nondisabled identities to our practice. Without cultivating self-awareness, we can reinforce assimilationist and ableist ideas for children and teach to a norm that doesn't serve our students.

Exploring our own identity and learning to discuss identity helps us understand the world and better differentiate for each child. We often hear equality framed as treating everyone the same and ignoring differences. Educators who do not differentiate based on thoughtful understandings of who children are and what they need erase children's lived experiences rather than celebrate or affirm them. Identity work allows us to see the impact of race, disability, language, and other social identities.

My relationships, family, and community have played a significant role in shaping my understanding of identity. Exploring my Chamorro ancestry and embracing Indigenous values shaped my disability identity, while connecting with disabled communities helped me find pride in that identity. That learning has been essential not just personally but to understand and resist the colonial and ableist practices that continue to shape early childhood education.

Blood: Learning from Family and Ancestry

Like many other Black and Brown people, I was not taught my history in school and only later learned how my family's story fit into a broader cultural context. I didn't learn about the colonization of Guam until adulthood, about our ancestors' beliefs, and how colonization erased so many sustaining ways of being and knowing.

The Chamorro people, the Indigenous people of Guam, are believed to have arrived around 2000 BC and built a thriving culture. Colonization began with the Spanish in 1521, who committed near-genocide. Chamorros faced cultural suppression, language was prohibited, Catholicism was forced to replace native spirituality, and traditional matriarchal systems were dismantled.

Yet cultural resistance persisted in families like mine. My Grandma Taitingfong remained a matriarch even after moving stateside, where she was expected to assimilate and teach her 10 children to do the same. She ran our family, organizing over 40 cousins, and passed on values of care, interdependence, and collective responsibility through how she lived and parented.

During WWII, my grandparents witnessed another attempt to erase Chamorro culture. My grandmother told stories of internment, punishment for speaking Chamorro, and death. After the war, the Guam Organic Act of 1950 made Chamorros US citizens but with limited self-government. It was also the era when the term "Guamanian" was created to describe those who called Guam home. These efforts to erase our culture impacted my family. Guamanian was the first term I was taught to describe us. Guam is the western word for Guåhan, a term whose erasure denies us the context and knowledge of the Indigenous name Guåhan, which means "we have" and reflects our connection to the island's abundance.

When my grandparents moved stateside after my grandfather joined the military as a steward, they didn't teach their children their home language. They hoped to live the American dream, a dream with no space for Guåhan. My family has since had the privilege to rediscover the importance of language.

Following models of Chamorro resistance, the grandchildren have been able to work to relearn the language collectively. My cousin is now teaching a class online to family, friends, and the greater social media world (San Nicolas & Santos 2025). By connecting around Chamorro language and culture, we've been able to share stories and trace the ways our matriarch passed down these values.

Today, many Chamorros still fight for cultural preservation, adapting cultural practices, and continue to struggle for self-determination in a multitude of ways. This knowledge of who I am has helped me discover the patterns between the cultures I am a part of. It took an understanding of what my people had been through and stories from my own family to map how I arrived here. This knowledge created a desire for people to be who they are and to belong. The opportunity to reclaim parts of myself allows me to see the importance of the exploration of identity in early childhood. It took generations to recover and reclaim our identity as a family. Our journey of reclamation could have started much earlier had I had a classroom where adults honored our ancestry and made space for family and cultural history.

Learning Who We Are: Ancestry as a Tool for Belonging

My experiences exploring and claiming my identity directly impacted my success as an educator. Building comfort and fluency around talking about identity helped me better support children in exploring their own. Asking questions of my family helped me ask the same of my students' families. Seeking out disabled role models taught me that identity is something we build together. As an adult, reflecting on where I learned these lessons—and what was missing—showed me just how important it is to intentionally bring identity into the classroom.

Understanding how to talk about identity, both my own and others', has been one of the most important parts of becoming the educator I am. Claiming my ancestry reshaped how I responded to the constant question, "What are you?" In the United States, non-white children are often asked this, whether or not they have had the chance to explore an answer. As a child, I repeated the percentages my parents gave me: 50 percent Guamanian, 25 percent Portuguese, 15 percent Scots-Irish, and 10 percent English. Over time, those numbers lost meaning. I started asking who the question was for and why. It was about others and their comfort. This helped me think more deeply about how we use labels in the classroom.

I learned how I wanted to share my identity with others from my immediate and extended family. Sometimes I say I am a disabled, Brown Chamorro woman or I am mixed race. Or my family name is Taitingfong. Or my dad is Chamorro, and my mom is white. I say I am disabled. My disabilities shift in how they affect me and how closely I match a diagnosis. I have learned the power of these descriptors, and when and with whom I want to share them. Understanding the meaning of these words in different contexts helped me navigate a world that strips power from anyone who is not white or nondisabled. It made me a teacher who pays attention to how language shapes the way adults perceive children. This helps me support children and families navigating labeling and diagnosis. As a teacher educator, I help new teachers honor a family's concerns about systems not built for their children while also supporting them in getting the services they need.

My family's stories of resisting racism and my own experience navigating both racial privilege and discrimination helped me grasp how race and ability intersect. My grandma Taitingfong shared stories of being in Mississippi in the '50s and '60s where white people stared, unsure whether she should walk her Brown body through the front door or the back. She refused the back door, and because of all I had learned, I had pride in her resistance while also understanding the privilege she held in being able to make that choice. It helped me to understand the way my mother's whiteness protected me, through my light skin, her insistence that NO ONE should treat me differently, and her indignance when they did.

More lessons were learned when I went to an all-white middle school, where many children were taught racism implicitly and explicitly. Implicitly, from the total absence of people of color among the staff, in textbooks, on classroom walls, and the stories we were told about history. Explicitly, I listened to classmates repeat racial slurs without consequences, teachers dismiss racist comments as jokes, and lessons that framed non-white cultures as dangerous, delayed, or full of deficits. In those spaces, I was not seen as white, and whiteness did not protect me. These lessons supported me in interrogating my own biases as an educator, becoming practiced in the discomfort of asking about my privilege and showing others how to do the same.

As an adult, I began learning from my ancestors and bone relations. I read more about race, listened to stories passed down, and studied sovereignty through Dr. Haunani-Kay Trask, a Native Hawaiian activist and educator, who reminded me that "cultural people have to become political" (1999). I read W.E.B. Du Bois and began to see how racism and ableism collude. I studied the work of other professors and activists, including Ed Roberts, Harlan Hahn, Simi Linton, and Stacey Milbern. Milbern's words stayed with me: "I would want people with disabilities twenty years from now to not think that they're broken" (2019). That shaped how I began to speak to children and myself.

Disability as Identity, in Practice

In my inclusive classroom, I worked as a general and special educator, yet I avoided saying the word "disability." Society had taught me it was a word tied to pity and brokenness. Even as I began to challenge my own quiet biases, I met many families hoping early intervention could remove a label they feared. For families who had already experienced marginalization and discrimination, "disability" brought more fear. That fear made it hard to talk about disability as a valid, valuable part of identity. But the more I reflected, the clearer it became that we needed to talk about disability, openly and affirmingly.

I could not do that work without tackling my internalized ableism. I had to expand my ideas about disability, embracing it as more than just a label tied to ableism and discrimination. Disability is not something to be feared; it's a part of who people are, and it brings creativity and unique strengths. Disability justice frameworks pushed me to envision a world built for everyone.

All my reflection on how I show up in the world has prepared me to help children navigate how the world shows up for them. When children entered my classroom, they were just beginning to make sense of who they were in the world, and I wanted them to know that their identities were expansive, not limiting, and they had options, possibilities, and the freedom to explore who they were without restriction.

While I had long understood the importance of teaching about race and culture as part of our identities from my own lived experiences, I hadn't yet fully understood how disability was a critical part of identity. Without that awareness, I couldn't help my students explore or embrace disability as part of their own identities. Until I embraced my disabled identity, I couldn't support theirs. I learned I had to build deeper connections with my own disability identity and theirs.

These connections to race and disability allow me to create classrooms where children are proud of who they are. That means rich representation: baby dolls that reflect the racial diversity of the class, and assistive communication devices for the dolls. It means reading stories about many kinds of people and families and spending intentional time with books like *We Move Together* (Fritsch et al. 2021) to talk about disability, community care, and complexity. I support teachers in learning about identity so they can become powerful collaborators in honoring all parts of children's lives.

Bone: Understanding the Body, Disability, and Indigenous Knowledge

To help children resist the harm of ableism and colonialism, we must first recognize how deeply these forces shape our world. Colonialism and ableism both shaped how society understands disability and care. Missionaries framed Indigenous people as childlike and in need of saving, just as disabled people are often seen as dependent, incapable, or in need of charity rather than autonomy. Relational caregiving was portrayed as burdensome, while nuclear family structures were promoted as superior. The medical model of disability reinforced these ideas, defining disability as an individual problem to be fixed. It positioned disabled people as broken and reinforced institutionalization, segregation, and systems where an outside authority determines who and what is normal. These values continue today in education. In early childhood special education, many systems that aim to support disabled children are still rooted in Western, medical, and deficit-based models. Disabilities are defined and treated through standardized evaluations and developmental milestones that reflect white, Western, and middle- and upper-class norms. These tools assume that children learn the same way and on the same fixed timeline. This often excludes children from services or places them on paths that separate them from their peers.

Segregation and rejection based on narrow ideas of normalcy affect how children see themselves. By the time disabled children reach later grades, many have already been disciplined, excluded, or told (directly or indirectly) that they do not belong. Without affirming language and representation, children internalize dominant narratives that uphold whiteness, nondisability, and Western ways of being as superior.

Learning from Our Indigenous and Disabled Ancestors

Knowledge of Indigenous cultures and disability can empower educators to resist these messages, reframe deficit thinking, and build classrooms that affirm every child's identity. Many Indigenous cultures reject individualistic and deficit-based ideas of disability. The te reo (or Māori) word for autism, 'Takiwātanga,' means his or her own time and space. An acceptance of autism as a way of being. In Chamorro culture, the concept of inafa'maolek, meaning "to make good," emphasizes harmony, mutuality, and reciprocity. These frameworks define disability relationally, not in isolation. Patty Krawec, an Anishinaabe-Ukrainian writer and activist from the Lac Seul First Nation, shared that there is no word for "disabled" in Anishinaabemowin. As she explained, "words follow concepts, so a friend of mine who studies and teaches the language set off on a quest to find out what the Anishinaabe concept of disability is. An inability, or refusal, to meet your clan responsibilities" (2021). This framing does not ignore impairment but instead locates disability within a collective context of responsibility and care. These ways of thinking center the community, not the individual, and resist colonial ideas of productivity and worth.

Indigenous ideas about community and disability helped me challenge previously unexamined biases in my classroom. I started small, focusing on what I could shift in our daily routines. Together, my students and I cocreated community agreements assessing what our classroom needed to feel caring, how we would treat each other, and what we would do if harm occurred. We revisited these agreements, adjusting as our needs changed. We explored the natural pace of the classroom by allowing time for transitions and rest while keeping a predictable flow of the day. I intentionally normalized having different needs and meeting them collaboratively. Fidgets were available, break options were offered without needing to ask, and children saw that there were many valid ways to learn.

I also changed how I approached Individualized Education Programs (IEPs). When discussing why a child qualified for services, I talked openly with families about how assessments might or might not reflect their values. I asked questions to understand what they wanted for their child. Accepting that children may learn on different timelines gave me more flexibility to cocreate meaningful goals.

As a teacher educator, this learning has been endlessly useful. I help others understand the history and ongoing impact of colonialism and ableism in education so they can push back, advocate for themselves, and support the children they work with. That makes all of us stronger educators.

Built: What Disability Community Taught Me

The COVID-19 lockdown took many things away but also gave me opportunities I never expected. As I struggled to navigate my changing disabled identity, I found community in new ways. The shift to online spaces allowed me to reconnect with peers in my doctoral program. I taught a class on race and disability during a time shaped by lockdowns, vaccine resistance, and uprisings following George Floyd's murder. I joined Zoom classes with other Chamorro people across the diaspora to learn about culture and language. I built new relationships and learned deeply from them. In a world slowed down so much that coyotes wandered campus, the stillness gave me time to find my footing. I began to understand my body, mind, and relationships differently. Those lessons became essential to centering disability justice, collective care, and expanding how I approached inclusive education.

Disability, Community, and Identity

The year before COVID-19 lockdowns, the demands of doctoral school and full-time work led me to burn out. Every day as I coached teachers across my city, I saw the same patterns unfold: Black and Brown children, especially those with disabilities, were treated as problems. Teachers imagined a "somewhere else" that would be a better fit. Perceived disability was used to justify segregation and removal. It was exhausting. I knew what was happening was built on decades of exclusion, particularly for disabled children of color. In grad school, I was learning the theory, but I already knew the truth: "somewhere else" didn't exist. Every child deserves to stay and learn in their community.

At school, I was learning more about how racism and ableism intersect and how deeply they shape the experiences of children and educators. While I was witnessing these injustices in classrooms, my doctoral program gave me the language to describe what I already knew: Racism and ableism work together to justify exclusion. DisCrit (Disability Critical Race Theory) helped me name what I was seeing. It showed how nondisabled, white, Western norms define what is considered "normal" or "valued" in schools—and how that disproportionately harms Black and Brown disabled children (Annamma et al. 2016). Even as I gained this theoretical grounding, my lived reality as a disabled doctoral student often felt disconnected from the institutions that claimed to support inclusion.

The stress of full-time work and school worsened my chronic illnesses. I learned that my disabilities and impairments are dynamic. Eventually, I took a leave from my doctoral program and reduced my work hours. After years of fighting for disabled children's accommodations, I couldn't access my own. There were days I couldn't get out of bed, read, or meet the demands of work or school. I was forced to slow down. I had to reevaluate my worth outside of productivity. I had to live by the principles I was learning from other disabled people.

Relearning Myself, Reimagining the Classroom

During this time, I began truly listening to disabled voices and experiences. I listened to audiobooks and podcasts from bed. I learned from Leah Lakshmi Piepzna Samarasinha how care work could be radical rather than viewed as a burden (2018). Through the Disability Visibility Podcast, I learned from other disabled people how accessibility is an act of love rather than a checklist, and how disabled people create culture. I learned how the medical system itself can be disabling as I navigated specialists. As I lost days then months to pain, I discovered crip time and Chamorro ideas of time, mo′na. These frameworks made sense in my life. Crip time, like Indigenous time, resists the Western focus on linear progress. Time is circular. Lessons repeat and return. These ideas honor slowness, adaptation, and interdependence. Others had walked this path. When I shared my struggles and disabilities, disabled peers in my program welcomed me. I learned so much from listening to how others moved through the world. I was lucky to be valued not despite my disabilities but because of them.

With this community's help, I learned to recognize myself as whole. My internalized ableism had been shouting about failure. But this community helped me see that my changing body and mind were not broken—they were different. They didn't match the rigid schedules of capitalism or graduate school. I saw how interdependence needed to be a focus, not just personally but in classrooms. Coaching educators, I saw how "difference" was misread as "deficiency," especially when Black, Brown, and disabled children didn't meet milestones or behave as expected. I began to reframe those perceptions. These children belonged, even if their participation looked different. Belonging does not depend on being the same.

Shifting away from rigid ideas of independence toward collective care allows all children to thrive. Western education, especially special education, often equates success with independence, regulating emotions, and completing tasks alone. But disability and Pacific Islander cultures value interdependence. Caregiving is communal. Support is expected and shared. By redefining success as interdependence, we teach children to work together, build relationships, and support one another. That fosters stronger, more inclusive communities. Normalizing shared support disrupts deficit-based models. It challenges the idea that some children's needs are "special" and therefore expendable. Indigenous and disabled communities offer examples of mutual aid and collective care that help us reimagine what classrooms can be. As my own needs ebbed and flowed, I saw that I needed others. By believing I am not a burden, I can say with confidence that the children we advocate for are not either.

I had time to understand why these views matter in classrooms with disabled children. They reshaped the lessons I teach to future and current educators and gave me lived experience to bring into those conversations. Embracing expansive ideas of time, disability, and interdependence has been essential not just for me but for anyone committed to justice. Schools built around nondisabled, capitalist ideas of time and success cause real harm. When we understand that, we can recalibrate. We can resist in small and big ways and help children do the same. We model that by knowing ourselves and expanding what is possible in education. When we stop chasing assimilation and instead build classrooms where every child, especially disabled children and children of color, can thrive as their full selves, we create spaces where all children are seen as whole and deserving of the time they take to learn.

Identity as a Tool for Liberation

My work to understand my own identity is not over. Identity is malleable and constantly reinterpreted. We return to it with new learning and build on it in community. In a time when disabled rights are under attack and diversity, equity, and inclusion are being weaponized by government bodies, it is easy to internalize messages that tell us we are alone and do not belong. But resistance has never been possible alone. It is only possible through collective care and interdependence.

The more I explore how colonialism and ableism intersect, the more I see what I had missed, not only in myself but in the children I taught. We need each other to build strong, affirming, collective identities, and that work begins with exploring our own.

We know from Black liberation and disability pride movements that building collective identity is a powerful tool for resisting oppression (Bell 1992; Mingus 2011). From Harriet Tubman, whose brain injury and later epilepsy shaped her understanding of freedom, to Stacey Milbern, whose activism helped define disability justice, disabled leaders have shown that disability is not a deficit. It is a source of creativity, resilience, and community power. Educators must share these histories and possibilities with disabled children. These are the stories they need. When we teach children that disability is not something to overcome but something to take pride in, we offer them both resilience and belonging.

I have spent years working with children labeled the hardest to teach. I turn my dreams toward them. I want them to experience belonging in ways I never imagined for myself. I want them to learn together, see their histories reflected in their classrooms, and know that their identities are powerful. I want them to show up as their whole, authentic selves and be embraced because of who they are, not in spite of it.

Reclaiming Indigenous and disability justice ideas helped me unlearn the Western belief that worth is tied to productivity and that disability is a problem to fix. I see it differently now. Disability expands us; it deepens our relationships, strengthens our communities, and makes us more creative. I more easily recognize who belongs in my life and who accepts me as I am. I have learned to make space for uncertainty. Indigenous communities have long resisted colonization. Disability communities continue to resist ableism not by trying to fit in but by redefining what it means to belong and to have value. Bringing these lessons into the classroom helps us build spaces where all children can thrive, not by shrinking themselves to fit systems but by reshaping systems to honor all of us.

We cannot move toward liberation alone. We learn from our families, our ancestors, and the relationships we build. Taking time to understand my own identity helps me imagine how children can do this work and why it must begin early. It shapes my values around family, community, and education. Learning from Indigenous and disabled identities helps me design classrooms where interdependence is the norm, where every child is valued for who they are, and where identity is a source of strength, connection, and liberation. When we engage with our shifting identities, we open space for children to do the same. Through this work, we do more than survive systems that were never built for us. We begin to build communities where everyone belongs.

So Many More Voices . . .

I'm so proud to be a Chinese American who's an adoptee with disabilities. But I haven't always been proud of my identity. I was outplaced to special ed schools that were mostly all White as a child. I learned at one of the schools that racism was ok. I learned in history class that people like me were perpetual foreigners and we didn't belong. That staying silent was better than speaking up about racism.

But after 2021, I started to reconnect with the Chinese culture. I even learned there were other Chinese adoptees like me in American history like Chow Manderien, Joseph Pierce, Edward Day Cohota, Lue Gim Gong, and Vincent Chen.

Tina Zhu Xi Caruso
Boston, Massachusetts

CHAPTER 4

Learning Myself Through the Eyes of Others

CARYN PARK

For most of my adult life, when asked about my Asian American identity, I had more questions than answers to offer. As a teacher-educator whose primary work was supporting teachers to become culturally responsive reflective practitioners and social justice educators, I felt I shouldn't be feeling such discomfort around talking about my own identity. It wasn't for lack of reflection on the subject of Asian American-ness; rather, this identity and this label have not seemed mine to claim, especially the *American* part of it, since I was born in South Korea and still hold Korean citizenship. Despite having lived in the United States for 40 years, I often don't feel that I truly belong.

When Debbie LeeKeenan invited me to join the AANHPI Voices project, my first thought was, "I can't possibly!" But I am glad I ignored the voices of self-doubt and just started joining her Zoom meetings to meet other interested colleagues. There was so much I still had to learn and process (about myself and about AANHPI identity) through this project, but it was reassuring that having more questions than answers seemed to suit Debbie just fine. This would be my chance to really lean into *all the questions*!

I use this chapter to share about some defining moments and key influences in my (ongoing) personal journey of AANHPI identity development. Beginning with my family's intergenerational experiences with migration and colonization, and my personal experience as a child of immigration moving between two cultures, I touch on some of the concepts introduced in Chapter 1 of *conditional citizenship* (Lalami 2020) and the model minority myth, and go on to discuss the impacts of learning the history of racism and US imperialism on my Asian American identity development. Amidst the contradictions and tensions that shape the politics of AANHPI identities, which I found so clearly articulated by Jeff Chang (2016) and whose work I engage with deeply in this chapter, there is also the possibility for collective resistance to oppression and the creation of more expansive identities and solidarities (Thanh 2025), which, as educators, I hope we can support and cultivate in ourselves and in young people. The other authors in this book illuminate many promising paths for doing this, and their stories have inspired and informed this chapter, as have the many AANHPI friends, family, and colleagues whose stories have also shaped who I am.

Family Legacies: Stories of Migration and Cultural Survival

I spent my childhood in two different cultures, and this has mattered a great deal in shaping my identity and imagination. I was born in South Korea only three decades after the end of the Japanese colonial period. I grew up with my grandparents' and other elders' stories about how they were punished as kids for speaking Korean at school, and about relatives who risked their lives to support the independence movement. The Korean War began only five years after independence, taking a country already devastated by colonization and dividing it into North and South, with each side being claimed by feuding Western powers. Both of my parents were born that same year—one a few weeks before and the other a few weeks after the war broke out—and they told me stories about how my grandparents were forced to flee to the southern coast and raise their young children in refugee camps for the next three years, and how they grieved the loss of loved ones left up north that they ultimately would never see again.

Migration is a theme in many of my family members' stories. Grandpa Park grew up in Pyongyang (North Korea), and Grandpa Kim in Harbin (Manchuria), but both married women whose families were from the South. My grandfathers were both migrants, displaced and disconnected from their families of origin by colonization and war. They encountered barriers to establishing roots in the South but managed to have enough professional and economic success that my parents both grew up middle class for the most part and were well educated. Sometimes I wonder if the stories of my grandfathers may have influenced my own parents to more easily take the leap to uproot our family and move to an even more distant land to pursue graduate study.

When my family first arrived in the early 1980s, Iowa City, our small Midwestern college town, was 94 percent White (Goudy & Burke 1980). The locals frequently stared at me openly, asked where I was from, or asked whether I was Japanese or Chinese. Asking where I was from reminded me that they saw me as a foreigner, and asking if I was Japanese or Chinese reminded me that I was from an insignificant place—how mad that would have made my grandparents! The only representations of Koreans I saw were on reruns of the sitcom M*A*S*H, where we were depicted as dirty, desperate, and tragic people who depended on the beneficence of American saviors. When those Koreans showed up on the television screen, I couldn't change the channel fast enough.

I was 5 years old when we first came to the United States, and over the next few years I gave up nearly all of my home language and cultural identity to fit into the dominant culture, a process that Cummins (1984) termed *subtractive assimilation*. High levels of assimilation are associated with "negative mental health outcomes, including depression, anxiety, and low self-esteem" (Cheung & Swank 2019, 99), while embracing bicultural identity is a protective factor linked to greater resilience and better outcomes such as less substance abuse, better coping skills, decreased conflict with parents, and fewer depressive symptoms. I, unfortunately, was a textbook case of subtractive assimilation—torn between two sets of cultural expectations competing for my loyalty instead of being able to integrate them in a harmonious way. I gave up my home language and closeness with my parents and even longed to pass as White.

Internalized racism is another term that describes my early socialization into dominant culture—learning to see my Korean-ness as otherness, as shame. I measured my difference against White middle-class norms so that when a friend told me in sixth grade, "I don't think of you as Korean," meaning it as a compliment, I took it as such. This is an unfortunately common story I've heard among other Korean Americans of my generation.

In 1987, after struggling unsuccessfully to keep me and my brother connected to our language, culture, and family bonds, my parents moved us back to Korea. I attended all of middle and part of high school in Seoul and was given the opportunity to relearn my language and study Korean history, literature, and the cultural achievements of my ancestors. After years of learning who I was in relation to people who saw me as *other*, my identity was reshaped by being immersed in Korean society, where I was part of the dominant culture. Although it felt like a punishment at the time to be uprooted and have to start over in a place I had forgotten, in hindsight, it was the return to my roots that helped me to find family and familiarity in myself rather than only otherness.

How general perceptions of Koreans have shifted over time has also influenced my identity. Today, South Koreans have more control over how they are represented in the media. Now, each time a new Korean show pops up on my streaming service, or a K-pop song plays on the radio, it feels like a little bit of healing for the little girl who felt so flooded with shame when reruns of M*A*S*H came on the television.

Asian Americans in US History

Asian American identity was not something that was available to me growing up in my small Midwestern town in the 1980s. The term itself didn't exist in my vocabulary. My teachers at school used the term *Oriental*, and even the Korean grocery store in our town called itself an "Oriental market." I didn't understand what the word meant and thought it referred to Korean, Chinese, and Japanese people. I completely missed that it had been a term originally used to refer to Western Asia (or the Middle East) and that inherent in the word is an exaggerated otherness seen through Western eyes (Said 1978). Having access to Asian American identity might have been a powerful antidote to the otherness that I associated with my ethnicity back then.

But what is *Asian American* identity, and how was it forged? Can there even be such a thing today, given the vast diversity of people of Asian ancestry who inhabit the United States? Having access to historical knowledge that extends beyond the history of White people in this country is of critical importance in answering questions about Asian American identity. My perspective on not only Korean Americans but also America itself has been transformed as my historical knowledge expanded.

The recorded history of people of Asian descent in the Americas dates back centuries to when Spanish trade ships brought Asians—both free and enslaved—from India, Japan, and the Philippines to Mexico between the 16th and early 19th centuries (Luis 2024). The first significant wave of Chinese immigration to the United States occurred in the mid-19th century California Gold Rush, only to be shut down abruptly with the Chinese Exclusion Act of 1882 as anti-Asian sentiment intensified in the Western states. Asians were the first group to be excluded by law from immigrating to the United States—we were the first "illegal immigrants." Additional laws such as the Tydings-McDuffie Act of 1934, which denied Filipinos US citizenship, and the 1942 executive order that forced Japanese Americans into concentration camps make it clear that Asian Americans have long been seen as "conditional citizens" (Lalami 2020), whose status and belonging in this country are never guaranteed, regardless of their legal status.

This history cannot be looked at apart from the history of racial oppression in the United States as a whole—from the brutal removal of Indigenous people from their traditional lands, Jim Crow segregation following on the heels of Reconstruction, the Mexican-American War that ended in the forced annexation of what we now call the US Southwest, to US imperial and ideological expansion into the Pacific Islands (and South Korea). Although it has taken different forms, the violent history of racism and colonization connects all peoples of color in the United States, as does the history of resistance against it.

The Beginnings of Asian American Identity

"Asian American" was a political identity forged as part of the great wave of identity-based movements that rose up during the Civil Rights Movement. Historians such as Claire Jean Kim (2023) have documented how some Asian Americans who had lived through the earlier waves of White nativism distanced themselves from the Black freedom struggles. But in the late 1960s, young Americans of Asian descent formed "a movement that denounced white supremacy and called for solidarity with other communities of color" (p. 242).

Asian American Studies departments popped up in California and spread to universities across the country during this time as extensions of broader social justice movements, creating spaces for ethnic consciousness-raising and leadership training, and where scholars and students connected with working class communities, rejecting the expectation to assimilate and instead "fostering self-determination through a Third World consciousness" (Zhou & Ocampo 2016, 5).

Cultural historian and hip-hop music critic Jeff Chang (2016), of Chinese and Kānaka Maoli descent, writes with nostalgia about those formative years of Asian American identity: "Back then the term was still a courageous provocation, like a black leather jacket or a brown beret" (p. 139). For these descendants of working-class East Asians, Asian American identity was a "powerful metaphor for their struggle against White racism" (p. 142). Chang remembers the first Asian American Studies course he took in college, where students from different Asian backgrounds came together "trying to figure out what they had in common with the person sitting next to them. Together you were going to learn how to be Asian American" (p. 140). I love the excitement, hopefulness, and sense of possibility in his descriptions.

In those early days, the Asian American identity movement consisted largely of people born and raised in the United States. Due to decades of restrictive immigration policies, the foreign-born population had reached an all-time low in 1970 (Moslimani & Passel 2024). In contrast, today over half of Asian Americans are first-generation immigrants (foreign-born) (Krogstad & Im 2025). This fact—combined with the increasing barriers to teaching accurate and complete history in our schools today—means that many young Asian Americans have little to no personal connection with the history of Asian America or how this identity is fundamentally connected to civil rights, feminism, and Black Power movements (Eng & Han 2018).

I was one of those individuals Eng and Han (2018) described, having spent much of middle and high school in South Korea learning world history and Korean history but not Asian American history. I later took classes in college that first exposed me to historical events in which Asian Americans played a significant role and got my first glimpse of all that I didn't know. I needed to learn a lot more to feel a stronger connection to this history, but I recognized the significance of what I'd been missing all those years of growing up "Oriental," feeling foreign and disconnected to the historical narrative of this country.

Contradictions of Being Asian American

The contradictions of Asian American identity never felt more acute to me than the year-long period beginning with the COVID-19 pandemic, the racial reckoning following George Floyd's murder, and the Atlanta spa shooting in which six of the eight victims were women of Asian descent. One minute, I was afraid to walk through the city by myself for fear that I would be harassed by people who thought Asians were to blame for the pandemic. The next minute, I was in the streets marching alongside thousands of people seeking justice for Mr. Floyd and countless other Black victims of state brutality. Then, in March of 2021, with the murders of those aunties, like whiplash I was reminded that anti-Asian hate was real.

It was also during this time that I clearly understood what it meant to be a token minority. As the only full-time faculty member of color in our education department, my presence spared us from appearing all-White. If we were interviewing a prospective applicant of color for admissions, I was invited. Anything DEI-related had to include me because, well, no one really had to explain why. Yet on more than one occasion, faculty and students made comments in my presence about us not having any faculty of color. During a faculty search process, White colleagues remarked that we shouldn't hire faculty of color without being able to support them adequately. Too caught off guard to respond, I hoped that someone in the meeting would point out that *I* had been hired into this all-White department. These microaggressions—some that were even intended as anti-racist—made me feel invisible. But how could I be invisible *and* be the token minority? I was a token that held no value.

Being labeled as "over-represented" in various fields is also discombobulating. In my experience, being "over-represented" means there are more people like me than are "needed." I was once invited to interview for a position in a department where they already had one Asian American female professor. By the second time I was mistaken for her by her White colleagues, I knew I had no chance of being offered the position. More than my own disappointment, I felt a pang of sadness for the Asian American professor whose colleagues couldn't tell her apart from a stranger. Being an Asian American token minority means that you barely count as a person of color, because you are perceived as "White-adjacent," but if there are two of you then you'd be "over-represented." Such are the contradictions of Asian American privilege.

How Conditional Citizenship and the Model Minority Myth Uphold Racial Oppression

I became a legal permanent resident of the United States (aka, green card holder) over 20 years ago, but in order to attain US citizenship, I would have to give up Korean citizenship. This is a big deal for me—I would need to *feel* American first. When I refer to myself as a Korean American, or Asian American, it comes with self-consciousness and feelings of being an imposter. Despite having children who are citizens and a career in teaching (American students) and preparing future teachers (to teach in American schools), I still feel a pit of anxiety in my belly each time I get into the passport control line after flying back from overseas. I hesitate before attending protests, imagining getting handcuffed and taken to the Tacoma detention center instead of the King County jail. Although I have supported political campaigns, I have never made a call to the legislators in my district, afraid I'll be told that permanent residents don't have the privilege of political participation that citizens enjoy. Can I call myself Asian American if my legal status excludes me from fully claiming the "American" part of that identity? If I don't feel that America wants me?

Lalami (2020) writes that conditional citizens have to demonstrate their "contribution" to society to prove their worth and display their loyalty because it can be questioned at any point. When our belonging can be challenged or even revoked because of our race, when 9 out of 10 Asian Americans report having personally experienced discrimination, and when these experiences are frequently related to being perceived as foreigners (Ruiz et al. 2023), we have to wonder how this perpetual state of not-belonging or belonging-with-contingencies impacts us.

Growing up in Iowa, I didn't have to be told explicitly that my best option was to leave as little trace of my difference as I could, to become a good little Asian girl, a model minority. Several chapters in this book discuss the myth of the model minority and the pressures that some of us internalized and had to break free from (see Chapter 1 and Chapter 12 for an in-depth discussion). The model minority myth not only keeps us compliant and self-policing but also pits us against other groups of color in an effort to justify blaming Black people in particular for their suffering. Jeff Chang (2016) writes pointedly about this painful positioning: "What does it mean to be the evidence that racism is not real?" (p. 144). Reminding us that Asians were able to gain the rights of birthright citizenship through the Fourteenth Amendment, he states that "the very idea of an immigrant or an Asian American is predicated upon the freedom struggle of African Americans" (p. 149).

The involvement of some Asian Americans in the Harvard and UNC admissions cases in 2022, which effectively ended affirmative action in college admissions, was a devastating betrayal against the broader coalitional anti-racist and social justice movements that have continued since the Civil Rights era. Although journalists have pointed out that the Asian American students recruited by Edward Blum's group, funded through conservative think tanks, were ultimately just used for publicity purposes (e.g., Kaur 2022), I was painfully reminded of Chang's (2016) indictment to Asian Americans that "You were part of the ruination" (p. 148), when some of us were willing to use our power "to make things worse for other communities of color" (p. 154). It's hard to describe the waves of grief and anger that come over me to see the dismantling of decades of hard-fought battles by recruiting people who look like me. "You want to walk away from being Asian American" (p. 155), wrote Chang a decade ago, and the resonance triggers today a shame that hurts more than being excluded.

Kim (2023) warns that if Asian Americans only notice and resist our structural disadvantages relative to White people, we may fail to notice and resist anti-Black racism, remain silent in the face of mass deportations of Latine people, dismiss how we are implicated in the genocide taking place in Palestine (which Viet Thanh Nguyen [2024] reminds us is part of Western Asia), or turn away from the international refugee crisis. Efforts to protect the narrow interests of the smallest definitions of "we-ness" will get us nowhere. Instead of such a limited solidarity born of scarcity and zero-sum thinking, Nguyen (2025) calls for an *expansive solidarity*, "wherein kinship grows between unlikely others in an ever-widening circle" (p. 44). Such an expansion is dangerous to the status quo—when Asian Americans can recognize both the victim and oppressor *within ourselves*. "Expansive solidarity helps us recognize that we can be both in turn—even at the same moment" (p. 55), and it is in this recognition that the contradictions of Asian American identity cease to hold us back, releasing the possibilities for our outrage toward injustice to extend farther outward.

Becoming AANHPI

Even with the excitement and optimism of the early days of Asian American identity formation, Chang (2016) recalls that there was a sense of "instability" inherent to the census category of AANHPI that attempted to include groups who shared few commonalities:

> Panethnicity, you learned, was a creation of the state—a provocation turned census category. The state had been blunt and overboard. It lumped all kinds of people of Asian and Pacific Islander descent together. It created new margins . . . (p. 140)

Despite the dilemma surrounding the question of "Who is us?," Chang (2016) describes this panethnic identity formation as having signaled new possibilities and hope for a generational shift in intergroup relations:

> Building Asian Americanness was a bottom-up project of unity in diversity. But also, what could be more 'E pluribus unum' than people from all these ancient warring cultures figuring out how to get along on American soil? (pp. 142–143)

Whether the AANHPI census category is little more than a top-down classification that has outlived its usefulness, or an expansive coalition identity that holds potential for strategic and substantive collaboration, there is clearly much work to be done in order for AANHPI to become an identity that all of us who are brought under its umbrella can choose to embrace. Chapter 2 in this book documents a conversation that took place with our Native Hawaiian and Pacific Islander (NHPI) authors and addresses important aspects of this issue. Asian Americans must take a more active role in reimagining what a shared identity could look like, rather than assuming that Native Hawaiians and Pacific Islander Americans would be seamlessly included into the fold. Indeed, assuming that some of us can represent all of us has led to harmful erasures with real-world impacts on NHPI children and families, and we hope that our book and the conversations that come out of it can contribute to repair and toward building AANHPI identity into something the Census Bureau may never have intended—something with meaning, self-determination, and true collective power.

There are, to be sure, histories that connect us. Many of us, our families, and our ancestors have been impacted by Western imperialism, including US imperial expansion in the Pacific, and European imperialism in Western Asia and the Indian subcontinent. The important differences between us are how we are positioned and position ourselves in relation to colonization today—with some of us who are Indigenous and others of us who are voluntary and involuntary settlers, we may have significantly different perspectives on the US government and what citizenship means to us. Our differences are opportunities to share our stories and visions for a better future for our children, families, and communities. We need identity coalitions that don't require ignoring our histories or minimizing present-day tensions—coalitions that can expand to hold us all.

Contradictions of Identity as Spaces of Possibility

In their book *Racial Melancholia, Racial Dissociation*, David Eng and Shinhee Han (2018) note that a key difference between first- and second-generation immigrants is the extent to which individuals see themselves as part of a collective, with a shared history and future. Immigrants who have not grown up understanding the racial history of the United States, who were members of dominant ethnic groups in their home countries, initially have little context to help them make sense of the experiences of exclusion and discrimination they encounter, and the racial melancholia this can cause. In my own case, I have elements of both first- and second-generation characteristics, in that unlike many of my friends or my children who were born in the United States and identify primarily as Asian American, I have experienced what it feels like to be a member of the majority group in a society whose language, culture, and identities are dominant and center in all aspects of social life. Here in the United States, I am someone who made the conscious choice to reside in this country, unlike my children who had no say in the matter and have no other place to call home. I imagine it might hurt more to experience exclusion from the only home you've ever known. I have another option I can choose if the racial melancholia ever gets to be too much: I can return to South Korea. My sons have no such option. As a mom, this breaks my heart a little. I wish there was a place on this earth where they could take it for granted that they belong.

They teach me that my perspective is mine, but not necessarily theirs. The first time someone called my younger son by an ethnic slur, he didn't come home crying. In fact, I only learned about it months later, because, as it turns out, for my American kid it was just another day. I've come to understand through my children's responses to racial exclusion, through reading every story told in this book, and through my reflection and writing process for this chapter, something that my kids, that Jeff Chang and other AANHPI thinkers figured out years ago, as the "In-Betweens," Asian Americans are familiar with living in the spaces between privilege and oppression. The contradictions of AANHPI identity—being both privileged and oppressed, held up as model minorities *and* as perpetual foreigners—can offer opportunities for us to recognize the incredible complexity and full humanity inherent to every person.

> To see beyond their own pain toward other people's suffering, toward the real justice they and those with whom they share this vision might be able to create together . . . When they choose to fight, because you know that someday they will have to, you hope it will not be merely for greater numbers and more power if those numbers lead away from equity, if that power is used to perpetuate injustice and inequality. (Chang 2016, 156–157)

How, as educators, can we ensure that the children in our care—when the time comes and they have to fight—will know what to do, and choose equity for all? How can we, as teachers, parents, teacher-educators, policymakers, and community leaders, serve as true and authentic models of the citizens we hope they will become?

Grounding ourselves in the history of our people and our relationships to other people of color is critically important. This allows me to accept that although my people have been colonized by other nations, now I am a settler colonist on the traditional lands of the Coast Salish people. As I struggle with being showcased as the token minority while simultaneously feeling invisible and devalued in my workplace, this country's history and present remind me that it was multiple layers of economic, educational, linguistic, and light-skin privilege, and decades of efforts of Black and Brown activists and organizers opening doors for it to be possible for someone like me to hold a university faculty position in the first place, while too many of those doors still remain closed for too many others.

As a child, learning myself through the eyes of others caused me to see my differences as deficiencies. Today, learning myself through the eyes of AANHPI authors such as Jeff Chang and Viet Thanh Nguyen, the authors who contributed to this book, and my AANHPI family, friends, colleagues, community members, and my own children, has been a transformative and healing experience of expansive identity and solidarity formation.

So Many More Voices . . .

I am a Korean-born, transracial adoptee, raised in a White, Jewish family. For far too many years, I felt that I was not "enough." Not Korean enough, Asian American enough, or Jewish enough. However, now I know that the more I stand in my power in the different communities I am a part of, I diminish my impostor syndrome and hopefully mitigate those feelings in others like me.

Liz SoHyeon Kleinrock
Author, Consultant, Educator
Teach and Transform
Washington, DC

CHAPTER 5

Searching for Who You Are

Three Generations of Educators

BY KIRA LEEKEENAN AND DEBBIE LEEKEENAN

For many of us, families, be they chosen or inherited, offer close connections and a sense of belonging that is timeless. Family members may share traditions, like the one month-of-life naming celebration in Chinese families, where our photo was taken. They give us visible heirloom artifacts, like this four-generation photo, and less visible messages about values and ways of being. Both traditions and heirlooms remind us of family once they are gone. They also connect us to race, ethnicity, culture, and language. They situate our identities in a sociocultural history that connects us to centuries-old ancestors. But what happens when our own specific history comes from diverse races, ethnicities, cultures, and linguistic backgrounds? How do we find ourselves when the communities that make us who we are teach conflicting values, behaviors, and traditions? This essay explores the ways in which three generations of women from the same family search for identity and belonging in society through their work, their interactions with each other, and their internal process.

Introduction

Mabel G. Lee, Debbie LeeKeenan, and Kira LeeKeenan are three generations of Chinese/Chinese American women in the same family who have spent their careers as teachers, striving to change the status quo. Mabel is Debbie's mom and Kira's Paw Paw. After Mabel passed away, Debbie and Kira started sharing stories with each other that illuminated the interconnectedness of both their careers as justice-oriented teachers and their process for naming, claiming, and understanding their racial identity as Chinese Americans. This essay starts with the story of Mabel, whose story was told through the practice of oral tradition, and is written as remembered by Debbie. The tone of Kira and Debbie's stories are different as they benefit from the natural conversations and reflection that come from writing together. This process allowed us to see the connective tissue between making sense of our

Four generations of LeeKeenan women (2004).

racial and cultural identities and finding places to belong. While we never had these conversations with Mabel, from how she talked about teaching and her students, we feel comfortable saying that she did find a "sense of home" in her role as an educator.

Searching for belonging is often how you find out who you are. Across our family's stories, we have learned how complicated and dynamic the process of understanding one's racial identity can be. Even within one family, our stories of racial acceptance and searching for belonging are so different. We invite you into our family to learn about the varied trajectories that took us into our careers as teachers and how those paths shaped our understanding of self.

Mabel: "I am going to be a teacher" (written by Debbie)

Mabel Gwon Lee (1923–2013) was my mother and Kira's maternal grandmother (in Chinese we say "Paw Paw"). She was born in the North End of Boston, Massachusetts, in the back of a Chinese laundry but lived her early years in Hong Kong, Guangdong, China.

Mabel's parents, my Paw Paw (婆婆 maternal grandmother) and Gong Gong (公公 maternal grandfather), came to the United States in the early 1900s for a better life from Hoiping, Guangdong, China. The Chinese used the term Gum Shan, or "Gold Mountain," to refer to San Francisco, and generally the western coast of the United States, often the first point of entry for many Chinese coming to America. While North America was referred to as the land of gold, the Chinese immigrants arriving since the late 1800s had a more difficult life than they had in China, experiencing prejudice and exclusion and difficulty making ends meet.

Gong Gong (公公) and Paw Paw (婆婆) started a Chinese laundry business first in Boston, then later in New York City, where I was born. The laundry business was hard work, and the family lived in the back to save money. Gong Gong (公公) worked in the front of the store and engaged with the customers since he could speak English. He also sorted clothes and wrapped packages. Paw Paw (婆婆), who could not read or write in Chinese or speak English, did all the physical work in the back—washing clothes, hanging them to dry, and ironing. Mabel told the story that after her mother gave birth to her and each of her four siblings, she got out of bed immediately to work in the laundry. This strong work ethic was forever woven into the family's fabric.

Mabel was the second oldest in her family and the first of her generation to go to college. Her parents insisted she live at home while attending college so she could help with the family laundry business. So, she folded laundry each day while attending Hunter College and then became a New York City public school teacher. Mabel led the way for her sister and her many nieces and nephews to attend college.

Mabel's first job as a teacher was working with gifted children at Hunter College Elementary School. While she enjoyed these children, she wanted to work with children who had more challenges, who were immigrants like herself. She got a job at P.S. 33 in New York City and ended up teaching there until she retired. She writes, in a personal reflection for a religious retreat, "I wanted to work with poor children, families who needed help, children with social emotional challenges, and learning difficulties. For more than 30 years I worked hard and gained satisfaction in ministering to the needs of these children." Teaching was her calling.

Debbie: Who am I?

Though I was born in New York City, I felt like an outsider while I was growing up. I was different, and that was a problem. I am Chinese American, born of an immigrant working-class family. My grandparents fit the image of stereotypical Chinese immigrants; on my father's side they opened a Chinese restaurant, on my mother's side a Chinese laundry business. At home, my parents spoke exclusively in English to me and my brother because they wanted our family to be "American." Yet my grandparents who lived with us spoke nothing but Cantonese.

I learned to live with contradiction, recognizing that "who I was" and my search for belonging was a messy process. Several memories stand out: Growing up in the 1950s, I never saw myself in the learning materials and language of school, the teachers, the administrators, or the photographs and pictures on the walls of the building. I read *The Five Chinese Brothers* by Claire Huchet Bishop (1938), illustrated by Kurt Wiese. The illustrations were cartoonlike figures with bright yellow skin and slanted eyes. I remember thinking, "No one in the family looks like this." "Why did they call us the yellow race? Yellow is the color in the crayon box. My skin is tan."

When my family moved to the suburbs of New Jersey looking for better schools, on the first day of third grade on the playground, a child came up to me and said, "Last year we had a Mexican; what did we get this year?" I remember the dead silence. No one said anything, not the children, the teachers, or playground monitors. Everyone just stared. I felt ashamed and alone. I knew then I would be a teacher one day, and I wouldn't let anyone be treated this way or feel so bad.

In high school, my friends were White and Jewish. I did not want to have Asian friends. I never thought of myself as Chinese in public; seeing other Chinese people was like seeing myself in the mirror, and I didn't like it. My parents encouraged me to spend a summer in Taiwan during my teen years, hoping that time in the "motherland" might make me more comfortable being Chinese. Yet that experience made me even more confused. While I looked Chinese, I did not speak like the girls in Taiwan or even walk like them. I did not feel like I belonged there, and I did not feel like I belonged in America. Everywhere, everyone just stared. Not Chinese enough, not American enough.

While these themes of searching for belonging, feeling ashamed and excluded, and denial and confusion around my Chinese identity were challenging growing up, over time I learned to be bolder, stand stronger, and advocate for myself and others.

Kira: What are you?

I was recently at a security checkpoint, in line with friends to see Janet Jackson. The security guard looked at me and said, "What are you?" I smiled and said, "I'm a human being." He said, "No, I mean—"I cut him off. "I know what you mean, I'm Chinese and White." He smiled widely. "I thought so; you look just like my wife." My friends in line were appalled that someone would ask me, "What are you?" I was shocked that they were shocked. I get asked that all the time.

The first time I remember being asked this question was when I was 16, but it was long before this moment that my racial identity caused feelings of isolation and confusion. My dad's family is White, his ancestors immigrating from Ireland. My mom's family is Chinese, her ancestors immigrating from China. In hindsight, race was central to our family dynamics, but as a child I just felt tension and confusion. Race and culture shaped big childhood events like holidays and family gatherings. Christmastime brought big family banquets on my mom's side with lots of second cousins and distantly related aunties I didn't really know. I remember dumplings and Chinese pastries, bright colors, murmurs of Chinese leaving watermarks on these memories. On my dad's side, family meant aunts and uncles and first cousins only. I remember feeling closer to this side, but I also think I knew that my dad's family wielded more power and privilege, and I desperately wanted to understand how to fit in. I now know that interacting with our extended family was jarring for my parents; not just me. But we didn't talk about it. Today, we know how important it is for children to see representations of themselves in books, pop culture, and in society. It is just as important for families to see representations of themselves. Early on in my childhood, race and culture didn't feel like safe topics to broach; my parents struggled to find peace within their divergent cultural backgrounds, and we lacked models of similar families. We needed to be seen as much as I, as an individual, wanted to be understood.

Additionally, any confusion I felt around my own racial and cultural identity I guarded inwardly, leaving memories to be analyzed later as an adult. An example of one such memory comes from when I was a young child. I remember vacationing with my cousins on my dad's side of the family and their friends showing expressions of shock when they found out my cousins and I were related by blood. The fair skin, blond, and reddish hues of my paternal cousins did not resemble my darker coloring anywhere. I loved my cousins and wanted people to look at us and see us as family. Unfortunately, we can't change how people see us. These early experiences, which were marked by outsiders making sense of what my racial identity meant, left me feeling like my identity as a Chinese American individual was something I had to overcome, and wished to minimize.

As I entered adulthood, I became more comfortable living in the space of racial ambiguity. I am not White passing, but I confuse enough people that I don't feel the same sort of discrimination other racial categories face—people just can't "place me." I know now that this is a privilege I grew up with. I also now recognize that it has created a sense of displacement for me. I didn't have a racial community that I felt I belonged to.

Mabel: Highlighting Children's Own Stories for Learning (Debbie)

A child's story about going on a trip.

My mom was my first teacher and role model. I remember her saying she had the best job in the world and that she loved her students. When I was 5 years old, she would show me pictures of her students when they went on field trips. I also remember her doing a lot of prep work for her classroom at night. While watching TV, she would cut out pictures from magazines to create games for her students. When my mom died in 2013, I found many teacher-made materials she had saved for over 60 years as I was cleaning out her house. The paper was yellowed from age and practically disintegrating, but the cutout magazine pictures were still there. I also found a collection of classroom books with dictated stories and illustrations by the children. One of them included crayon drawings by her children on a field trip to the zoo and the children's dictations under each drawing handwritten by my mother. Another book was about their favorite foods at home. These language experience books were stories and illustrations made by children based on their own experiences from their home and lives. Mabel was responsive to children's interests, hearing their stories, foregrounding their experiences as relevant and important. Did my mom save these books for me to find many years later? These artifacts from her teaching were an "heirloom," highlighting her commitment to a culturally responsive pedagogy, way ahead of its time.

Mabel cooks fried rice with children in class (1930).

Debbie: Becoming a Mixed-Race Family

I began my college years in an identity crisis. I became an Asian Studies major at Oberlin College in part to explore my own roots and learn more about my ethnic identity. I joined the Asian Studies group to find a community.

I also met a White Irish American who became my life partner. For the most part, both our families accepted our biracial marriage, although there were objections on both sides by a few family members who predicted there would be trouble if we got married. As our family expanded to include our two children, we wanted them to be raised in communities and schools where they would be embraced for who they are. We were a mixed-race family encountering the world differently than other families. I looked for more diverse books that could provide mirrors and windows (Bishop 1990) so my children could see themselves represented and the world around them too. Holidays and cultural traditions were important for me to pass on. Kira and her brother were very excited to plan a special Lunar New Year activity to share with their preschool classrooms. We celebrated cultural and traditional holidays like Chinese New Year, Easter, and Christmas, and we had many extended family gatherings and ate cultural foods. However, the challenges and tensions of being different, of what it felt like to be mixed race, were never clearly articulated within the family. As Kira reflected earlier, we didn't talk much about our feelings and emotions.

Looking back, I now wonder why? Growing up, I never experienced talking about problems. In fact, I remember my mom saying, "Don't hang out your dirty laundry" and "Keep a brave face." However, I also experienced the cognitive dissonance of working hard to be the model minority and please my parents, and at other times fighting the stereotypical Chinese mode of being obedient, quiet, and passive. In adulthood, I was loud, enthusiastic, and an activist. "You don't act Chinese, Mom," my own children would say. A lot of conflicting emotions were not processed enough. It took many more years for me to feel comfortable being vulnerable.

Kira: Finding My Identity Home

In my early 20s I started my career as a teacher. My first job was teaching high school English in a Title 1 school that served mostly Latine and Black students. Teaching these students was one of the first times that I remember consciously embracing my Chinese Irish American identity, although the motivation was less that I was Chinese and more that I was not White. Students recognized me as a person of color—even though they also felt the need to ask me that question: What are you? They saw me as someone who was safe, someone who could possibly understand what it meant to be *othered* (Omi & Winant 2014). My development as an educator ran parallel to my understanding of my place within the AANHPI community. I began to see my "otherness" as a superpower, a way to connect with others who had also felt like they didn't belong. I'm grateful to have found teaching as a young adult, because I was hungry to belong to a community. I found that community in other educators who were committed to justice and equity-oriented teaching; I also found that sense of belonging with my students, other people of color.

As I made my way through a master's and PhD program, conversations about race were central to my continuing development as a teacher, teacher-educator, and researcher. Through academic lessons that began to connect identity and the sociocultural context in which the idea of races are born, I found the language that supported my teaching practice and an understanding of my experience as a biracial woman. I am so grateful for these conversations, as they made me a better educator, citizen, mother, daughter, sister, and friend.

Kira: Becoming a Social Justice Educator

As a teacher, and now teacher-educator, my commitments have always been focused on social and racial justice. I think of social justice as teaching and learning that intends to advance equity across social identity groups (e.g., race, class, gender, sexual orientation, ability), promote critical perspectives, and nurture social action (Carlisle et al. 2006; Dover 2009). In practice, this means questioning and acting in ways to change the inequities, hierarchies, and injustices that currently exist in our society. Racial justice means critically examining the ways that racism operates in our society, institutions, and in schools, within one-on-one interactions and making efforts to eliminate racism by intentionally acting in anti-racist ways (Kendi 2023). Both commitments are far from simple, but to delineate these terms into something very basic, very human, they mean that I always try to teach in ways that make visible those who have felt or feel invisible. This is why I associate my own awakening as a biracial, Chinese Irish American woman with my work as an educator.

In so many ways, the work I do to advocate for my students, specifically students of color, and to teach in ways that promote justice, equity, and anti-racism, is also advocating for myself and my right to be seen. Through inquiry, my students explore their funds of knowledge, their existing literacies, and the stories they tell themselves about teaching, learning, and school. A lot of my work with students involves unlearning the harmful discourses that tell us we don't have every right to show up as our authentic, complex, messy selves.

Debbie: Finding Belonging and Embracing Conflict

My cultural identity story and being part of our multiracial family directly influenced my educational philosophy and trajectory. My lived experiences with prejudice and rejection, identifying with groups that were marginalized, and having a strong sense of empathy resulted in wanting to be an educator who centered diversity, equity, and belonging at the core of whatever I did. I began as a Vista volunteer in North Philadelphia working with Head Start and later was an assistant youth director at a settlement house on the Lower East Side of New York City.

My teaching career began in earnest as a public school elementary special education teacher in Brookline, Massachusetts. This was one of my all-time favorite positions because of our principal, Alvin Fortune, a Black leader with great vision and presence. He created an inclusive community where we met regularly in dialogic study groups before it became popular to do that. Al Fortune was a role model, mentor, and outstanding example of an educational leader. It was also empowering that my first boss was a person of color.

During the next three decades, I found my voice as a social justice educator and became comfortable in my own skin as a Chinese American. As director of the Tufts University Eliot–Pearson Children's School, my core focus was creating a community of learners for children and adults while guiding the program through an anti-bias transformation over a long period of time. This process involved creating a safe and brave space for reflection, risk-taking, learning, and growth, and ensuring that all students, families and staff felt visible, valued, and validated. I learned quickly that I needed to model being vulnerable, so I began to share my personal stories about searching for belonging and going "public" with my identity journey. By sharing my stories, others became more comfortable sharing theirs, and the teachers' commitment to teach with an anti-bias stance grew.

Over my 17-year tenure at Tufts University Eliot-Pearson Children's School, the program became known for its anti-bias education. It also is powerful to see how the educators who worked there have continued to bring anti-bias work into their current roles and jobs. Simultaneously, I was fueled by a long-term collaboration and friendship with my mentor and colleagues, Louise Derman-Sparks and John Nimmo, as we chronicled some of the lessons we learned during our long journey as social justice educators in our writings (Derman-Sparks et al. 2023) and two films on anti-bias education. (LeeKeenan & Nimmo 2021, 2024). It is critical to find your allies to support and sustain you for the long haul.

While my Chinese culture emphasized not "rocking the boat" and keeping peace and harmony, my professional experience taught me that conflict, tension, and pushing against cultural norms is when change happens. Anti-bias and social justice work is inherently about change. There will be the inevitable dissonance and pushback when you are talking about diversity and equity, because we all have different identities, histories, experiences, and contexts, which leads to different perspectives, values, and beliefs—and we "carry our ghosts with us" (Lightfoot 2003). The intersectionality of our own social identities and lived experiences impact how much we can manage discomfort and risk-taking and balance them with the need for safety. We may have different viewpoints, but when we struggle together, and really listen compassionately, we are often surprised. We can always learn something, even if we don't always agree.

Conclusion

It wasn't until we wrote down our three stories that we started to see the similarities between them. Several themes stood out for us: the inherited struggle to claim who we are while wearing our "educator" hats, the blessings of tradition we get from our family, and the unspoken actions that we model—such as hard work, the preservation of cultural traditions, and education centered on social change. It was particularly interesting for Kira and Debbie to realize that they were most comfortable being loud, vulnerable, hardworking, and conflict-facing Chinese American women when working as educators. Our collective inheritance of becoming social justice educators was "passed down" through three generations by example, observation, experience, and support. This recognition also raises the question about what early narratives about being Chinese and female did we internalize and reproduce?

Many writers of color living in America have written about the challenges of growing up non-White in America. There is no "quick fix" for this societal reality, and it cannot be tackled by one person. However, one person, and even better, one family, can foster community and help each other feel seen, especially if that means feeling *seen* by others outside your family. Our stories collectively showcase different quests for belonging, but they similarly emphasize that creating learning spaces of belonging for students is central to our teaching pedagogies, *and* to our identity.

In these conversations about our journeys, we find and claim our racial and ethnic identities. The racial groups in which we belong are much more complicated than a census bureau can suggest. We can't rely on published texts to represent the many different identities that exist in our classrooms. What is published is woefully behind the many ways we present ourselves as human. Our identities shape how others interact with us, how we interact with the world, and how we perceive our students in either a positive or negative way. We as educators and teacher-educators need to create opportunities to talk about our intersectional identities, model vulnerability for students and preservice teachers, and create opportunities for students to explore their social identities in ways that support belonging. As educators, this process of making sense of our own racial and ethnic identities is one of the most important lessons we can *give ourselves* and teach to the next generation.

Authors' Note: Writing this essay together has been a gift to us. Our stories are also an heirloom gift to our children and grandchildren. Through our stories, we have found moments of awakening. Hearing these stories for the first time brought new perceptions of each other and a new sense of appreciation for and belonging with each other. This naming, claiming, and understanding of one's racial and cultural identity in the context of family is a complicated and messy process. It is also one that we continue to embrace and explore. Since each generation brings their own context and experiences to these journeys, we look forward to bringing future generations of LeeKeenans into this conversation.

CHAPTER 6

Weaving a Lei of Kuleana, Empathy, and Commitment

DONNA ELIZABETH KALEIOKALANI REID-HAYES

In Hawaiian tradition, the concept of moʻokūʻauhau, or genealogy, is taken to mean more than the generational map or lineage of our families (Saffery 2016). We think of the many genealogies that weave through our lives—kūpuna (ancestors or elders), mentors, education, careers, opportunities, and even trauma and tragedy. Each offers something to the overall moʻolelo (stories) of our lives.

I am an educator. I work with 5- and 6-year-olds in kindergarten. I am of Native Hawaiian and Caucasian descent. I was born in Hilo on Hawaiʻi Island and was raised mostly in Honolulu on the island of Oʻahu. I was proud to be what I called "part Hawaiian" without a deep understanding of what that meant. I was a blonde, blue-eyed Hawaiian, wondering if I was Hawaiian enough and too timid to seek entry into my own culture. As my doctoral research into Hawaiian Culture-Based Education and Indigeneity developed, I could see how my approach to education was shifting. I found that my self-identity as a Hawaiian was shifting. Eventually, I would give myself permission to embrace my Native Hawaiian identity. I would finally say, "I am Hawaiian."

I am inspired by Hawaiian scholars Mehana Vaughan (2016) and Makalapua Alencastre (2015) to think of moʻokūʻauhau as the weaving of a beautiful and intricate lei. As a lei maker gathers materials for the lei she will weave, she is careful not to take more than she needs. She looks for the right combination of blossoms, ferns, and leaves to create what she envisions. We gather the stories, experiences, and relationships that impact who we are and who we will become. We are each weaving a lei, resplendent and uniquely our own. It is critical that we honor that work within each other.

Each child comes with their own moʻokūʻauhau, both familial and experiential. Their stories, family history, and cultural traditions are carried within them, influencing their actions and attitudes. I share the metaphor of weaving a lei with families on Back to School Night to help them grasp the concept of moʻokūʻauhau. A child is born already weaving their own lei, developing a sense of self in connection to their experiences and their culture. As educators, our task is to offer opportunities and challenges as blossoms for the child to weave into their lei. As I awakened to my own cultural identity, I saw clearly the need to honor each child's unique journey into self-discovery and agency.

In education today, we are seeing a focus on curricular objectives, data-driven practice, assessment, and children being reduced to a series of data points. We are losing sight of the greater importance of education: developing and empowering a learner to pursue their own ideas long after they leave our classrooms. In the busyness of school, we need a reminder that we are nurturing children to grow into engaged, autonomous individuals who can thrive in a complex world. Will they know who they are?

Will they feel valued? Will they believe their ideas are worthy? Each time we honor the initiative and individual thoughts of a child, we build upon the idea that they are deserving, capable, and enough.

I have three moʻolelo that I offer as provocation. Each of us read stories from our unique kuanaʻike (perspective). My hope is that these moʻolelo encourage you to think about your own moʻokūʻauhau and what drives your actions. What is the lei you are weaving, and what will you add next? In understanding more deeply our own unique perspective, we are more likely to support our haumāna (students) and their ʻohana (families) in delving deeply into their own moʻokūʻauhau and their own identities.

Moʻolelo: My First Days of School

We had just moved to Honolulu from Hilo. Tears were flying in all directions! My first day of kindergarten! "You didn't say goodbye!" "Wait! I need another kiss!" My heart pounded, my mother was trying to smile, to be encouraging, but nothing calmed me. Eventually, we left . . . walking to the car . . . we had failed.

I went home to my new house to climb the shower tree in the front yard. My heart began to calm, my tears dried, and my mother went into the house to gather laundry to hang on the line. I didn't know what to do. I had gotten what I wanted. I was not at school, but now what? I climbed higher and higher until I reached the spot I had claimed as my own, scanning the street and getting to know my new world.

We headed to school the next day to try again. My mom was holding her breath, trying to be brave. She pulled at my hand, rushing me along the sidewalk outside the fence. She pulled me through the gate, letting it slam behind me. To me, she seemed shaken. We walked to my classroom. Miss Tan loomed over me.

"Good morning. Come on in and say goodbye to your mommy." The tears began again as I looked at the children already playing—building with blocks, painting at an easel, laughing with friends. The same panic returned. I knew no one. My heart pounded. I couldn't let go of my mom's hand. She tried to pry my fingers from hers, but my crying got louder, more fitful. I clung desperately to her hand, and again we left, retreating to the parking lot. Back to the safety of our house and my tree.

Finally, on the fourth day, we entered with more strength. My mom seemed to have a plan. I wonder now if she had talked to another mother for advice or if she and the teacher had made a decision together. She walked me to a small, friendly-looking child.

"This is Kathy. She lives in our neighborhood," said my mother encouragingly. She placed my hand in Kathy's hand and fled! Years later, a mother myself by then, I learned that she ran to the car, tears streaming down her cheeks. This time seemingly successful, she returned home to the laundry and my tree, empty in the front yard.

Memories of those first days encourage me to crouch down, opening my arms for a hug. "Good morning. I'm Mrs. Hayes. You can call me Aunty Donna. I'm so excited to meet you." Some parents push their children forward.

"Say hello to your teacher." Some offer a handshake or a hug. Some are nervous, wondering how the goodbye will go. My memories guide me, softening my tone, and slowing our transition to say goodbye to parents.

"Tell mom to be good! We are going to have a fun day!" To the parents, "We will take good care of him, not to worry."

My first full day was a blur of painting, laughing, stories, and snacks. I loved the blocks, drawing with crayons on large sheets of paper, making books, and singing songs with our class. Kathy became my friend and my entry into this new world of school. A world I would come to see as a second home, a haven, a place of excitement and growth. I would reside there quietly, at the fringes, always a bit cautious before joining in.

The 5-year-old in me thinks carefully about what I will offer the children on their first day. There will be a bit of paint, some great stories, gentle hugs, and time to listen to each other—time to begin to form the relationships that will be so important in our work.

My classroom asserts its identity, uniquely set in Hawaiʻi—with paintings of kalo (the taro plant) and an ʻauwai bioswale (a vegetation irrigation channel) for children to explore. The images offered in this story remind us that the learning environment we create reflects our values and our beliefs (Biermeier, 2015). These images are meant to provoke and inspire. This moʻolelo drifts between the present and the past as I carry the history of this place and of my own ʻohana with me into my teaching. I think of those who traveled this path before me, and my awareness of the connections to our collective past encourages me to consider each child and the histories they carry within them. I am humbled to honor those who have come before us.

Moʻolelo: A Feeling of Place

I am sitting in a preschool classroom in Reggio Emilia, Italy, sketching what I see. My fingers ache to touch the colored plastic cylinders, the slices of gnarled wood, and the flower heads that are drying on the table. My own classroom creeps in at the sides of my view—oil pastel drawings of Night Blooming Cereus created so carefully by the children in the first days of school line the walls. Their bold strokes are standing out on a black background. A hint of pink tinges the edges of some petals. A bee climbs over a stem. The children are learning to observe closely. We display their work as important pieces of art so they will see their capability. The beauty of their efforts lifts their shoulders and brightens their eyes.

Child doing a close observation drawing of the Night Blooming Cereus.

A photo captures a child looking intently into the center of a blossom growing on the rock wall surrounding our school.

Time mingles: my Tūtū (grandmother) as a young girl, laughing with friends just inside that wall, the blossoms wilting as the sun rises in the sky. I see her long skirt swaying as she makes her way to the classroom carrying books clasped to her chest. These drawings and the huakaʻi (trip) across campus tell the children they are part of something larger, deeper than what they fully comprehend. They are connected to those who came before them and to those who will come long after they have left this place. They are nā keiki o ka puna hou (children of the new spring).

The chatter of our group of visitors brings me back to the strange and inspiring setting. I realize I have been gathering experiences, coming to Italy to seek out blossoms that will add texture, color, and fragrance to the lei I am weaving. My lei is my own, uniquely woven, intertwining my experiences to create my particular worldview. I am aware of the blossoms, the beauty I am taking in; however, I am oblivious to the seeds that have embedded themselves in my heart, waiting for a later date to unfurl. I am unaware of the lei that is yet to be brought out into the light.

As I chat with others in my study group, some are making lists of what they will need in order to recreate a Reggio look in their classrooms or to replicate projects we have seen represented here. I know we cannot recreate Reggio Emilia in our own schools, but we can be inspired to create our own schools for the democratic education of children within our own contexts and our own cultures. Schools where children are researchers, autonomous learners in their own right. Schools where beauty, nature, the arts, family, and community sit at the center of learning environments to inspire and capture the learners' imaginations. Schools that embrace their place, the community, and the culture within which they exist.

At home, as you reach our classroom door, your eyes are drawn to photos. Children laughing in the loʻi, a look of concentration as a child counts multicolored buttons, parents and children crossing a river together, a tiny hand exploring the texture of a yellow-green kalo leaf, two boys building a dam with smooth stones in the ʻauwai, and a child beaming with pride at the top of the pole. The word inspire is prominently defined "to fill someone with confidence and a desire to do something, to breathe, to give breath to life."

The tone is set. The identity of this space is clear. This is a place of children. They are encouraged to be adventurous, creative, and independent. There is joy on their faces, light in their eyes. Process documentation dots the cabinets sharing their work, their wonderings, and their explorations.

Entering the room captures the senses. Bold paintings of kalo line the walls. Close observation drawings of leaves hang from the ceiling, displayed in family groupings, sometimes three generations together. Their perspectives are often shared, each artist creating their own interpretation of the leaf in front of them. The room is set up for exploration, inviting small hands to turn over sea glass, noting its uneven shape and heft, or experience the texture of monk seal fur. Rich to the senses, enticing the eyes and hands, this environment invites builders, observers, experimenters, artists, and creators. Children are playing. Some children are drawing and chatting with friends while others are outside gathering leaves to create designs around rock sculptures in the ʻauwai. A pair of boys carry geometric creations across the grass to share with friends in another classroom. The teachers are difficult to spot. One is in the studio helping children cut cardboard with an electric saw; the other is playing a game with a small group.

There is an energy that a visitor might not notice at first glance. The children gather supplies for themselves—some are active with friends, while others find time alone with a new book. The visitor lingers near the door, happy to be an observer, but if he lingers long enough, he will be eagerly invited to become part of the play. He will lean down to pick up a block and add it to the top of a tower and laugh as a child tries to build on from this new height. He will find himself in the midst of playing, no longer an observer but a participant, a fellow learner engaged in the exploration of that moment. My Hawaiian kuanaʻike is evident in the way I welcome parents, siblings, and kūpuna into the learning. I know they hold valuable insights into the child's life. The children and their ʻohana become family, forever part of my moʻokūʻauhau. I know that I am also being woven into the child's lei and the lei of their ʻohana. Might their view of the child and their own kuleana (responsibility and privilege) towards learning shift? I know our shared experiences will impact my teaching and my learning in unforeseen ways.

Moʻolelo: Ka Papa Loʻi o Kānewai

In Hawaiian culture, there are protocols that help focus interactions and learning experiences. In developing these protocols with children, we help them embrace cultural practices and acknowledge and embrace the cultural practices they may have in their own families.

Children begin to step up onto the bus. Keola pushes a heavy paper sack towards the driver. "Thank you for driving us!" he says quietly. The bus driver seems surprised. "For me?" "Yes," I say. "A little lunch from us." "Mahalo," he says with a gentle tone of gratitude.

"Mahalo!" "Thank you!" "Bye bye!" The children spill from the bus onto the pavement. We make our way down the steps, the kumu (teacher) waiting to welcome us. Our group stands tall, feet planted. We remind family members, "Hats off and stand with the children." The alakaʻi (leaders) begin:

> Eia no mākou nā keiki o ka punahou
> Hoʻomālamalama e mohala ai . . .

The kumu reply with an oli (chant) that speaks of this place, its importance, and meaning in connection to this area. We gather to hear moʻolelo of Kāne and Kanaloa and how they found water here. The adventure begins. We walk upstream, alongside the river, to learn about how the farmers diverted water to irrigate the kalo growing in the loʻi (taro patch). The ʻauwai flows alongside our path. "Look at those roots!" a child exclaims. "Look at the tree roots dropping down from the hillside above our heads." "Are there fish in the ʻauwai?" "Does this stream go to the ocean?" "Is this the stream from Mānoa Falls?"

Their curiosity reminds us how important it is to venture beyond the walls of our campus to explore their community and to ground them in their unique home.

We return to the loʻi, retracing our steps along the river. Then it is time to step into the loʻi.

Our kumu shares the importance of stepping in with good intentions, of entering this work with an open heart and a sense of respect for the kalo as the older sibling of the Hawaiian people.

Small feet step in; toes disappear into the rich mud. Squeals of delight and surprise erupt as the children feel the cool squelch of mud between their toes. Family members begin to step in. For some this is a completely new experience. At the edge there are a few children who hesitate. We encourage them by reminding them that this is our work for the day. A hand clenches mine. Jamie is unsure about this, but she knows it is her kuleana, her work to do. She is brave and will respect my firm request.

Uluwehi quickly plunges in, sinking up to his knees, then crouching down to feel the gentle embrace of the mud. His smile tells us he is comfortable in this space, in this work. He begins to mound mud at the base of the kalo as he's been taught. His parents work alongside him.

Class and families working in the lo'i.

Seeing this 'ohana reminds me of a parent describing their child's curiosity piqued by planting kalo in our garden and her interest in adding it to their garden. She pretends to make poi for the family at home. These are the moments that let me know we are awakening something in our children.

Here in the lo'i, we reconnect to the story of Hāloa, one of the Hawaiian creation stories. We are reminded of our connection to the land and our kuleana (responsibility and privilege) to care for this place as it nurtures and feeds us.

As feet are rinsed in the clear, cool water of the 'auwai, we prepare to leave this place for now, our thoughts moving toward the rest of our day. I step onto the bus feeling lifted; our work is satisfying. I believe it is my kuleana to inspire, provoke, and help to build a sense of place and purpose in our children. To help them embrace their home, this 'aina (land), and the culture that surrounds them.

Closing

As educators and scholars in the Hawaiian context, Sumida and Meyer (2008) suggested that if we "awaken our intellectual growth as teachers, we, in turn, do the same for our students, and for the larger educational community of learners" (p. 344). They stated, "Education, in its highest form, liberates human potential through transformational teaching and learning experiences" (Meyer et al. 2018, 17).

Grandparents and child painting en plein air together.

As I took time to reflect on myself and on my strengthening relationship with my Hawaiian identity, my commitment to my culture and to my haumāna evolved. At each turn, my haumāna benefited from my emerging understanding of the importance of self-reflection to our growth, identity, and strength. My growing sense of who I am as a Hawaiian pushed me to embrace my kuleana to ground these children in the values, culture, and beauty of Hawaiʻi. It is my kuleana to support the children as they begin to explore, acknowledge, and embrace their own cultural traditions and attitudes. I worked to offer opportunities to explore their home and their developing sense of self. It gave me added strength to support their curiosity, their agency, and their individual approaches to our daily work.

In embracing the importance of our own kuʻu home (beloved home), we can grow to understand how others value and cherish their own beloved homes. In growing to appreciate the beauty of our own families and our own cultures, we can grow to understand how others cherish their own cultural identities and traditions.

I have learned that developing empathy and an attitude of acceptance and openness to a culture can help children embrace the cultures of others as their world broadens. Our work as educators is to prepare our haumāna to go out into the world in a way that is pono (righteous and just). Learning to accept ourselves and to understand what drives each of us enables us to value that journey in others.

So Many More Voices . . .

Between Two Worlds: An Asian-Adoptee Experience

I am a Korean American adoptee, raised in a White family in predominantly White communities. A child of the '80s and an Asian American female and a transracial adoptee, I grew up without any mirrors in school or mainstream society. My sense of belonging has often been tenuous and grasping. I was either *too Asian* for my White friends and family or *not Asian enough* for my Asian American peers who were not transracially adopted.

As a younger adult, I was self-conscious about not being Korean "enough." In college, I joined the Asian American Student Union (AASU) and quickly found I had no shared cultural, familial, or immigration experience with other AASU members. In Asian-dominated spaces, I felt my whiteness as an adoptee acutely—and often with shame—like an impostor who belonged there even less than in White spaces. I also began to see how I benefited from White privilege: I was treated as a "safe" person of color, not only because of the model minority myth but because White-dominant culture was, in many ways, my own.

My Korean American adoptee identity has been elusive and ever-changing for me. Yet, finally at 50 years old, I claim it fully for myself. That journey started in 1999 when I lived in Korea for three months in my 20s. I was finally surrounded by others whose faces were similar to mine. I looked in the mirror and recognized the face looking back at me as just a *normal* face. It was the first time I didn't wish that I were White.

My identity journey came full circle when I recently returned to Korea after 26 years as part of a government-sponsored adoptee program, along with 75 other adoptees from around the world. A friend summed up that experience perfectly: I left Korea with an adoptee community behind me and a solid knowing that I am Korean and I am American too.

When I became an educator, I realized how children make meaning of themselves in our classrooms. I wanted to be the teacher who uplifted and honored the histories, perspectives, and voices of children like me, who lived their lives in relation to a dominant narrative that never includes them. I wanted to share my transracial adoptee identity with students and families to affirm both nontraditional family structures and multiracial families where children do not look like their parents. I have usually been the only Asian American and/or educator of color in the schools I've worked in, adding another layer of tokenism and pressure to represent all Asians and/or all people of color, which has sometimes fed into my impostor syndrome as well. Yet, as I look back on my career, I feel proud to be an educator who is a Korean American adoptee and the mirror for children whom I wish I'd had growing up.

Rebecca Slaby, Executive Director
Amazeworks, Minneapolis, Minnesota

CHAPTER 7

My Journey

Koko Samoa and Community

SALA SATARAKA

About Me: Bitter to Bold

Any time I attempt to describe myself, my values, the work I do for a living, or my culture, I immediately think of food. One of my favorite sweet dishes as a child was Koko Alaisa (Samoan Cocoa Rice). Traditionally, this comfort dish is made with roasted cacao beans that are hand-ground into a coarse paste, rice, and coconut milk. While there are other variations, Koko Samoa (cocoa) is the central ingredient. It is often brewed into a hot drink to share at family gatherings, village meetings, or simply to enjoy.

Growing up in Hawai'i, I learned to make Koko Alaisa using Hershey's cocoa powder and processed white sugar—ingredients my single mother could afford with food stamps. It wasn't until I was older that I tasted Koko Alaisa made with Koko Samoa. My young Americanized tastebuds went through a shock! What I once experienced as bitter and chalklike is now a bold, earthy flavor I can fully appreciate as an adult with a more experienced palate.

I am a Samoan Pacific Islander, queer, neurodivergent mama, born and raised on the island of O'ahu, Hawai'i. My relationship to my identity has evolved over time. I began identifying as a Pacific Islander in my mid-20s while working at the University of Washington (UW) Seattle. In my early 30s, I was diagnosed with ADHD and later self-identified as autistic. Growing up in Hawai'i, you didn't need to categorize yourself based on race, but ethnicity. Moving to Seattle in 2007 was a major culture shock.

At Seattle University, I often found myself explaining who Samoan people were and proving that Samoa is a real place on the map. At the small Jesuit Catholic university, I met only six people who identified as Pacific Islander—two Samoans, three Hawaiians, and one Chamorro. Thankfully, I found community through the Office of Multicultural Affairs Department's (OMAD's) immersion program for first-year and transfer students of color. It was there that I added "BIPOC" (Black, Indigenous, and People of Color) to my growing menu of identities. Although this community brought joy and meaningful experiences, I still often felt alone as the only Pacific Islander in many spaces. Back home, my struggle was legitimizing my Samoan-ness as someone who enjoyed cocoa powder straight from the box and couldn't speak Samoan. On the "mainland," I was fighting for recognition of my people's very existence.

I found relief in 2016 when I began working at UW Seattle and met my first Pacific Islander colleague-turned-friend at a staff committee meeting. He invited me to other spaces where there were other Pacific Islander staff, faculty, and students. It was in these spaces that I learned what it truly meant to be Pacific Islander—and how deeply connected our peoples are through ocean, land, and shared cultural practices and values. This period continues to serve as an anchor, reminding me of who I am and who I come from as I navigate predominantly White and whitewashed spaces.

My Identity and Profession: Cooking Time

My identity as a Pacific Islander shapes my professional life in profound ways. It wasn't until I began seeing a Samoan therapist in 2020—the only one in Washington I could find online—that I discovered a new path toward reconnecting with my Samoan roots. At the time, I was struggling with my identity, viewing myself through others' eyes and feeling perpetually "not enough"—not Samoan enough, not Pacific Islander enough, not neurodivergent or queer enough. Through our sessions, I started to understand how my upbringing and lived experiences were deeply woven into my ongoing struggle with cultural identity and mental health.

One session, my therapist asked a seemingly simple question that shifted everything: *What does being Samoan mean to **you**? What values do **you** embody from Samoan culture?* I had never considered that I could define this for myself or even have an opinion on what being Samoan meant. The idea that I could shape my own understanding of Samoan identity (while still honoring my family and culture) felt both liberating and painful. I still sometimes sit with the sadness of knowing how many years I spent trying to mold myself into whatever version felt most palatable in each space I occupied.

This internal negotiation continues to surface in my professional life. The lack of representation of Pacific Islander educators and leaders in the education field has, at times, fed my impostor syndrome—a false narrative that told me I did not belong in certain careers, roles, or institutions. It emerged in the careful way I chose my words while advocating against ableist and racist policies and challenging toxic work environments, afraid of being labeled "too much." It appeared in meetings where I accepted watered-down compromises while urging organizations to include children's books that reflect diverse family structures, such as same-sex parents households, amid the ongoing vilification of LGBTQIA+ communities. When I look back on these moments where I wish I was bolder or stronger, I slow down and think of Koko Samoa. I imagine pouring a warm cup for my younger selves, reminding them that bitterness does not mean something is wrong; sometimes it simply means the flavor is unfamiliar. Not every space I'm in will be ready for the warmth, depth, or richness that I will bring, and that's their journey.

When I finally began answering my therapist's question, the values surfaced like familiar tastes I had forgotten I knew. I named what I love about Samoan culture: our sense of humor, the fullness of our "aunty laughs," our deep love of family and community, the grace of our dances set to slit drums and guitar, and, of course, our delicious food that brings people together from everywhere.

This is where my work as an educator meets my Pacific Islander identity. I believe nurturing relationships with children, families, and communities is much like cooking a meaningful meal. You start by listening—learning the history of the dish and who it is meant to feed. You gather the right ingredients and tools, trust those who have cooked before you, and invest time, patience, and care. You taste as you go, adjust when something is off, and accept that no two kitchens—or classrooms—are the same.

My first experience working with preschoolers was in 2012 as an AmeriCorps member with the Washington Reading Corps program at Solid Ground. I supported a morning preschool program at a nonprofit in SeaTac, Washington. I will never forget the first Samoan child I worked with. She was a joyful ball of energy and called me "Aunty," a term of respect for your elders in Pacific Island cultures. After a few weeks, I stopped seeing her. I learned that she was disenrolled due to attendance policies tied to government assistance requirements—policies that often make it difficult for some families to stay enrolled. At that point in my career, I didn't yet have the understanding or experience to name what I was witnessing: a system that valued rigid and often outdated measurements over nourishment and care.

How time is perceived and valued in my multicultural family continues to shape my personal and professional life. Pacific Islanders (like many other BIPOC cultures) value time spent with family and community, connecting over conversation and food. My Japanese American side of the family shared these values but placed a stronger emphasis on timeliness, often attaching shame to lateness. Having parents who also work in a deadline-driven profession deepened this internalized pressure around timeliness and attendance. Much like my transition to appreciating Koko Samoa for its complexities and rich flavors, learning to sit with my own discomfort and unlearn practices that perpetuated shame and Western ideologies was a bittersweet process that continues to guide the way I navigate the world and this work.

Having this as a backdrop, and working with young children and families from diverse cultural experiences and values, was a challenge for me when I started in education. I didn't realize how much this would also inform the way that I parent my now 10-year-old daughter, who is also autistic and has ADHD. It has been a wonderful and often difficult journey navigating complex education and special education systems. Neurodivergence and disabilities were not topics you would commonly hear at the dinner table of a Pacific Islander family, making my village smaller and experience lonelier as I attempted to advocate for resources. As I mentioned earlier, Pacific Islanders are community-oriented, which made this journey even more difficult. I have been working in the education field for almost 20 years—from preschool centers to nonprofits to higher education—and I still struggle to understand what resources exist and where to look in these institutions and systems that are not designed for Pacific Islanders, or people with disabilities and complex needs. Pacific Islanders often make up less than 1 percent of any US institution's population or are aggregated within the "API" or "AANHPI" umbrella, and so are not considered in critical decisions, leading to underresourcing and negative impacts on issues like our education and health.

There is still little research that tells the full story of Pacific Islander students' experiences in the US education system, and what does exist is often difficult to access. As a result, many Pasifika children and families remain overlooked in educational research and policy. In August 2024, the Pacific Islander Community Association of Washington (PICA-WA) helped make these experiences more visible through the publication of the *Washington State Native Hawaiian and Pacific Islander Community Data Report 2019–2024*. In the Holistic Education chapter, the report highlights a sobering reality: Many Pasifika children begin school already behind, with only 34 percent entering kindergarten ready during the 2021–2022 school year (Pacific Islander Community Association of Washington, 2024). The report makes clear that this is not a reflection of students' potential, but of the systems meant to support them, and it calls on leaders and policymakers to center Pasifika youth and families by investing in NHPI educators and school leaders, supporting immigrant families, ending disproportionate discipline practices, and improving culturally aligned, disaggregated data collection and reporting.

What I've Learned: Cooldown Period

In 2025, I started a new role in the Youth Development and Expanded Learning field at School's Out Washington. I have never worked for an intermediary non-profit, but it has offered me opportunities to see how critical expanded learning opportunities are for young people, families, and communities. Much like the early learning field, many of the youth-serving programs offer wraparound services and aim to address the whole child. Working in preschool centers, elementary and middle schools, afterschool programs, higher education, and now in expanded learning, I see how fractured and separated the care of children has become. If only we collaborated and came together to help youth. If we followed them across settings, the outcomes would be so much better.

For this reason, my message to others in the field is as you advocate together for a better world for children, think of it like cooking a meaningful meal. Listen, gather the right ingredients and tools, trust those who have cooked before you, and invest time, patience, and care. You taste as you go, adjust when something is off, and accept that no two kitchens or chefs are the same. Families should be treated as the head chef of their kitchen. We are guests. The feedback you receive might hurt your feelings at first, but the change it makes in you will last a lifetime. Be sure to pass it on; knowledge and wisdom should never be hoarded. Give access to all. That is where change comes from. Faʻafetai tele lava.

CHAPTER 8

Envisioning Just Futures Through My Phoenix Eyes

JAMIE CHO

It's 8:00 a.m., and the sun is rising as I walk across the University of Washington Seattle campus, using a maps app to navigate to the building where I am teaching. Walking into the large lecture hall for 120 students, I take a deep breath. I look at the young faces that look back at me wondering who I am and what they can expect this quarter.

I start class with my story. I grew up in Orange County, California, and in elementary school in the 1980s, I was one of the few Asian children at my school. In my class, there was only one other Chinese American boy. Frequently, on the playground, my peers would pull up the corners of their eyes to make fun of my almond-shaped eyes. I felt self-conscious and ashamed of my smaller eyes and humiliated to be the subject of ridicule. But I didn't tell the adults. I silently endured.

My eyes have been a symbol of my identity, perceived by others to symbolize my foreignness, even though I am American. The frequent question "Where are you from?" may stem from curiosity about my ethnic origins, but as a microaggression insinuates that I don't belong. As a child, I felt shame for being visibly different in school, and it made me want to hide. I wished that I could look more like the quintessential Barbie—white[1], blond, and blue-eyed.

My mother said I had phoenix eyes, the classic eyes of Chinese beauty. She said they stood for loyalty, honesty, and wisdom. I didn't understand then, but my journey of self-discovery led me to see the wisdom from my mother's perspective. My eyes are part of a legacy inherited from my ancestors. They carry their stories, sacrifices, and successes that I bring to my work today.

My Inherited Eyes

My parents came to the United States in the 1970s. My father, Jerry, came to pursue his PhD in engineering at the University of Houston. My mother, Jenny, who was a teacher in Taiwan, came a year later. I was born in Texas as my father was completing his doctorate. Two years later, when my parents were expecting their second child, my sister, they were living in Utah. We didn't have any extended family to help out when the baby was born. My maternal grandparents advised my parents to go back to Taiwan for the delivery so that they could help out with me, their 2-year-old. It is a common Chinese practice that after the birth of a child, the mother will be well taken care of by a family member or nurse who supports the needs of the infant and the mother.

1 I use the lowercase "w" in "white" when referring to the racial category, to decenter whiteness and disrupt the dominant focus on the white gaze (Howell et al. 2019), and to foreground the stories and experiences of Black, Indigenous, and People of Color (BIPOC).

There are many taboos during the first month after birth, such as avoiding showers, remaining indoors, and eating only hot foods. Women are given lots of healing and nutritious soups and herbal remedies. Often, it is another caretaker who is meeting the feeding and diapering needs of the infant to let the mother rest and recuperate. So, my parents went back to Taiwan for my sister's birth. This is why I am the only person in my family to be a US-born citizen. It was often said in my family that I could be president.

On Saturdays, my entire family went together to Chinese school. It was housed in a Buddhist temple where our Chinese lessons were followed by religious teachings. My mother worked as the administrator at this school, and she was an example of an innovative and collaborative leader. My beautiful mother was, and still is, outgoing and talented. As the administrator, she would take on many tasks, including acting as master of ceremonies whenever there was a school assembly, cultural celebration, or religious event. In this temple, in this Chinese school, I felt completely "at home." I was surrounded by people who knew me by name, largely because they knew who my mother was. These people, who had eyes like mine, often code-switched between Mandarin and English. Many of the other children attending Chinese school shared my identity, ABC, or American-born Chinese. We had the common experience of looking Chinese and behaving as Americans, having never lived abroad. None of us liked learning Chinese because it is a very difficult language to learn and involves a lot of rote memorization of characters, stroke order, and the correct tonal marks. However, the community that was created in and between classes was the incentive to attend. In this Chinese school, I felt I could be my authentic self.

As expected of me as the firstborn girl in my family, I worked hard, graduated in the top 10 of my high school class in 2000, and went to the University of California, Berkeley, also called Cal, its familiar nickname. When I visited Cal for the first time, I loved it. The campus was majestic with its large trees, and I felt like it was exactly what college should be. And it was. In college, I was challenged to learn about perspectives I had never considered. I had amazing professors who asked me to think critically. Every day there was a protest at the south entrance of campus, and folks shouted their views on the corner of Bancroft and Telegraph. Cal was the birthplace of the term Asian American, created to build solidarity among folks of Asian descent. This environment, with its constant questioning and encouragement to challenge the status quo, was also the birthplace of my criticality. It was here that I first learned to examine ideas deeply, to not take information at face value, and to develop my own perspective through thoughtful analysis and reflection.

The Bay Area became my home for over a decade. As a freshman, I met my husband, a Korean American man. We lived across the hall from each other in the Unit 3 dorms. After we graduated, I continued with my doctoral program in special education. Looking back on graduate school, I miss how much time I had to think. In that respect, it was magical. It was also a formative time of growth for me, and a lot of that learning I attribute to my colleague, Emily Nusbaum, who was the only other graduate student in our cohort. Needless to say, we became fast friends, and she introduced me to the world of disability studies. She helped shape my thinking to be more critical, more inclusive, and more anti-ableist. I graduated with my PhD in 2008. At that time, I was six months pregnant, and I walked across the stage with my son in my belly. I think that means he has an honorary doctorate.

My Eyes Symbolize Vulnerability and Honesty

Six years later, still in the Bay Area, my son started first grade. Our first house was in the suburbs, three blocks from our local elementary school. On the first day of first grade, as my son was walking to line up outside of his classroom, I saw a child, another first grader, pulling up the corner of their eyes and laughing with the peer next to them. I was shocked to see those same racist taunts I had experienced still circulating on his elementary school playground. As an adult now, I spoke up and talked with the teacher and principal, who then led discussions with the children.

I tell this story to my undergraduate students to let them know that racism still exists. It is not a thing of the past; instead, it is very real and alive. It continues to affect me, my child, and all of us. I share my stories with students to model vulnerability and honesty. I also share this story to invite students to think about their experiences in school. These moments on the playground, when no adult was watching, are formative experiences. My own experiences of being teased are memories that still linger with me decades later. Coupled with my children's experiences compel me to teach in ways that disrupt the status quo and challenge students to dream and imagine transformed systems.

When my daughter was 6 years old, she and I read Joanna Ho's children's book *Eyes that Kiss in the Corners*, and I cried. The eyes that had provoked playground teasing and ridicule were the subject of a popular children's book. It is the validation I never received at school. During the pandemic, at a time of heightened anti-Asian hate in this country, I was approached by my daughter's elementary school to offer a workshop focused on talking about race with children. Attendees received their choice of this book or other diverse books. It is with hope that I do this work to change the narrative so my daughter and all children in the future who have eyes like mine will describe them as "eyes that kiss in the corners," and part of the legacy that we receive from our elders.

In my courses, I model the types of practices I hope my students will take into their future classrooms. For example, I have used ungrading for all my classes, including the large undergraduate courses, to shift power and ownership of grades to students. I explain to students that I believe they do not have to prove their worth to me and that their learning should be internally motivated. I ask them to imagine our time together like we are taking a cooking class, focused on the process and not the product, and taking some risks together as a community. When some students express discomfort with uncertainty about whether they will get a 4.0, which I think is part of this learning experience, I ask them to reflect on why they feel that need for perfection and why they don't think they can trust themselves to be a good judge of their work and effort. Combined with flexible deadlines, the option to revise assignments, and accessibility for everyone, most students feel less pressure and less stress and can focus more on learning. I believe that students need to experience what abolitionist education can feel like so that they are released from the socialized experiences of "doing school" and can enact more equitable ways of teaching and learning.

Every quarter I have a student who says to me, "I've never had an Asian teacher before," and I can see that it is revolutionary to learn from someone who looks like me, who has a job that they now might consider. Teaching students to view events and experiences through a critical lens is very rewarding. The students who tell me our class "blew their mind," or who linger after class to continue the discussion with questions, are folks who are grappling with their place in this system. Those students who embrace their responsibilities, change their life—quit a job not aligned with their values, switch majors to pursue something more fulfilling, decide to become a teacher or advocate—signal to me I am doing something right and pouring into students in a way that nurtures their activism.

My Eyes Symbolize Loyalty and Authenticity

Teaching for social change is a calling that I have happily assumed. That work doesn't only happen within classroom walls or on a college campus. I believe that a lot of the "teaching" I do happens in short conversations with one person or a small group of people. I attribute this type of teaching to my maternal grandpa, my 外公 (wei gong).

Once a year in the late spring, my maternal grandparents would come from Taiwan and spend four months with us. It was a fun time for my family having long-term guests, and because my grandparents helped around the house, my parents were more relaxed. My grandpa, who was a military man with a shaved bald head and a big belly, had a commanding presence but was also joyful and quirky. For example, from his military training, he preferred a hard pillow. So when he came to stay at my house, my parents would stack two phone books tied tightly with rope for my grandfather's pillow. My grandfather also was a collector. On the weekends, my family would scour swap meets and thrift stores for special ashtrays. My sister and I would pride ourselves on spotting the unique ashtray hidden among a bunch of junk if it passed my grandpa's inspection. My grandpa was not a smoker, but he had hundreds of one-of-a-kind ashtrays that he meticulously cataloged and stored. My fondest memory of my grandfather is when he was writing at his desk and I would stand behind him, rubbing his shaved head, which felt simultaneously soft and spiky.

My extended family in the 1990s. From left to right: my sister, me, my grandfather, my mother, my grandmother, my dad [從左到右：妹妹、我、外公, 媽媽, 外婆, 爸爸].

In the afternoons, my grandparents would come to pick my sister and me up from school. They often were waiting on the playground when the bell rang. They didn't speak English, but my grandfather would engage my classmates in a game. He would hold up his right hand and count in Mandarin, 一, 二,三,四,五 while showing the corresponding fingers, and then he would count in English, one, two, three, four, five. My peers would count along and cheer when my grandfather recited the numbers. This became a daily ritual and something my classmates looked forward to.

During my grandparents' stay, they would make traditional 饅頭 (steamed buns) made from fresh ingredients. My grandfather would stand on a stool in the kitchen so he would tower over the counter and use his hands to knead the dough. Then, he molded it into an oblong shape, and we would wait impatiently for it to steam. Then when they were ready, the neighborhood children would come quickly into our kitchen for a freshly made bun before going back outside to play.

In the company of my grandparents, it was completely okay to be different. It didn't matter that they didn't speak any English. Through their example of showing up as loyal to their authentic selves, I believe they taught children at my school and in my neighborhood that difference can be fun, and delicious.

My Eyes Symbolize Courage and Wisdom

My adult experiences have, in many ways, mirrored my childhood experiences. While I grew up and still walk with a lot of privilege, in terms of education, class, heteronormativity, etc., I find that my Asian eyes, or Asian-ness, still define my experience in this world, professionally and personally. In the field of early childhood education, which is still a white woman–dominated discipline, I see that there are not many people who look like me in professional spaces. While commitments to anti-racism are often talked about, the undercurrent of complicity to the current norms still exists.

Recently, I was invited to facilitate workshops with early childhood professionals and social workers through the Seattle Chinese Information Service Center. In one workshop, we discussed the meaning of the Chinese proverb 枪打出头鸟, which can be translated to "shoot the bird that sticks out." This common saying originates from a story about a hunter trying to shoot a bird. In the dense forest where the hunter is searching, there is a bird perched visibly on a branch in the trees, making it the obvious target. The meaning of this proverb is that it can be dangerous to be different, or too unique, and the lesson is that it is better to conform and be the same as everyone else. These Chinese ideologies play very well with the model minority myth that paints Asian Americans as obedient, docile, and quiet.

But I'm not. As a higher education professional, I have been that conspicuous bird, because not only do I contradict the stereotype of an Asian American woman, I also stand out as an outspoken advocate. I am very kind, humble, and certainly respectful to others. However, I bring a critical perspective to discussions, and I am not scared to advocate for myself and others. I believe because of the privilege that I enjoy that it is my responsibility to leverage that privilege and say or do the things that are harder for others to do because they have more at stake. I also believe that speaking up when I have been slighted and harmed is a generous gift that allows others to do better. However, in some spaces where social justice is presented publicly as a vision and mission, behind closed doors I have faced racism in the form of microaggressions, gaslighting, and punishment.

Throughout my professional career, I have held titles that positioned me as a champion for equity and justice, roles that, on paper, suggested a commitment to transformation and accountability. These titles inspired me to rise to the challenge, to live into their promise, and to claim the responsibility and privilege they carried. And yet, while outwardly the title suggested my job is to do the work of justice, when I had private conversations with folks, or suggested changes to policy and practice, I was questioned, undermined, and made to be the villain, revealing the deep discomfort institutions have with actual change, especially when it threatens entrenched power structures or challenges the performative nature of their proclaimed value.

Advocating for myself and for my students is a double-edged sword in the context of the model minority myth because I am perceived as too pushy, disloyal, and ungrateful. My image has been distorted as incredibly powerful and threatening, forcing others to do things that they do not want to do. These are racist tropes that stem from xenophobic ideas of "yellow peril" and sexist ideas of ambition. What a white man does every day without question becomes fodder for others to question my place and integrity within an institution where I have done amazing work. I am not credited for my outstanding course evaluations or for teaching 10 classes and over 150 students a quarter. Instead, I am judged for my lack of complacency. As an Asian American woman in academia, I am expected to be humble and grateful for what I have been given.

My Phoenix Eyes Envision Justice

In 2023, I gave an EduTalk, a College of Education version of a Ted Talk. I wrote the script and had it reviewed by many of my colleagues, and then began rehearsing for three months. Every day as I drove to work, or when I was driving to pick up my kids from school, I would recite this five-minute talk to myself. When the day arrived, I went to my local hair salon to get my hair and makeup done for the event. The stylist, a Vietnamese American woman, says, as blunt Asian aunties do, "I used to have eyes like yours—small with a single eyelid—but I got surgery in Asia and now they are much better." She goes on to suggest that next time I am in Asia, I should get double-eyelid surgery to have bigger, more beautiful eyes. Her intent is kind. She is not insulting me but making a suggestion she thinks I will appreciate. What she doesn't understand is that while I may have been insecure about my eyes, and they may have been the reason I was "different" as a child, at 42, I have no intention of changing my eyes. They are a part of who I am.

Hours later, I get up on stage, stand on the circle rug, and proclaim, "I am a walking counternarrative." I explain to the audience, and future YouTube watchers, that I defy the stereotypes of an Asian American woman because I dare to speak up, challenge others' assumptions, disrupt microaggressions, and call folks in to do better. I share that I teach because I believe teaching is a form of advocacy that invites the next generation to think and act in ways that disrupt the status quo and move us all toward more equitable systems. I teach because it's one way that I resist people and systems that tell me no, stop, or you can't. I know that what may not be possible for me, when a system is too big for me to change, I can share with my students and have them carry the vision forward.

Me on stage at EduTalk 2024, themed Thriving Generations.

The wonderful thing about being bolder, braver, and living in your truth is that you meet people who see you for exactly who you are, and they appreciate you. These people remind me of my worth on the most difficult days and stand with me when injustice occurs. They also call on me to advocate for those who need support. For instance, as a respected advocate in the school district, I had the privilege of supporting a Chinese American mother who was fighting for her son, who had been unfairly punished by a middle school administrator. It took a year, many emails, phone calls, and meetings, as well as thousands of dollars to a lawyer, but we won. It didn't undo her son's trauma, but he saw how many people believed in him and knew he was not deserving of the punishment he received.

I have also had the tremendous honor of advocating in a case of anti-Asian hate where a racist white neighbor was targeting her older Asian immigrant neighbors. Besides writing declarations for the court and op-eds for the newspaper, I was privileged to walk alongside two courageous survivors and a generous team of pro bono lawyers and volunteers. It is incredible what can happen when a group of committed individuals collectively fight for justice. It may have been a long and frustrating battle against inequitable systems, but these folks who were all strangers in the beginning, I now proudly call my friends.

Every win deserves celebration, even when they feel small and take forever. Lawyers advised us it would be impossible to remove the racist neighbor from the homeowner's board of directors, yet a court did just that and issued a 10-year protection order. We rented a room in a Chinese karaoke restaurant and sang loudly and uninhibited. We sang for all the pain and frustration, and we embraced for our victory. Our joy is hard fought, so in these moments, we are reminded that joy is also resistance, and resistance is survival.

Some stories stick with us over time. One Chinese story that has stuck with me goes like this: Once there was an elderly man named 愚公 (Yu Gong). He lived in a small village at the base of two towering mountains. To reach the next town, he had to climb these two mountains, a long and arduous journey, which limited the village's access to vital resources. One day, Yu Gong resolved to move the mountains. The villagers mocked him, believing his idea to be impossible. Undeterred, Yu Gong explained that while he might not achieve this goal in his lifetime, he would start digging and pass the task on to his descendants. He was confident that, over generations, the mountains would eventually be moved.

This is one of the classic parables meant to teach children the importance of hard work and perseverance. It also conveys the cultural values of steadfastness toward a goal and the need to labor for the greater good. When I share this Yu Gong story with my undergraduate students, I highlight its parallels to our ongoing struggle against oppression in this country. It's a lifelong endeavor, and while we may not see the fruits of our labor, we do what we can and pass the responsibility to the next generation, and the one after that. In this commitment, we hope our collective work will ultimately lead to liberation for all. I invite students to join me in these commitments and take action toward a just future.

Cumulatively, the many experiences of bias, racism, and disrespect that I have experienced as an Asian American woman has been exhausting. During the pandemic, I met with a therapist, and she said, "What does it cost you to not speak your truth?" At that moment I had an epiphany. It hurt to be dismissed, ignored, and discredited, but it hurt me more to be silenced or to censor myself. That day,

I decided I would be bolder and braver. I committed to living my life aligned with a vision of social justice, hoping that one day all children will walk free in this world.

As a child, I couldn't understand what my mother was teaching me about my phoenix eyes. My eyes seemed too different, too foreign. Through my journey of self-growth, I have come to see my eyes as a strength. They have come to stand for loyalty, honesty, and wisdom, as my mother said. They have given me the capacity to be loyal to the cause of social justice, honest and vulnerable about my experiences, and brave and wise enough to know that my life can be lived for the purpose of a vision. Phoenixes are magical creatures that represent rebirth, and I believe my experiences have made me become the educator and advocate that I am. I dream of a phoenix-like revolution in our school systems and in our country that centers children and their families. My eyes may have been the reason for being teased, but they are also the eyes that watched my children's first unsteady steps, read the book that validated my daughter's inherited eyes, and represent a vision that challenges my students to be advocates, allowing me to bear witness to oppression so that I can labor for justice.

CHAPTER 9

Koʻu Inoa, ʻO Wau Kēia

My Name, This Is Who I Am, the Shaping of My Kanaka ʻŌiwi Identity

ALETHEA KUʻULEI SERNA

O Kuʻulei Koʻu Inoa: Kuʻulei Is My Name

> "Kuʻulei. My beloved wreath of flowers. Wherever you go, you will share love with whomever you come across and entreat others with joy."

My mother had first revealed her full manaʻo (intention/thoughts/meaning) for the meaning of my name, *Kuʻulei*, in a congratulatory card when I graduated with my master's degree in education. Only knowing the literal translation, "*my beloved lei*," for most of my life, finally learning my mother's deeper intention for my name, and in a way, my life, was like a special coming-of-age moment. I grew a greater appreciation for my name, my mother, and my ʻohana (family) as I reflected on how my personality and life experiences were prophesied by this name chosen for me.

In this chapter, I share the story of my name and how my parents' manaʻolana (expectation/hope) for me has been hidden within it. My parents' expectations and hope for me, manifested through my name, have guided my life through experiences of love and care from my ʻohana and community since my early childhood until today. My name is included in my moʻokūʻauhau (genealogy/family story), and my kūpuna (elders) raised me to fulfill my kuleana (responsibility) to uphold our kānaka ʻōiwi (Native Hawaiian) and ʻohana culture and values. I share the influence of my name story and my moʻokūʻahau on my decision to become an early childhood education teacher-educator as well as its impact on my educational practices.

Koʻu Inoa, Manaʻolana Koʻu, Mau Mākua Iaʻu: My Name, My Parents' Hope, and Expectations for Me

In Hawaiian culture, an inoa (name) is a precious personal possession for an individual. It is causative, a force and living entity that could influence health, happiness, and lifespan. Hawaiian mākua (parents) choose a name with careful thought, family consultation, and, ideally, supernatural advice, such as receiving a name via a dream or praying to a "higher power" (Pukui et al. 2002). It's the responsibility of mākua to teach the significance of the name, "for children will eventually walk away from their most sacred inheritance if meaning is not established in terms they can relate to and sustain their culture" (Titcomb et al. 2019, 186).

In alignment with this, my mākua selected my name carefully as if it was a prophetic ideal for my life. Ku'ulei, I was to share love everywhere I go and would cheerfully ask with a positive and encouraging attitude. My brothers always put me up to ask my father for money when we were in high school for entertainment, because they knew that I could entreat my father to give all of us the money we needed. I recall colleagues sharing with me that they observed that people would do anything for me, if I ask. I don't believe it is always true. However, my friends, family, and colleagues always believed it. My parents nourished that meaning and helped it to become manifest in my life until they finally decided it necessary for me to understand not only the meaning of my name but also their mana'olana placed in that meaning that would hopefully shape my character for my life's purpose.

Ko'u Inoa and Ko'u Mo'okū'auhau: The Pride and Mana (Power) from My Inoa to 'Ohana

Ticomb et al. (2019) state that "name, genealogy . . . are foundational aspects of Kānaka 'Ōiwi identity" (p. 186). Inoa (one's name) is important in understanding one's purpose in life, how mo'okū'auhau (genealogy, family story) is important in understanding one's *kuleana* in the community (Titcom et al. 2019).

Upon this new revelation of the full meaning of my name, I became more cognizant of my actions and interactions with people and circumstances in my life. I realized that what my parents desired for me had been and was constantly becoming manifest in my life. I began to reflect on my childhood and how my 'ohana also fed into the hope for who I was purposed to become through my name.

I became their *Ku'ulei*, developing into the person that my parents had hoped for, the one who shared love and entreated others with joy. I was able to quickly connect to my kūpuna who took care of me. I was a joyful and loving child who entreated my kūpuna to provide me with the best care possible. I honored and welcomed my caretakers by listening and participating in their daily lives.

My parents made sure that I knew my 'ohana members and our mo'okū'auhau. Ever since I was a young child, we attended as many family gatherings as possible in order to stay connected and know members of our 'ohana. Those gatherings had a hundred or more people in attendance. It was tradition and a sign of respect to greet our family members, especially our kūpuna, with a hug and honi (a kiss). Greeting our 'ohana in that manner allowed us to feel more comfortable around them and learn who they were in relation to our mo'okū'auhau. Most importantly, the 'ohana would recognize us as a part of their mo'okū'auhau.

Our lives were extensions of my kūpuna's life story, their mo'okū'auhau. I was to perpetuate and carry our family legacy through my name, Ku'ulei, to share love and entreat others with joy. I represented my 'ohana and their names. This kuleana helped to shape a part of my identity.

Ko'u Mo'okū'auhau: 'Ohana Roots, I Am Grounded

> Your mo'okū'auhau is a genealogy, or mo'olelo (story or history) of your family that traces back to your ancestors. Genealogy is the record of your kūpuna from whom you received some of your talents and mana (divine power or authority or privilege).

> These stories contain ʻike kuʻuna (inherited knowledge). They teach who your family is and what is important to your family. These stories also teach values and guiding principles, which aid you in decision making. . . As the moʻolelo (story) guide your actions, they form your character and define your self-identity. (Kamehameha Publishing 2025)

To kānaka ʻōiwi (an Indigenous person of Hawaiʻi; Native Hawaiian), knowledge of one's ʻohana and their moʻokūʻauhau is invaluable. Like knowing the meaning and intention of our inoa, it is imperative for one to learn their moʻokūʻauhau to understand who they are, where they come from, and their kuleana in life. Immediate or extended, ʻohana must remain close to one another. In one's moʻokūʻauhau, an individual discovers their mana.

I am a proud kanaka ʻōiwi. My birthplace is Honolulu, Hawaiʻi, on the island of Oʻahu. Since birth, I was raised in Hālawa Heights. I am a proud great granddaughter, granddaughter, and daughter of the Hukiku-Flores-Distajo and Dart ʻohana (families). My father is Antonio Distajo Jr. of Hālawa, Oʻahu, and my mother, Flaviana Keakalaulono Dart of Keaukaha and Waiakea Homestead, Hilo, Hawaiʻi. My father is of Native Hawaiian and Filipino descent. My mother is of Native Hawaiian and Caucasian descent. I am proud to be of mixed ethnicities. However, despite being multiethnic, my ʻohana raised me to strongly identify with the ʻāina (land) of my ancestors' birthplace, which is Hawaiʻi. They raised me to take pride in our Indigenous heritage and values.

Both of my parents were first-generation college graduates, my father a civil engineer and my mother an educator. They were Native Hawaiian college graduates in the late 1950s during the time when Hawaiʻi was colonized and illegally annexed by the US government (Nasser 2021), until Hawaiʻi's statehood in 1959. My parents' educational accomplishments took place when the use of the Hawaiian language in schools was banned and most of what Hawaiian children learned at home was not reflected in Hawaiian territorial schools. My grandparents were of the working class. My paternal grandfather, Antonio Distajo Sr. was a business owner, owning a well-renowned local barber shop, Aiea, Oʻahu, and my grandmother, Mary Kuipua Flores, worked at a pineapple cannery. My maternal grandfather, William Gulstan Dart, was a supervisor at Hilo Electric Light Powerhouse Company and a pastor of two churches in Hilo and Pahoa, on Hawaiʻi island. His wife, my grandmother, Elizabeth Keakalaulono Tucker, was a stay-at-home wife and parent, who was a mompreneur, selling her high-in-demand baked goods, as well as an ordained minister.

I have received some of my talents, mana, and purpose from my moʻokūʻauhau, like my high value for education. Both sides of my ʻohana highly valued and deemed education as a means to forward the next generation toward a better life and greater opportunities. My grandparents sacrificed to ensure that their children, my parents, were able to access higher education and excel into a life that was successful. My paternal grandmother once told me that she raised my dad, her eldest child, and his brother to mālama (to take care of) others, especially his ʻohana and eventually them in their elderly years. My father recalls that his parents were not wealthy but worked hard to provide money for him and his brother to attend the engineering college at the University of Hawaiʻi. My mother's parents also supported her and her sister, allowing them to leave their island home to attend the college of their choice. It was no different for me and my siblings. In our early childhood, it was assumed that there was an expectation for us to pursue higher education, have a career that would provide us with the means to raise our own families, and continue to perpetuate the reputation of our family's story.

My mo'okū'auhau also recorded the importance of my 'ohana's Christian faith and spirituality. Kanaka 'Ōiwi tend to be very spiritual people, acknowledging spirituality as a social norm. My ancestors were Christians, as many Native Hawaiians were. In our mo'okū'auhau, my ancestors experienced supernatural occurrences, such as miraculous healings, after praying to Ke Akua, which led to their conversion. My family members also established Christian churches on the Hawaiian Islands and became clergy. My mother's parents were pastors. My father's 'ohana were also founding members of the First Hawaiian Pentecostal Full Gospel Assembly church in Honolulu, and his brother was the senior pastor of that church. This mana was also passed to me, as I also became an ordained pastor in 1991 and continue to serve in my church like my grandfather once served.

I am very proud to be a descendant of a rich genealogical heritage displayed in the lives of my kūpuna, and it has shaped me into who I have become today. Now that I am older and have my own children, I have become more aware and appreciative of my mo'okū'auhau, the genealogical stories of our family traditions and history. These mo'olelo highlight my family's 'ike (knowledge) and mana, which are my inheritance. They have provided guidance for the values that I have adopted and now live. I am grateful for the "full circle" moments when I realize that I have manifested my mo'okū'auhau, subconsciously and consciously, in my actions and choices throughout all aspects of my life, relationships, education, profession(s), etc. My kuleana to our family history and the reputation of our name have defined my identities and the intersectionality of those identities.

> O Alethea Ku'ulei Keakalaulono Distajo ko'u inoa. 'O wau kēia (This is who I am). I have the power of my inoa, my 'ohana, and Ke Akua (God). I am an intersection of multiple identities birthed from my 'āina (land), mo'okū'auhau, and life experiences to fulfill my purpose while I have breath. I am a kanaka 'ōiwi (Native Hawaiian) of mixed ethnicity, a wahine (woman), daughter, granddaughter, a widow, a mother of three beautiful, loving, and intelligent kaikamahine (daughters), a sister, an auntie, a friend, a colleague, a mentor, a pastor, a professor, and an educator. This is who I am.

Hālawa to Hilo: The Experiences of My Child Care on the 'Āina of My Kūpuna, Bridging Generations

I am the lei of my 'ohana. I am the pua (flower) of my family. I am pua lei.

Children are often referred to as *pua* (flowers) in Hawaiian culture. The Hawaiian Dictionary defines pua lei as "cherished blossom or child" (Pukui & Elbert 1986, 346). As highlighted in the definition of pua lei, Hawaiians loved and cherished their keiki (children). It was common for extended families to help parents care for keiki. I was fortunate to be born into a very loving and supportive 'ohana.

From Hālawa, O'ahu

I was cherished in Hālawa, O'ahu. Hālawa was the beloved home of my father and his kūpuna. Instead of formal preschool, my mother chose to allow my tūtū lady (great-grandmother), Annie Anahiwa

Hukiku, and my grandmother's sister, Aunt Delores Anahiwa Flores, to provide child care for me while she and my father worked. My grandmother, Mary Kuipua Flores, would also provide care whenever she was not working. My early childhood experiences in Hālawa were so joyful and warm. Education and academic accomplishments were important to my parents; however, at this stage in my life, they felt that ʻohana identity was more important. My mother told me that our kūpuna were able to teach us about our Hawaiian heritage and ʻohana ways, values, and morals.

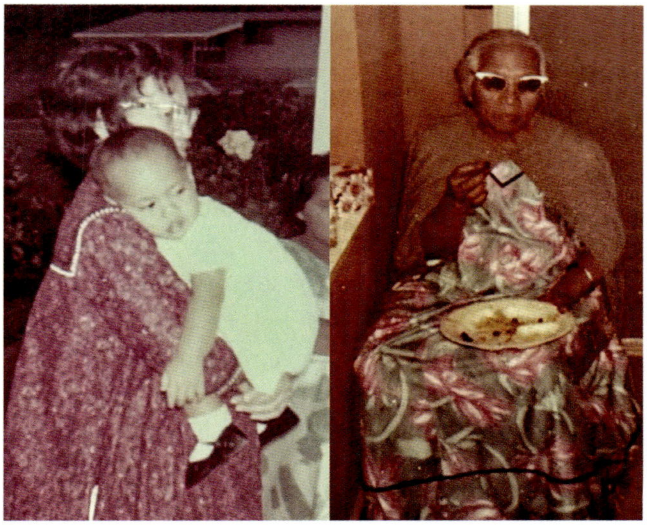

My paternal grandma, Mary Kuipua Distajo, holding me on my first birthday party (left) and her mother, my tūtū (great-grandmother), Anahiwa Hukiku Flores (right).

My mother recalls that my tūtū's home was always the gathering place where family and friends came and went. My paternal grandparents also lived next door to my tūtū, which made that home more special because her family lived nearby. I feel privileged to know that my child care took place on the ʻāina of my extended ʻohana, connecting me to the natural environment. As a child, I took full advantage of the nature around my tūtū's home, such as sitting by streams with an abundance of opai (tiny crayfish); playing in her yard; picking "*dragon eye*," a sweet lychee-type fruit (aka longan), to eat; and riding my cousin's jeep in the neighboring cane fields. I remember relaxing on my tūtū's lanai (outdoor porch).

Another of my most precious memories of my early childhood was the food my tūtū fed me. It's funny how food becomes nostalgic in many cultures. It was no different for me. My tūtū didn't feed me baby food from a bottle, but rather fed me food that gave Hawaiians sustenance for many generations before Western contact: iʻa (fish), poi (mashed taro), and hua kai (scrambled egg) soup. It was like soul food. Up until my college years, my grandmother and her siblings always called me to their table to offer me their secret stash of Hawaiian delicacies. They offered me special species of raw poke iʻa (cubed fish) that was not offered on the buffet line for everyone else. I always felt honored and special that at family gatherings, my kūpuna invited me to partake of the food that they had brought to share only among themselves. This is such a haliʻa aloha (fond or loving recollection) for me.

Enjoying these experiences during my early childhood years with my kūpuna involved observing, listening, and doing, which are traditional patterns of education for Hawaiians (Chun 2011). Observing my mother's choice for my early childhood care allowed me to connect with my ancestors and affirm my cultural identity as a kanaka ʻōiwi—more specifically, identifying as a valued member of my ʻohana. My inoa, Kuʻulei, manifested the reciprocation of love given and returned to me by my tūtū, grandaunt, and grandmother. I am a descendant of my Hawaiian ʻohana and so blessed to learn their heritage and values.

To Hilo, Hawaiʻi

Hilo was a town located on Hawaiʻi island. We traveled there by airplane often in my early childhood and elementary years. Hilo was the birthplace of my mother and the place where my maternal grandparents lived. My grandfather, Grandpa Hilo, as I so dearly called him, was such a tremendous spiritual force and influence in my life until he passed in my eighth grade year. Every winter break after Christmas and most summers, my mother took us to visit her parents on Hawaiʻi island. I loved it there. My grandmother, whose name I carry, passed away when I was 7 years old. However, most of my early memories were of my Grandpa Hilo. I spent most summers with him and, sometimes, I would stay with him alone while my family flew home to Oʻahu. My Grandpa Hilo was a quiet man of action. He would take really good care of me. He made breakfast for me every day, if my mom's brother didn't beat him to it, and cooked his special chicken bone soup, my favorite meal each time I visited. I remember that he took me to Woolworth's to buy the best fried chicken in town. We would eat our chicken together and save the bones for his special soup. Yikes, now I realize that my grandfather used those bones to make a special soup that tasted so good. Yummy! In addition, my grandfather made my favorite berry jam using the fruit from a tall tree that grew in his yard. I loved spending my school vacations there in Hilo.

In my elementary years, I was able to observe my grandfather's faithfulness and steadfastness to his calling as a minister of God. I remember passing his bedroom in the morning, catching a glimpse of my grandfather on his knees praying or sitting on his bed reading his Bible. My grandfather was a man of few words. However, he never failed to serve the people and to provide for their natural and spiritual needs. Grandpa Hilo would often pick up other kūpuna to give them a ride to church because they didn't drive. Also, every Thursday night, my grandfather traveled 45 minutes one-way to another town to hold a church service for a few people, maybe two families at most. As a child, I felt that the car ride on a dark road was boring and way too long. I often wondered why my Grandpa Hilo would travel so far with only a few members. However, my grandfather was committed to minister to people in need. He would encourage everyone in attendance with a sermon and then pray for them to be strengthened until the following week. Then he would do it all again, never complaining.

My Grandma Hilo, Elizabeth Keakalaulono Dart (left), and Grandpa Hilo, William Gulstan Dart (right), were renowned pastors in Hilo, Hawaiʻi.

This is my moʻokūʻauhau of my Christian faith and service to others in need. My observance of my Grandpa Hilo living the life of his conviction, not to please others but to please his God. He passed this down to me. My grandfather would often ask me at a young age to participate in parts of his church service, like singing a special song, leading the congregation in hymns, or leading testimonials. My grandfather normalized my participation in leadership and service at a very young age. Due to his confidence in my ability, I soon gained confidence to also serve God and others, helping them in whatever ways that I could. Today, I am an ordained minister. This is one of my identities, and I am proud of it.

From Hālawa to Hilo, my kūpuna nurtured and demonstrated extreme care for me. Those interactions fed into my lives. My kūpuna lived by example, modeling lifestyles of Hawaiian values, such as aloha (love), hoʻokipa (hospitality), onipaʻa (perseverance), poʻokela (excellence), and pono (uprightness). They identified my special gifts and nurtured them by providing opportunities for me to practice. My kūpuna were the strong but quiet lifters, the encouragers that modeled total acceptance of me in my early childhood. They made me feel special and helped build my confidence to do whatever I put my mind to. It is evident that my kūpuna set the foundation for my moʻokūʻahau that has guided my actions and formed my character to help define my identity. They always esteemed me as their Kuʻulei.

Moʻokūʻauhau of Aʻo and Alakaʻi: Educational Servant Leaders

> Aʻo is the Hawaiian word for education that implies both to learn and teach. This sense of receiving and giving emphasizes that the ideas of relationships and belonging are the primary actions in Hawaiian culture and society. (Chun 2011, 84)

I come from a long line of educators and servant leaders, in traditional and nontraditional settings. This is my moʻokūʻauhau in education and service. In my early childhood, I observed and experienced through my parents' lives that education and service to others were very important. My mother was a music, English, and Spanish teacher in the Hawaiʻi Department of Education, a Sunday school teacher, and a choir director in our church. My mother, like her father, picked up children and their mothers or grandmothers from federal housing who often didn't have a ride to attend church. I remember my mother taking them to eat at McDonald's after church before taking them home. My mother would also take us to visit people in convalescent homes and hospitals to bring gifts and show them that they are not forgotten. My father, although a civil engineer by profession, was also a US Army Reserve officer who served as an instructor and educator in his field. My dad also served in ministry and conducted early church services for prisoners in the local jail before attending regular church each Sunday.

My father, Antonio Distajo Jr.; my older brother, Anthony Kehau Distajo; and me (left). My mother, Flaviana Keakalaulono Dart, my older brother, and me (right).

My parents and kūpuna placed a confidence in my early childhood that made me feel like I could accomplish anything. I observed their diligence in child care, education, and their Christian faith. I developed an aspiration to care for children, too. So I made the decision to become an educator and, later, a teacher-educator. Also, my ʻohana taught me the importance of my inoa, my moʻokūʻauhau, and understanding its relevance to my life. This influenced my passion to promote education and total well-being for kānaka ʻōiwi children and youth. I continue to engage in this work by supporting kānaka ʻōiwi children, their families, and community through educational grants that provide professional development and resources to schools. I am also the proud mentor of kānaka ʻōiwi scholars and graduate students. I develop caring educators who teach kānaka ʻōiwi keiki. I am proud to fulfill my kuleana that will perpetuate their lineage and moʻokūʻauhau.

Holomua: Advancing ECE Teacher Education and Leadership

"He lei poina ʻole ke keiki: A beloved child is a lei never forgotten."

> "Lei. Figurative. a beloved child, wife, husband, sweetheart, younger sibling or child, so called because a beloved child was carried on the shoulders, with its legs draped down on both sides of the bearer like a lei." (Pukui & Elbert 1986, 200)

In Hawaiian culture, keiki are revered and precious like lei who adorn their ʻohana members and are an extension of their legacy. I was blessed with familial interactions that never made me feel forgotten. They provided me with early learning experiences that were meaningful to my Hawaiian heritage. I experienced kūpuna believing in me, imparting their love and wisdom into me by sharing their moʻolelo, and the importance of our genealogy. My ʻohana always recognized my potential for becoming a leader and lifted me until I reached those higher heights. I was my ʻohana's beloved lei, their *Kuʻulei*, imparting love and wisdom into my life.

As I reflect on my early childhood and the exemplary, but not always perfect, lives of my kūpuna and mākua (parents), I realize that I have been blessed with the wealth of opportunities to "live out" the intersections of my identities that have been shaped by my moʻokūʻauhau. These identities have influenced my pursuit of becoming the best educator and early childhood teacher-educator. These early childhood experiences as a kanaka ʻōiwi have helped to inform my professional decisions, manaʻo (thoughts), and practices for early childhood education teacher education.

> E hana mua paʻa ke kahua mamua o ke aʻo ana aku ia haʻi
> Build yourself a firm foundation before teaching others.
> Ōlelo Noʻeau #276 (Pukui 1983, 34)

My early childhood experiences have built a strong foundation in my life to teach others. Those experiences taught me the importance of ensuring that early childhood education educators incorporate culturally responsive pedagogies in their practices. For example, the traditional patterns of Aʻo (education) in Hawaiian society/culture were nānā (observation); hoʻolohe (listening); hana ka lima (doing); reflection; and questioning (nīnau) (Chun 2011). We need to support teaching and learning that reflect strategies on how children from different cultures best learn and apply those to our own praxis.

My experiences of my ʻohana practicing Hawaiian tradition and values in their daily lives have also taught me the importance that early childhood education educators should be trained to engage and strengthen relationships with children's families, familiarizing themselves with the children's home culture. This is valuable to Indigenous families (Grace & Serna 2012; Sole et al. 2024). I was fortunate to be immersed in the traditions of my ʻohana every day in my early childhood years. I did not have to mitigate between home and the preschool culture that may have possibly negated my home culture and ʻohana values. Early childhood education educators should always seek to build pilina (relationships, connections) with children and their ʻohana.

As a teacher-educator, I would like to also develop creative leader mindsets in early childhood education educators/professionals, such as optimism, creative confidence, empathy, and ambiguity to name a few (Douglass 2017). My kūpuna were also optimistic and built confidence in me. I recall my parents and kūpuna not allowing me to feel bad about being left-handed or having a high forehead. I was told that left-handers were smart, and my forehead indicated that I was going to be very intelligent. I chuckle now but am grateful to my ʻohana for always encouraging me with optimism. My parents were also great at making me look at circumstances and people from multiple perspectives. I was taught to withhold judgement until I understood the entire matter; in other words, "don't judge a book by its cover." This taught me to be empathetic to others many times. I believe that early childhood education educators should model and practice these attributes. Because I observed and experienced such great care as a young child, I came to love working with children and serving others.

Lastly, my early childhood experiences provided me the security to be totally accepted for who I was. I was often supported to accomplish my goals and succeed. My gifts were identified and encouraged by my ʻohana. This has impacted me and given me a strong desire to help all keiki identify their unique gifts that make them special in this world. I want to help children actualize those gifts by providing them opportunities to experience self-efficacy, like my grandfather offered me when he allowed me to lead singing in his church service. I want children to feel celebrated and have total acceptance of who they are, where they come from, and the value they have because of their uniqueness. We can model total acceptance of students, their families, and their communities by allowing them to share their moʻokūʻauhau. Indigenous parents want children to learn their Indigenous history and identity (Sole et al. 2024). In listening to children's moʻokūʻauhau, early childhood education educators can help them identify the mana and talent unique to them and their ʻohana. It is my hope that early childhood education can give our children more opportunities to develop a greater sense of cultural and familial pride, connection, and purpose to something greater than themselves.

So Many More Voices . . .

As a Japanese Filipina mixed-race American, my identity is unfinished. I carry histories of colonization, war, and racism—of atrocities survived and committed, and of joy, culture, and the gift of knowing my ancestors. Some days I feel grounded; other days split. I'm learning to stay with the tension, learning alongside my children.

Gabrielle Kazuko Nomura Gainor
Dancer, Activist, and Communications Professional
Seattle, Washington

CHAPTER 10

Immigrating to America

A Filipina's Story

ROSEMARIE RIDEOUT

My story is about the challenges and successes of an immigrant who comes to America with a dream and a hope for a better life. This is about a girl who grows up in the rural Philippines and her father's desire for a better life for her than he had. It is also a story about the challenges a first-generation AANHPI person faces in the American system of education, the challenges of experiencing racism and exclusion, and the challenges of being an outsider struggling for recognition and acceptance.

I was born in July 1987 in a small fishing village located on the largest island in the Philippines. Our island, Mindanao, is known as "the Land of Promise" and is one of over 7,000 islands that make up the Philippines. In addition to this large number of islands, there are also over 100 different languages spoken in the Philippines. We are one nation with many different cultures, but a common heritage of colonialism, religion, family, and poverty.

My father was a fisherman with a third grade education. He came to Mindanao when his family home and cropland on the island of Cebu was destroyed by a major typhoon. Everything was lost, and while some stayed to rebuild, Papa left for Mindanao—for the Land of Promise. That's where he met Mama, and the rest is history as we say.

Mama has a sixth grade education, and like most Filipino women, was content and happy to be around family. She washed clothes for neighbors and had a small sari store in our squatter home. On our island there is little in the way of industry or work. Fishing and farming are the main industries. But you have to own a boat to fish and land to farm. Our family had neither when Papa arrived. When I left in 2015 to come to America, Papa had just passed away. His only possession, his boat, had been sold to pay his medical bills. We never had much. Papa always taught us to work hard and share with those around you. And, Papa knew the value of education—when it came to our education, he was without compromise. He demanded that we continue our education and move past him and Mama. He knew the value of what he never could have, and he was determined to avoid letting us go down the same path he had followed. Papa was a visual learner, like me. "To see is to believe" was what I recall growing up, and these are words that echo with me today.

Our daily life was one of survival. If Papa caught fish, we ate. If Papa caught a LOT of fish, we had some extra money to buy some extra things. If Papa couldn't fish for a few days because of bad weather, we had to borrow rice from the neighbors or we didn't eat.

But we were always happy and positive. I lived with hundreds of other children, and we played together and made our own toys and games from whatever was around us. We never had store-bought toys, books, paper, or pencils. Only a few families had TV. When someone had a happy event, they shared what they had with everyone around. When Papa caught a lot of fish, we shared first with our neighbors, then ourselves, and then sold it to the market if any was left over.

I didn't realize it at the time, but all of this helped to prepare me for a career in early childhood education. I had several aunts and cousins who were teachers, but I had no dream that one day I could be that person, no dream that one day I would see reflected in the children of Reggio Emilia, Italy, my childhood from Santa Cruz, Davao del Sur, Philippines.

Rosemarie's parents with their grandchildren, on her mother's birthday.

Understanding Philippine Culture and History

The Philippines became an independent nation at the end of World War II when the United States granted our independence. Before that time, we were the property of the United States, having been "won" as the spoils of war from Spain after the Spanish-American War of 1898.

Rosemarie (in purple, about 13 years old) with her extended family and friends, with a Lechón (traditional roasted pig).

During the time of Spanish rule, Dr. Jose Rizal was a writer, doctor, and activist who advocated for the free education of all people, to lift all Filipinos out of the poverty endured under the Spanish colonial rule. He is called the Father of the Philippines. He was executed for his views and work, and it is due to him that our nation considers teaching an honorable profession and the tradition of teaching started in my family.

When I grew up in the 1980s and '90s in our squatter home located 100 meters from the Gulf of Davao on the Pacific Ocean, we lived in economic poverty. Squatter homes rarely have running water, toilets, or electricity. It is a home that you do not own. But the home itself does not make a family or a culture; the people who live in the home create family and culture. And our home was strong and we were rich because of Papa, Mama, and all those around us. I never knew we lived in poverty because we had family and friends and freedom to explore the whole village, the ocean, and everything around us.

Culture is important to understand as a part of a person's story. I'm describing my culture and my upbringing because I am not alone in making this journey. Sometimes I feel alone in the early childhood education profession because there are few colleagues who share my story and my culture. More on that later. . . .

As a child, I didn't enjoy school. I felt that being confined in the walls of the classroom wasn't really learning. Because I am a visual learner, school was tough for me to handle, and I was not the best student. The teaching was all in English (our official language), but no one spoke or read English outside of school, and I had no support for using English at home. Since our parents were not literate in English, we never "studied." I remember many days in the classroom when I would look outside and think of being free from school, going to the ocean or just being with my friends and learning about life.

Our public schools had limited supplies of books. If you wanted one, you had to be present when they were handed out, or else you ended up copying everything or writing what the teacher said. Most of the classrooms were without electricity, and there was no technology. Corporal punishment was legal and common when I was in school (it no longer is).

Although my family valued education, our circumstances made it difficult for me to be successful in school, and as a young child, I couldn't see the value of sitting inside where it was hot and boring. One time my friends and I didn't come back for the afternoon session. Our teacher found us by the beach and told our parents what happened. My papa was disappointed and angry with me, because I didn't use my talents and disrespected all he had done for me. I promised Papa that I would do my best from that point forward.

I stuck with school, graduated with my high school diploma, but could not continue to college. Unlike in America, there is no financial aid system to help you pay for college. I worked for a while in a fish cannery, but the work was not for me. There were limited work opportunities around me, and I felt no sense of direction. The Philippines is number one in the world with the largest percentages of citizens who work and live overseas. At any one time, there are over 10 percent of our citizens (10 million people) working and living abroad in more than 200 countries. This is because of the limited opportunities at home. Our people work in jobs that many people won't do in our host countries, like maids, caregivers, nannies, clerks, and waiters. Many ships and cruise lines employ Filipinos.

I was heading for that life until the internet arrived. At age 20 (2007), we got our first cell tower in our village, and that changed everything for me and my generation. Three years later, I met my husband on an international dating site. He had one question for me: "What is your biggest desire?" I told him how much I wanted to continue my education, and a few months later I was able to enroll in a technical school (STI-Digos). Two years later we were married in the Philippines, and our son was born 10 months later, in 2012.

In 2015, when our son was almost 3 years old, I obtained my green card and came to America. We moved into my husband's family home in Flint, Michigan, with his 100-year-old mother. This was culturally appropriate for me—we always have our family together in the house. I didn't understand it was not always viewed that way in America! In the Philippines, we have multiple generations in one small home. It took me a while to realize that it was different in America.

Having never traveled outside the Philippines and only recently taken my first plane flight, coming to America for the first time was overwhelming to me. I remember thinking how fast things moved and how big the houses were. I really didn't understand why only two people would live in such a big house. My husband had arranged for our son to attend preschool in a parochial school near our house. When I visited there, I was in awe of all the resources for the children. I had never seen anything like this.

Knowing our son was in a good preschool setting, I started on my own journey. My story is about my experiences immigrating to a new country. I learned some helpful strategies that I would share with anyone in my situation:

1. Find a community of your culture near you. I found a Filipina friend at the local mall, and my husband found a local Filipino association that helped me greatly.
2. Visit your local community college. I had no understanding of the American education system until I visited Mott Community College, which changed everything when I realized there was a path to get my degree.
3. If your English skills are below average, find a local literacy program for help. This helped me greatly when I was getting started.
4. Understand that most American educators want you to succeed! In my first class at the community college, my professor was Filipino. He was one of many "lucky" events that happened along the way.
5. Take advantage of mentors who come your way. Many Americans want immigrants to succeed and are willing to help.

"Bloom Where You Are Planted"

A few words about living in Flint, Michigan. One thing that happened to me when we arrived in 2015 was we were told "don't drink the water." I had just come from a country where we didn't drink tap water either, but I was surprised to find that in Flint, in the United States of America, we couldn't drink the water. People were telling me that we might get sick or lead poisoning, our hair might fall out, rashes and itchy skin would happen. People lined up for hours to get free water at churches. This was very strange to me, and yes, my hair got thinner, I had rashes, and our son tested positive for lead exposure (he's going to be fine). All of the schools have installed special water fountains with filters. We still drink bottled water at home. It is just a fact of life for our daily routine in this community. While we are being told that the water is "safe" to drink, many (including me) are drinking bottled water even to this day.

Once I started my schooling in early childhood education, I also began working in different early childhood settings in the area. The first thing I did was volunteer at my son's parochial school, to help out in the pre-K program. What I observed (and felt) with the teachers and other parent volunteers was that I was not welcomed by them. It was awkward and I did not understand. They would talk among themselves and did not include me in what they were talking about. If I came close, sometimes they would stop talking, so I thought "maybe they are talking about me?" I was shy and thought my accent must be so bad, my English must be hard to understand. This made me feel very uncomfortable. I did not really know what to do to overcome this.

Thankfully, our son was well liked, and he spoke less English than me at this age. Our son came to America speaking a mixture of mostly Visaya with a little English. Some of the children found it hard to communicate with him. I would try to speak English with him, but sometimes I had to use Visayan because I did not know the English word. Visaya is not well known outside the Philippines, and many English words don't translate directly into Visaya. Our son was able to overcome this language barrier. He learned English quickly and was involved actively with other children.

Then one day a new teacher arrived. Her husband was a native Filipino! She was excited to have our son and me in the classroom. I could tell that the other parents started to observe that she was spending more time with me and asking me questions about the Philippines and my family, although this didn't change the way the parents treated me. Whenever adults talked with me, they were polite but not warm. I wondered why I was rarely asked about my family, my country, and my journey to America. We were never invited to anyone's home, never asked to go out after school or on a weekend, never involved in any birthday parties or play dates outside the school. It made me feel like we were "different." This was a new feeling I never had before.

Instead, I was asked how I met my husband. Most assumed he was in the military, but when I told them we had met on an online dating site, the conversation usually stopped. I learned that Americans stereotype younger Asian women who meet men on dating sites as scammers. I learned that they think that the only reason I was in the United States was to get citizenship. They had a hard time believing that two people could actually meet online and fall in love, much less get married, have a child, and want the same things for their family, such as a life in America.

When I was first admitted to the United States in 2015, I was a permanent resident (a "green card" holder). When I applied for US citizenship, my husband and I were nervous, though we tried to keep our faith strong. What if the United States would not approve me for citizenship? What if my husband died suddenly and I was deported? What if I was accused of a crime because someone didn't like me and I was deported? It is hard to explain to an American citizen all of these thoughts you have when you are waiting for your citizenship chance in the United States. Recent events in America have made this very clear to immigrants.

Why is this important, and why mention it? These worries affect what you say and what you do. You might not want to speak up because you don't want to make trouble. Maybe you are shy around strangers who speak a different language, and you're not really sure if you should get involved in a discussion. You think "maybe they don't like foreigners." Or maybe it's hard to understand what they are saying because you are listening to them speak English and then trying to translate it into your own language and it's hard to keep up. All of these are real feelings which can affect you in the workplace.

Navigating College for the Immigrant Student

In March of 2025, I graduated with my BAA magna cum laude from Central Michigan University. My major was early childhood learning and development; my minor was in family studies. I was blessed with wonderful advisors and supportive professors. The best advice I received was from Dr. Cheryl Priest when I shared with her my concerns about my ability to understand English. She encouraged me to talk with each professor at the beginning of class and tell them a little bit of my story. That was one of the best suggestions ever. Every professor appreciated knowing my story.

The hardest part of American schooling for me was multiple-choice tests. Group projects were also difficult, because I am a visual learner, and when there were group meetings, everyone would talk at the same time. I could not follow the discussion because it was hard for me to understand what was being said, translate to my language, and then respond. I feared those situations. I did not want to hold people back, appear stupid or slow, or otherwise embarrass myself, so I did not try to change their behavior. I just didn't do well in those situations. I excelled in group projects in my home country, because we were all on the same page. For any immigrant coming to the United States, be prepared for this. I think it is especially hard for someone like me, an Asian person, because I was always taught to not question or create conflict.

Fitting into the American Early Childhood Education Work Setting

In my home country, we expect a new teacher to work closely with another teacher to get oriented and involved. This did not happen for me (or any other new hires, either) at my early childhood education jobs. As early childhood educators, we are trained in parental involvement and making children and families feel welcome in the classroom setting, so I was surprised at how little sense of belonging I felt in my work settings. The adults I interacted with didn't want to know about my personal life or experience. There were times in the first few years of work that some of the staff would make a plan for getting together after work. I wasn't included.

Because of my English skills, I am still learning which words to use, and I can get frustrated when I can't get the right word in my head. It might take a little patience to listen to me at first. But the isolation I felt definitely affected me in my work settings. In some instances, parents would not want to talk to me and would bypass or ignore me to talk with an American-born teacher or aide. In other instances, I was excluded from meetings and discussions about important things. At staff meetings I did not speak up because it was hard for me to follow what was going on. I asked my early childhood education center director about this and told her that I felt like I didn't know how to get into the discussions. I had much that I wanted to share. For the next couple of meetings, I was asked to contribute, but nothing really changed. She soon stopped asking me to be involved, so I just stopped participating. I know that was wrong, but I felt like I wasn't welcome to speak up.

Don't get me wrong, there have been great mentors. It has taken a while, but finally I am gaining courage to speak up, and sometimes I am listened to. The children love me. They are the easiest part of my job. Their parents and guardians are less tolerant and in some cases rude to me. What I never know is how to overcome this, because there is no college course on "how to fit in as a foreign-born teacher."

Important Lessons Learned

I am very proud of my heritage and my family. I am very proud of what I have achieved. It's hard to grow professionally and personally when you feel isolated in your classroom and no one wants to ask you about your journey. If you're an educator reading this and you recognize someone you work with who is in a similar situation, please reach out and say words like "tell me about your journey to this classroom." We all have a need for connection, regardless of where we started or how we got here.

When I am in an early childhood leadership position, I will encourage my staff to learn about the *whole* child—we already do this in some centers by making home visits. But what about all the staff you interact with? Do you know them as *whole* people? Storytelling is also an important skill to practice with each other. We're great at reading stories to our students and great at helping them to imagine. But what about the stories *we* have from our own childhood? Some are very heartwarming, others are heartbreaking. But they are *our* stories, and telling them is a way to teach and learn from each other. But first someone has to ask me about where I grew up, and they have to want to learn. In the meantime, all I can do is bring in lumpia or some other native food—but that's not really what being from the Philippines is all about. Learning about the place someone comes from is important to understanding the person. It's the "home visit" that reveals much. My impression is that this is not so important to Americans, but family and home is everything to a Filipina.

Just as we want to welcome a child's full identity into the classroom, an educator's full identity can be connected to their work with young children. In the future, I hope I can support these connections as a leader in early childhood education.

Being the "first" at something is not always easy. I am the first in my family to leave the Philippines and move to a different country, the first to learn to drive a car, the first to own property, the first to graduate college. I will be the first to have something published in a book. The challenges for this Asian American Filipina have included the daily challenges every immigrant faces in the United States: learning new foods, new customs, different government policies, and all the cultural differences from my home country of the Philippines.

Nobody can ever take away my educational accomplishments, the pride I feel, and the pride my family feels for me. I sacrificed everything I knew, everything I was comfortable with, for the opportunity to learn and grow and make a different path for my family.

My inner pride sustains me daily. Nobody can take that away. As I have grown in my position at our Early Childhood Learning Center, a few of my colleagues have begun to make efforts to understand me and my background. I am not a person who typically talks about what I have accomplished or brags about what I am going to do. My philosophy is to do what I am supposed to do as best I can, and if someone wants to know me better, all they have to do is ask.

So, please ASK and I will TELL.

So Many More Voices . . .

> I think of the AANHPI identity as a bucket to hold us- but it is not all of us; it's just the surface. It does not capture the complexity that we all come with; people can be multiple things at once.

Charis-Ann F. Sole
Chapter Author

CHAPTER 11

Access to Education

A Refugee Immigrant's Journey

BICK HANG

Why I Am Here

I am a refugee immigrant from Vietnam. This became my identity at the age of 7 years old. When I was 7, it was during the time of the Vietnam War, and my family was living in Saigon. In 1975, when Saigon fell to the communist party, my family had to flee due to the work my father did for the South Vietnamese Army. There were seven of us in my immediate family—my parents and my five sisters, who were all under the age of 9—but we were also close with our extended family. We were just having a regular day until late afternoon, when my father came home and said, "We have to leave." He drove home in a big army truck, and we were fascinated by it because we had never seen it before. He tried to stay calm and made it sound like we were getting ready to go on a vacation trip. At that time, we didn't really know what was happening. I got the sense that my mother knew something else was going on, but she didn't say anything. My father asked us to grab whatever we could carry before getting onto the truck. My immediate family and 11 other extended family members climbed into the truck before my father drove us all back to the military base. Once we entered the base and passed all the checkpoints, I remember we all walked down to the beach to get on a military barge to evacuate us to another destination along the river.

At the next destination, we were surrounded by bombed-out abandoned buildings and empty military shelters with no electricity or good running water. As we took shelter at a nearby abandoned building, we continued to hear overhead bombings that took down more buildings, and people were scrambling to get their families to safety. We, again, had to flee and traveled on foot for days to find safer shelter. As time went on, we were getting farther away from our home, and the option of going back home was fading away fast. Our only option was to go back into the river and go out into the open water. It was no longer an option to go back home. We had lost everything, so our only option was to move forward, wherever that may be. There was no plan. If we go back home, my father would have been captured, sent to a reeducation camp, or executed—that's what happened to South Vietnamese soldiers who stayed behind.

The bombing never quieted down. My father negotiated with the boat owner, and our family got into the small and overcrowded fishing boat with many other families trying to flee to safety. A few days on the boat became so many long days, and I stopped counting. Drinking water and food became scarce, and people were dying of dehydration. I remember my mother giving each of us about a tablespoon full of water two to three times a day to keep our mouths from drying out and becoming dehydrated. At some point the boat had stopped working, and we were just floating in the open water. A couple of people had died, and the crew members decided to throw their bodies into the water so the sharks would no longer swim around the boat. I remember being so scared. Eventually, we were rescued by a cargo ship. The crew used a net to hoist up a few people at a time. Out of fear of being left behind, people panicked and started to climb onto the side of the boat and clung to the outer side of the net, fell, and drowned. Fortunately, all my family and extended family members made it safely onto the ship. Everyone who was rescued was housed below deck. At this point, we were so grateful for the rescue. I remember having sliced bread for the first time, along with some sort of porridge when food was offered. We didn't know where we were going but were hoping for a safe place.

Resettlement and the Value of Education

We ended up in three different refugee camps located on military bases to be processed to enter the United States: first in Guam, then in the Philippines, and finally in Florida. Because our extended family was so big, a total of 20, it took a long time to be sponsored. After about six months, we were finally sponsored by a Southern Baptist Church from Birmingham. We were brought to a rural farming area to stay in a hostel owned by the lead sponsor from the church. The adults in the family were tasked to install/repair barbed wire fences around acres of property for 75 cents an hour, but our family never saw the money. My parents were told that the paid income will be held for them and to be used during weekly grocery shopping trips with church sponsors; grocery lists were often monitored and limited. The children attended weekly in-home English lessons, and Wednesday was Bible study day for everyone, all facilitated by church volunteers. On Sundays, the church bus came to take us to church. Our family stayed there for almost a year before my father and uncles decided to petition the church sponsors for support to move out to the city to find jobs and enroll their children into regular school. The church sponsors were reluctant because it meant they would lose workers, but they helped our family to find housing in the city, and the children were enrolled into a nearby school.

The school population was mostly Black students; we were one of two Vietnamese families in the whole school. It was hard at first because we didn't speak or understand a lot of English. My siblings and I participated in the school's pull-out program (English as a second language—ESL) to get more one-on-one support to learn English. Math came easier to us only because we could understand numbers. When I hear someone say, "Asians are really good at math," I think about this and know this is a myth. We were not necessarily good at math, but numbers were the only thing we understood. Nevertheless, we enjoyed going to school because we didn't have the same opportunity in Vietnam. Back in our country, we were poor but didn't really know it. Public school in Vietnam was fee-based, and there were times we didn't attend school because my family didn't have money to pay the overdue tuition fees for myself and my sisters. I remember a time during a school day; my sisters and I were locked inside a principal's closet because my parents hadn't paid the monthly tuition. It was a traumatic experience. Once we came to the United States and found that school was free, we were excited about attending school. My parents understood and believed education was important. They put forth all efforts to ensure we went to school every day. We really appreciated the opportunity to attend "free" school. For a long time, we all would get perfect attendance every year. Once we became more fluent in English, we were driven to complete our education and graduated from high school and then went on to attend college. With additional hard work and support from my parents, my four siblings and I also graduated from college.

Becoming an Educator

I became an educator because school was always very important to me, and I remembered what it was like when I couldn't go to school. I understood the challenges of not being able to attend school on a regular basis. It was a privilege to have completed my education and earned a master's degree in human development with a specialization in bicultural, bilingual development in young children. My current work within early childhood education allows me to have positive impacts on young children's development, particularly for children who come into the learning environment with established home languages and home cultures. I currently have the privilege of serving as a curriculum and instructional coach for a team of 35 culturally diverse teachers within the Seattle area. I am always inspired when I see upcoming Asian teachers within the field of early childhood education. I get to learn so much from them and want to contribute to their professional development to bring out their best selves, fostering culturally responsive teaching practices so the children can get quality learning experience that best meets their learning needs.

How Others See Me

In my experience, when you say you're Asian American, many people don't think about whether you were born in the United States or are a naturalized citizen. You are always looked at as being different, a "foreigner" of sorts. When they hear you speak English well, they say things like "You sound so smart." This is a form of microaggression; people think they are paying you a compliment when they are being offensive. I tend to stay quiet and do more observing in new settings. This is sometimes mistaken for passiveness and weakness. I usually take time to formulate my thoughts and responses before they are shared in public spaces. I process and think through my response in my head before I speak; some people talk out loud to process their thoughts. For the community that knows me well, I am a strong partner and collaborator who takes into consideration the impact a decision may have at the collective verse at the individualistic level. When we cooperate and work together, more than likely the experience will benefit the group. As the saying suggests, a rising tide elevates all boats.

Strengths Uncovered

Despite the challenges growing up as a Vietnamese refugee immigrant, I have gained strengths from my Vietnamese identity. I have a deep understanding and empathy for the immigrant and refugee perspective. I draw on my own experiences to support teachers to think about how they can support children as they navigate the world around them. I try to model and demonstrate through my actions what it means to be present and resilient. As someone who is bilingual and bicultural, I understand that being able to navigate in and out of different cultures is a strength. In my coaching work with teachers, I encourage and foster support for them to be cultural navigators to bridge support for children and families to take pride in maintaining and preserving cultural languages and traditions. Family partnership can play a key role in building a strong learning environment for all children.

After all, families are their children's first teachers in life. They can serve as an asset within the school system if leaders are efficient in how they incorporate and collaborate family strengths in developing meaningful learning opportunities for our youngest and most formidable population.

Lessons for the Early Childhood Classroom

As mentioned above, family participation and partnerships are important ingredients in helping to meet children's learning needs for more positive outcomes. This is a low-cost investment for a high yield in return. Once families are supported to understand the power of their participation and involvement, the opportunities to share their skills and talents are endless. Families are a great source of support for children's development and transferable learning connections from home to school and school to home. Families can provide firsthand connections to home culture and language(s) that can be incorporated into the collective classroom learning environment. They are historians of their own families in language, traditions, songs, food, and stories. When those cultural aspects are included within the classroom setting, all children and families will benefit in learning and understanding about the larger "family community." When families participate as coteachers to support children's learning, children and families are empowered. I support and welcome these opportunities whenever they arise; this aspect of teaching continues to be my all-time favorite strategy to be in partnership with families. This inclusive and collaborative process also provides opportunities for the learning community to gain greater understanding of cross-cultural exchange and pollination, with a deeper appreciation for the similarities as well as how they can support one another to better understand cultural differences within the learning community.

Classroom teacher success also relies on continued, genuine support from leadership to ensure professional development and teacher care are at the forefront. The creation of a healthy community of educators will support and transform teachers' ability to exchange and cross-pollinate skill sets to be explored within the learning environment that best meet children's learning needs. These opportunities should include time for peer reflective practice, designated coplanning time, observation of each other's classrooms, a peer-mentoring process, and equitable pay. Just as we create and provide space for families to fully engage in their children's learning and development, we also need to do the same for teachers to grow and develop. Without such a support network, we will continue to operate in mediocracy or less than.

To better support the overall Asian community within the education system, a different process of data collection is needed to accurately reflect the needs of all Asian students. Asian Americans are not a monolithic culture. We need to disaggregate data differently to have a better understanding of needs and deficits of specific Asian groups. Education data generally show the Asian population as doing well and performing above average, but there are Asian children struggling who are overlooked within the education system. How can we collect data differently to identify and notate the struggles to better support their education journey? My education journey and professional career have not been without challenges; however, I love my work and remain deeply committed to advocating for children and families within an education system that truly supports and develops their learning potential.

CHAPTER 12

Being Asian in America

Connecting Stories Through Generation and Time

LISA LUKE LEE

> "To forget one's ancestors is to be a brook without a source, a tree without roots."
> — Chinese proverb, n.d.

I am a third-generation Chinese American, born in the state of Hawai'i in the late 1950s. I chose early childhood education as a career, one of the least desirable choices on an immigrant's path to financial stability and success. Not law or medicine . . . it wasn't going to impress my parents. From their point of view, early childhood education was an "if it makes you happy" choice. Forty years later, I am indeed happy that I made that choice—only now fully aware that I had the power to choose in a way that the Asian women who came before me could not.

In my 40-year career in early childhood education, I chose to work much of it serving immigrant and underserved communities. Over a decade of it was spent as the child care director at Wu Yee Children's Services in San Francisco's Chinatown. Most of the families were first-or second-generation immigrants from China, Taiwan, and Vietnam. A few private slots were filled by third-generation Asian families who wanted their children to have roots in the language and culture of their ethnic heritages. The home languages of the children were Cantonese, Mandarin, or Vietnamese. As a director and third-generation Asian American, I had the rare opportunity to understand their perspectives and experiences. As they shared their stories, hopes, and struggles, I learned about myself and the journey of my own family.

From One Generation to the Next: The Imprint of Matriarchs

My family spent Sunday evenings at my maternal grandmother, Popo (grandmother) Lee's house. Popo Lee's home was just up the hill from our home in Kalihi. At Popo Lee's house, a tiny pair of red embroidered shoes had a place of honor amidst the porcelain Chinese dishes in the living room cabinet. No one talked about them, but I knew they belonged to one of my mother's grandmothers. I didn't know my great grandmother's stories. I only later researched the painful ritual of wrapping the feet of young girls to stunt their growth and break the bones to achieve the admired three-inch lotus feet (Foreman 2015). While I grew up running barefoot on the beach, my great-grandmother grew up bound.

Friday was dinner at my paternal grandparent's house. My Popo Luke cared for 6 to 10 of my siblings and cousins during the day when our parents went to work. In my career, I would have called what she did unlicensed family child care. In my childhood, it was just Popo's house. She loved us fiercely. I took much of what she did for granted—she made our school lunches, sewed the family's clothes, tended the gardens, and cooked family meals. I believed she was self-taught. She found the freshest produce and best prices by looking at pictures and prices in the newspaper grocery store ads. She couldn't read, at least not in English. I didn't know then that reading Chinese characters was valuable. I could read when I was 5 years old. I believed her when she would declare, "Me no smart."

I heard Popo's stories in snippets of broken English—of traveling on a steamer ship to live a new life or having a baby upstairs of the Wo On Store in North Kohala. She sold her jewelry when times were tough and taught herself how to cook and sew. My popo was a picture bride, matched by her parents through a photograph to a man she had never met. She said goodbye to her mother at the age of 17 and voyaged across the sea to be the wife of the first son of a third wife, a life without status and a good share of hardship. Just one more woman who did not get to choose. My journey as an Asian American is tied to the women who came before me. The ability to choose, to find and use my voice as an early childhood leader and activist spring from their journeys. In my heart story, I often consider that I was set on this path by my Popos' who loved us so well in their homes. My Popo Luke made each grandchild feel like her favorite. She bought me my first book in a grocery store outing. I chose "Thumbelina," the story of a blond, blue-eyed fairy who married a prince on a lily pad. My Popo Lee, who was more assimilated, learned about being American from joining the Catholic Church, watching *Dark Shadows* (a soap opera about vampires), and scanning the *National Enquirer*. Popo Lee raised five of her own children and filled a bedroom with her grandchildren's school and graduation pictures. In her home was a shelf that had books of great American women like Jane Addams and Louisa May Alcott, who lived lives of service. My ancestral heritage is rich with their stories of endurance and love. They fill me with gratitude. Over the years I've come to appreciate my family, deceased and living, in all of their complexity.

Position and Point of View Separate and Connect Us

Every Asian American shares a family history as immigrants in the United States. The privileges we walk with, the opportunities afforded to us, the macroculture that surrounds us, and even the language(s) we speak are impacted by our generational position. Each of us is shaped by the regional and sociopolitical contexts that our generation experiences. Growing up, I was aware of the differences between my grandparents, my parents, and my own generation. I had to work to understand their choices from their perspectives and then to appreciate the internal and external pressures each generation has faced.

Like many ancestors of non-native people in the islands, my "fresh off the boat" grandparents came on ships as cheap labor to work on cane and rice plantations. No one told them that they would be settling, uninvited by the people who lived there first, on Hawaiian land. It was a time of the American settler colonization of Hawaiʻi. It was a time when White missionary families and American businessmen overthrew the sovereign queen and garnered economic and political power in the islands (Lagaso 2017). The European Americans were the bosses, and their presence established histories and color lines that exist today. The language of these first colonizers was English. Their culture would shape the island territory, its people, and all who came to settle there (and vice versa). To survive, my grandparents learned the language and culture of power. This new language (English) and way of succeeding was embraced and passed down to my parents. My parents would similarly pass these ways of being and knowing to me.

My parents were "American-born Chinese" (the ABC generation) who experienced assimilation and annexation of the islands by the United States of America. They lived through the bombing of Pearl Harbor and celebrated statehood. They were proud voters and engaged citizens in the newest 50th state. Unlike their parents who came to America for a better life, my parents embraced their American identity. Unlike other Chinese living in the mainland United States, they became part of a growing majority who had increasing economic power. Patriotism was popular and a way of surviving and belonging. Being successful meant living the "American" life and being model citizens.

My parents upheld Chinese cultural values of filial piety—having respect and care for parents and elders. They had duty and great expectations placed upon them as the second generation. They believed in the promise of education, sacrifice, and hard work. Through my parents' generation, our families emerged from the agricultural fields, sweatshops, and canneries to achieve the American dream. According to plan, they secured white-collar jobs which enabled them to purchase homes, take vacations, and access good health care. They worked hard to be upwardly mobile. They believed in the American dream, a dream that hid the white superiority secrets, colonialism, and the model Asian minority myth. They chose that dream for their children. My bilingual parents, thinking they needed to make a choice, chose the language of power for my generation. Cantonese, the language of my grandparents and ancestors in China, slipped away without knowing that it could have stayed even as a new language was embraced.

As third-generation Americans born and bred in the United States, we grew up as American as the apple pies my Aunt Nancy baked. While the Chinese side of me was rooted in my parents' mahjong games, shopping in Chinatown, and Lunar New Year celebrations, it was easy to grow up identifying everything we did as American. Unlike generations before, we had television and commercials to teach us. My meal of choice was hot dogs and Campbell's chicken noodle soup. Breakfasts were pancakes from a Bisquick box and birthday cakes from Betty Crocker. Our living room was filled with Barbie, her friends, and all her cars and homes. When we got our first TV, we cheered when "we beat the Russians" by landing on the moon.

As our family lived the American dream, I learned about and rooted for the White people on television. I cared for white baby dolls and cut out pretty dresses for pink-skinned paper dolls from *McCall's Magazine*. In short, I learned to identify as White American and thought of other people of color (who were mostly those "bad" people on TV) from the "American" point of view.

While it was a goal for my parents' generation to graduate from high school, it was an expectation for me to graduate from college. As a privileged Asian in Hawaiʻi, I attended private schools where we spoke proper English, practiced Catholicism, and went to college. After school, I hung out in libraries, my father's business offices, and my mom's City Hall workplace. From infancy, I absorbed the dominant American discourse that would open doors in government, businesses, and boardrooms.

In my early childhood career, and especially when I worked as an administrator, I was increasingly invited to sit at tables where policy and decisions were made. I didn't look like most of the people sitting in the meeting rooms, but I spoke English without a "foreign accent" and had ways of relating to others that was culturally familiar. I could access and read all the administrative, legislative, and programmatic policies that were only available in English. As doors opened for me and not others who looked like me, I grew to understand my own privilege and responsibilities as the only Asian American at the table.

In three generations, my family has thought of and declared their identity differently. Perhaps this is what happens when one's ancestor is an immigrant, made more complex by the experience of colonization and regionality. We are much more than we are perceived to be on the surface. My grandparents believed the annexation and overthrow of Queen Kapiolani was the righteous path to statehood. My parents celebrated and succeeded as a result of the colonization of the Hawaiian islands. They were proud of being thought of as a "model minority" (Ruiz 2023). I am undeniably American, but my experience and meaning-making as an American and as a Chinese person is very different from generations before me.

I learned to hold dissonance as normal—even as a strength. Although it was unconscious for a while, my Chinese roots run deep. For a long time, I lived with a divided identity—my Chinese self and my "American" self. For example, as a child, my American side raised her hand high to speak. My Chinese side was quiet as a mouse. My American side insisted on Campbell's chicken noodle soup. My Chinese side liked wonton mein (soup dumpling noodles). Today, I can appreciate and be at peace with my integrated identity as an Asian American, Chinese, American, female/feminist, former Catholic/Boomer/local Islander, third-generation Asian. Internal dissonance exists and yet each intersection offers connection and understanding of others.

Majority and Minority Matters

In Hawai'i, the Asian minority myth was made real when White business owners characterized Japanese and Chinese laborers as more deferential and hardworking. They were hired as cheap laborers in cane, pineapple, and rice fields. Some Asian Americans were portrayed to be more polite than others. Asians were often seen as a law-abiding group who had achieved a higher level of success than the general population. In truth, this myth pitted people of color against one another. Over time, Asian populations grew. Chinese and Japanese populations would be advantaged in hiring practices, educational access, and home-buying transactions. These Asians gained economic and political power second only to White people.

The model minority myth was not talked about in my family, at least not in the ways I have come to understand it from others. Although the myth persists, the term is not even recognized by 50 percent of Asian Americans today (Pew Research 2023). Perhaps Asians of my grandparents' generation looked away not seeing harm in thinking that some Asians were superior and more hardworking than others. Perhaps they believed that Asians were indeed better at math or that Asian family values were better than others. Perhaps they survived by not "rocking the boat." In truth, my settler ancestors also experienced hardships, unfair labor practices, and living conditions. As I did once, they likely went along with how the system worked in order to get ahead, unaware of the stereotypes that assumed excellence from some and failure from others. They just moved ever upward, never connecting their treatment to the hardship of others.

As an Asian American educator, I understand the Asian model minority myth from firsthand experience and through the eyes of those who benefit and those who have been disadvantaged. As an activist working with Whites and other people of color for greater equity, I have a responsibility to not contribute to ways of being that divide or do harm to others. As a director, I worried when teachers preferred being assigned to the "quiet" Asian kids over other children. As a policymaker, I advocated strongly for disaggregation of racial data that hid disparate results of Southeast Asian and Pacific Islander child outcomes. I spoke up against narratives that pitted people of color against one another. I acknowledge that having grown up in the majority population, higher than others in the Black/White color line, influenced how I was treated and how I walk in the world today. Understanding and educating others about the myth is important to me as it continues to thrive, impact educational systems, and hurt the community I claim to be a member of and the community I want to create.

Happiness and a Fourth Daughter's Choice

"At the preschool and kindergarten level, only 2.2 percent of teachers report to be Asian. In 2018, 5 percent of students in prekindergarten through grade 12—or roughly 2.7 million children—were Asian American" (Oh-Young 2022). This information comes as no surprise to me. In 1977, I made the choice to be one of those rare Asians who would choose early education as a career. The gap was less obvious in Hawai'i, where I was surrounded by Asian and Asian Pacific Islander colleagues. That said, one had to really go against the grain to pick not just education but early education.

For many immigrants, education is the path forward. The pressure on children to do well in school starts early. Many of my Chinese friends had parents who would pay them cash for every "A" they got on a report card. Although my parents never paid me for grades like other Chinese parents did, I knew they had sacrificed for my education. In our home, doing well in school and going to college was routine, like brushing your teeth.

Without being told, every Chinese child in my time grew up knowing what the "best" choices should be. One could be a doctor, engineer, or lawyer. Or you could be a business major as long as you could earn a lot of money when you were done. Being a preschool teacher earning minimum wage was not on that list.

But my American self was ok to go against the grain, and my parents had already fulfilled their American dream. I was their fourth and last child to graduate from college. In 1980, I earned my Bachelor of Arts with an elementary teaching credential and a specialization in early childhood education at the University of Hawai'i. In doing so, I became one of the rarest of oddities in that likely lower than 2.2 percent number, an American-born Chinese professional in early childhood education. Under the early leadership of Dr. Stephanie Feeney, my class was pushed to ask ourselves, *Who Am I in the Lives of Children?*, now in its 11th edition. We were molded by deep reflections and discussions of values, ethics, and professionalism. We had access to great teachers, cutting-edge theory, and practicum experiences. We were told that the fight for respect and worthy wages might be a career-long battle. I knew very early that I wanted to contribute to my field of choice. I had benefited from access to an amazing early childhood education credential program that was ahead of its time. Only years later, working on behalf of the early childhood education workforce, did I learn that the majority of Bay Area educators worked full time while attending early childhood education classes at night. The majority of Asians in early childhood education were immigrants, studying content in a language they were only learning. Some were teachers when they lived in China who were on career paths that were filled with barriers for their advancement. I learned again how privileged my path had been.

Regionality: Observations of Living on the Other Side of the Ocean

When I moved to California at the age of 21, I was the first of my family to leave the islands. Women were living their best liberated lives (like Mary Tyler Moore on TV), and I was excited to explore the world across the Pacific. I was often, and at times abruptly, reminded that where one lives influences how one walks in the world. In the states (as people from Hawaiʻi refer to the continental United States), I was much more aware of my "Asian-ness" both within and outside of the Asian community. I had grown up in a "melting pot" where my friends and neighbors were from a variety of ethnicities. My neighbors and classmates were Japanese, Filipino, Italian, Hawaiian, Samoan, Chinese, Portuguese, and mixed race. Interracial marriages were common and their hapa (mixed-race) children prized. Yet the melting pot was different in the mainland. I had moved to a state with great diversity, yet people related to one another differently.

I learned how people hung out with "their own kind." And among my new Chinese friends, I learned the differences between being ABC and "fresh off the boat" Chinese. Being labeled ABC, I became aware of how "American/Westernized" some of us had become. The duality of Eastern and Western values within me would become a lifelong lesson.

People of all ethnicities perceived me as Asian first, contrary to my childhood assumption of my identity as being simply American. I didn't know that to many people, "American" was defined as White. You learn that over time when well-meaning people continue to ask, "Where did you come from?" I was miffed that people would ask where I learned to speak English so well. Most people I met expected me to have an accent or to be meeker than I was. Once after a speech I had given at a conference, someone asked, "How did you learn to speak that way? Where did you learn to be so funny?"

Where did this kind of thinking come from? Was it just ignorance? It made me think of the privileges I grew up with as a majority population where no one questioned if I belonged. It made me question my own beliefs about others, and my beliefs about myself. I began to see what I had absorbed about others and what I wanted to unlearn as I worked with others.

Throughout my career, I grabbed every opportunity to continue to learn. From higher education at San Francisco State University, and graduate studies at Pacific Oaks College, I had access to continued learning. New knowledge came through participating in communities of practice such as BANDTEC (Bay Area Network for Diversity Training in Early Childhood) and equity-based professional development such as the California Association for the Education of Young Children Leadership in Diversity. Deep knowledge also came from serving on boards and state work groups which held commitments to diversity, inclusion, and education. In all these settings, I met many wise and inspiring people. So many heroes who contributed to my own learning.

Relearning, Reframing: Bananas and Boiled Eggs

One of my heroes, Grace Lee Boggs, said, "Being a victim of oppression in the United States is not enough to make you revolutionary.... The oppressed internalize the values of the oppressor. Therefore, any group that achieves power, no matter how oppressed, is not going to act differently from their oppressors as long as they have not confronted the values that they have internalized and consciously adopted."

At the age of 26, I became the naïve director of Wu Yee Children's Center in San Francisco's Chinatown. Despite my English-only background, my resume rose to the top as a rare Chinese candidate who was fully credentialed in early childhood. In my decade there, I navigated state and local licensing regulations, championed bilingual education and family support, advocated for the Chinese immigrant community, and fought for equal access to opportunity and wages for teachers. However, even with those efforts, I became truly successful when I realized how much I needed to learn to be culturally competent and relearn as an Asian and as an American. I'm forever grateful for the lessons and doors that opened for me there.

As the director serving an immigrant Chinese community, my title among the families was "Lǎobǎn" (老板/闆) [old boss]). Being Lǎobǎn meant that I was "in charge." In the immigrant culture, it meant that my decisions were never openly opposed even when they were foolish. It meant that "good" parents would discipline their children for not greeting me each morning as a sign of respect. Often it meant being held up as a successful role model for children to aspire to become like.

In over a decade of conversations, I would learn many lessons about power, perception, and identity. None would be more powerful than a conversation I had with a 4-year-old Chinese child. Like many of the parents, her mom worked in a sewing factory. This girl was well on her way to being bilingual. With the sureness of truth only a child can hold, she took me aside one morning. Looking directly into my eyes, she declared, "You are not Chinese." With a little "huh" from me, she continued to explain how she had come to this conclusion. "You don't talk Chinese, and you don't act Chinese."

After years of studying *Anti-Bias Education for Young Children and Ourselves* (Derman-Sparks et al. 2020), here it was—that magical, teachable moment. Besides being in awe of this child's observation skills and burgeoning identity formation, I thought about the assumptions that had led her to this conclusion. Classification by language—very cool. Classification by two attributes—by language and behavior—very, very cool. My reply seemed to suffice as a good beginning of a larger conversation. Acknowledging her astute observation, I shared, "Well, you know what? I am Chinese. I think I look like your mom too. My mom is Chinese and my father too. They spoke Chinese but I didn't learn like you do." Just like it says in the *We Are All Alike* book, "Not all Chinese are alike. We are the same, we are different"(Cheltenham 1991).

Over the weeks and years, I continued to recall that conversation and to realize how truly a magical moment it had been. It was teachable in a most reciprocal way. My Western ways of being in the world were visible to a 4-year-old child. I wanted to explore my identity as a Chinese person. What might I want to change? And could I learn to code switch and culturally swing within my own community? I was raised American, privileged as a majority population in the islands. What biases had I absorbed about people who looked like me? What would I want to unlearn? How might I grow?

Was I a banana? Yellow on the outside but white on the inside? Or a hard-boiled egg? White exterior with a yellow yolk heart?

Red Lipstick and Finding Voice

> You don't choose the times you live in, but you do choose who you want to be.
> – Grace Lee Boggs

My decade at Wu Yee cemented my career's focus on equity and bilingual education. My relationship with the families as partners and advocates for their children became a lifelong passion. My admiration for educators only multiplied by working alongside the dedicated and diverse staff who met challenge after challenge. When I left the administration of child development programs, I became the National Program Director of Family Support Training for the Parent Services Project, which took me to hundreds of communities impacted by poverty and institutional racism in over a dozen states. As my world became bigger, the lessons about building community, how change happens, and about bias and oppression as it was experienced across the United States grew more profound.

Leaving the Asian bubble in San Francisco afforded new experiences in different communities. It was unusual to see another Asian at an event outside of Hawaiʻi, California, New York, or Chicago. There were even fewer of us in academia or administrative roles, often working in isolation. In certain parts of the country, people would declare, "You are my first Asian person." In the early days of embracing my role as a leader in our field, I often felt like a crayon in a box. I would be asked to speak on a panel, do a keynote, sit on a board or task force. I sometimes knew and often wondered if I was included because the powers-that-be wanted Asian representation.

I often questioned if I was good enough, but I pushed myself to show up. During a time when Asians were fighting for representation, it felt rude not to participate. As a result of my choices, my academic resume never matched up to some of the experts I sat at tables with, and self-doubt would creep in. Before a speech, I'd head to the ladies' lounge to make sure I had my red lipstick on—a nod to the myths about powerful Asian women. It was like my secret power. It never failed to remind me that I could do what was needed—to be the voice of people who look like me but who weren't invited. Through my lips would come the stories of my grandmothers, the opinions of immigrant teachers who felt invisible, the questions of the families and their children who were losing their language and culture in their quest to belong. It was one way to be a bridge, and with it I carried the goal of having these very people sit at those tables.

The Mahjong Table in My Mind

As I have walked the world as an early childhood Asian American educator, activist, and leader, I have long sought out a beloved community. With a nod to my Chinese roots, I manifest a perpetual mahjong game happening in my head—like the kind my parents played late into the night with their best friends. The adults would spend hours talking about everything as the tiles clicked on the table. Seeing strategy and seeking wisdom. Grateful to be playing together. At the end of the night, they would tally up the winners and losers and paid money into a joint kitty—saving up to take their children to a fancy dinner. The goal was not to beat one another but to win together.

In my own journey, I am strengthened by my own mahjong game playing in the back of my mind and deep in my heart. The chairs are sometimes filled with the old aunties nodding and laughing at my predicaments. Like my mom, the aunties always have an opinion and push me to define my own. At other times, my grandmothers come forward with their winning hands doing whatever is needed to love me forward. As I have matured, my table has grown too. It is full of teachers, colleagues, and coconspirators who have inspired along the way. Parents who hold dreams for their families and children who have graced me with truths. Some days, it's Grace Lee Boggs, Yuri Kochiyama, or Audrey Lorde. They are talking and laughing, offering wisdom unasked for. They remind me that none of us are alone. I am grateful for the company.

PART 3

Connections to Our Practice

The contributions in Part 3 focus on the authors' experiences in their workplaces. From classrooms to universities, and non-profits to home visiting, the authors explore how their own ethnic and cultural intersecting identities impact how they teach, how they develop curriculum, and how they interact and support the children, families, and college students they serve. Inevitably, it is a reciprocal process where we also learn from the students and families in our programs and classrooms. The authors in this section span across Chinese, Filipina, Korean, Native Hawaiian, Indian, Japanese, and Pakistani ethnic heritages, bringing those life experiences and perspectives to their professional practices, embracing culturally responsive and culturally sustaining pedagogies in their work in the classroom and teacher education. The emphasis on family support and community, as well as the understanding of a shared experience, informs the creation of a caring and equitable learning environment for children and adults.

Many Asian American and Native Hawaiian, Pacific Islander (AANHPI) families now live in the diaspora away from their homelands. This presents unique challenges in keeping cultures and languages strong. Early childhood educators can provide support in overcoming these challenges. These author contributions shed light on how we can impact others directly in their roles.

Reflection Questions

As you read the chapters in Part 3, we encourage you to reflect on the following questions:

- How do you support the range of children and families in your programs that allows them to honor their cultural, ethnic, and immigrant stories?
- Does your setting reflect the cultural ways of knowing and being of the children? If not, in what ways can you bring these cultural ways of knowing and being into the early learning setting?
- Whose history is present in your curriculum? In your environment? Are children's ancestral stories a part of the curriculum? Can you think of any cultural/historical practices that support your professional efforts?
- As someone engaged in early childhood education, reflecting on the state of the world today, what role or responsibility is uniquely yours, given your distinct experiences and values in building a shared, hopeful future?
- How did you become aware of the model minority myth? How did you experience it, and how do you see it present in today's early education system?

So Many More Voices . . .

I've finally made peace with myself—I'm proud to be a professor who teaches child development with a funny accent. It's a part of my identity, and I stand tall in it.

Jenny Shu-Chen Yen
NAEYC AANHPI Interest Forum Co-Founder
Professor, California State University
Fullerton, California

CHAPTER 13

The Journey of Belonging

Resilience and Perseverance Among Asian Educators

JERRY YANG, SANG EUN CHOI, SARAH FONG, BANDI LIM PARK, JOSEPHINE PULIDO, EDNA JEAN VARGAS, AND YANLING ZHAO

In the mosaic of American early childhood education, the stories of Asian immigrant educators show a repeating pattern: a journey from fitting in to belonging. It is always a long process filled with resilience, courage, and perseverance. "Not giving up" is the most straightforward way to describe their stories. These newcomers accepted the challenges of immigration and have found unique ways to not only survive but also make this new country their second home.

This narrative weaves together the journeys of seven immigrant educators—Yanling Zhao (Angel), Bandi Park, Edna Vargas, Josephine Pulido, Sang eun Choi (Irene), Sarah Fong, and Cheng-Ta Yang (Jerry). We come from Chinese, Filipino, and Korean cultures, and our stories reflect "our own" unique approach to adapting to this new country. While there are differences across cultures, there are also similarities that are important to recognize.

Origins and Callings: Diverse Paths to Early Childhood Education

Each of us found our way into early childhood education through our own unique circumstances, but for all of us, our life experiences and the opportunities we encountered played an important role in triggering their innate potentials and passions to this field. We are all employees of Kai Ming Head Start, a non-profit organization serving the most vulnerable families with young children in San Francisco for 50 years. Jerry serves as the current executive director, while the rest of us work at the organization in various roles. The agency inherits and embraces its "Kai Ming" (啟明) name from a group of passionate young advocators in San Francisco Chinatown in the 1970s, symbolizing inspiration and enlightenment.

Sang eun Choi (Irene): Responsibility Toward Those in Need

Since I was young, I've felt a strong sense of responsibility toward those in need, especially young children and the elderly. This compassion likely came naturally from my family, who consistently cared for others in our community and donated to televised fundraisers supporting people without access to basic resources. During my college senior year in fashion design, I volunteered at children's facilities. One of the most impactful experiences was teaching art and math to a group of 6- to 7-year-olds at an orphanage in Seoul, Korea. Over time, I built strong bonds with the children and witnessed their growth, which brought me immense joy. While I taught children academic subjects, what they truly gained through our time together and social interactions was emotional security, which supported their development. I, too, grew alongside them. That experience made me realize that my true calling was working with children.

Motivated by this realization, I decided to pursue a career in art therapy. I believed that art could be a powerful medium to help young children express their thoughts and feelings and serve as a tool for healing. I planned to take courses in the United States in 2008 to prepare for my master's degree in Korea. However, life took a different turn. I ended up staying in the United States, got married, and worked as a graphic designer for a living. Even while raising my own child, I couldn't stop thinking about working with young children.

When I learned that City College of San Francisco (CCSF) offered free classes to residents, I saw an opportunity to return to my passion. I enrolled in early childhood education courses at CCSF, determined to realign my career with my goal of working with children. Balancing work, school, and family was not easy, but I felt fortunate for every opportunity and stayed committed to making a difference in children's lives through education.

Today, as a classroom teacher, I remain passionate about integrating art into my teaching. I use it to create an open, creative environment where children feel safe to express themselves. I also see art as a way to support families by blending my background in design with early childhood education. Even the family communication posts I create are designed to be visually clear and easy to read to help increase family engagement. Thoughtful design benefits not only the children but also their families. Through this approach, I strive to provide both care and meaningful connection to those who need it most.

Josephine Pulido: Shifting Educational Experiences into New Beginnings

My experience as an elementary school teacher in the Philippines significantly shaped my career aspirations. Before migrating to the United States, I dedicated 13 years in public education, gaining diverse experience across various grade levels, and culminated in a deeply rewarding year working with intellectual disabilities in a special education classroom.

My initial hope for a swift transition into teaching within the San Francisco Unified School District (SFUSD) proved unrealistic. While possessing a Bachelor of Arts in elementary education, my credentials as a foreign graduate had not yet been evaluated then to an accredited evaluation agency. A lack of US-based working experience also presented unexpected challenges. Recognizing the need to gain practical experience working in a diverse group and bridge the gap between my qualifications, I pursued a temporary, part-time work position in the hospitality industry. The work was quite different from teaching, but it developed necessary skills in communication, teamwork, and adaptability within a multicultural environment. It gave me the realization that teaching is definitely my cup of tea. It is not merely a profession, it is a calling.

I began volunteering in a classroom setting, a crucial step towards reentering my chosen profession. This experience not only refreshed my teaching skills but also provided valuable connections or networking opportunities within the SFUSD. I started working as a substitute paraprofessional at my daughter's school for a couple of months. Through this connection, I discovered CCSF's child development program. This led me to pursue coursework. Eventually, I enrolled in a Substitute Teacher Empowerment Program (STEP), which has been instrumental in facilitating my return in teaching while allowing me the flexibility I need. I have grown immensely as an early childhood educator. It is far more amazing and rewarding having the opportunity to see infants' development and grow from toddlers to preschoolers. I started as an observer; now I take pride in fostering environments where young learners can build strong foundations and acquire the necessary tools to thrive. Life does not always go as planned, but with hard work, perseverance, and determination, dreams can become reality.

Sarah Fong: From Art Student to Growing Young Minds

I previously worked in my family's fashion garment business in China. When I moved to the United States in 1993 after marrying my San Francisco-born husband, I faced numerous challenges adjusting to a new life. At that time, technology was not as advanced as it is today. There was no computer or mobile translation app, therefore no online tools to help with the transition, so the culture shock and language barriers felt even more overwhelming. Initially, due to my limited English skills, I had to rely heavily on my husband for everything, from grocery shopping and doctor's appointments to navigating complex government paperwork. I didn't even feel confident booking a hotel for a vacation on my own. I felt isolated and grounded at home most of the time, which made me feel both dependent and disconnected from society.

Eventually, I realized that I needed to take steps toward independence. I enrolled in English as a Second Language (ESL) courses at CCSF. It was difficult in the beginning, but over time, I found my confidence growing. With consistent practice and strong encouragement from my family, I gradually got better at communication in English. I began to manage daily tasks on my own and became more independent in my new environment.

My interest in early childhood education began unexpectedly through motherhood. When I enrolled my first child in the preschool classroom at Kai Ming Head Start, I was introduced to the world of early learning. I quickly became involved by serving as a parent representative on the agency's Parent Policy Council, where I participated in program-wide decision making. Through this role, I attended numerous workshops on parenting, child development, and family engagement. I was especially intrigued by topics like brain development, which helped me understand how children grow and learn.

This involvement led to hands-on experiences. I started volunteering in the classroom, which marked my first experience working directly with children in a group setting. One memorable day, I worked closely with a little girl who had a speech delay, autism, and a seizure disorder. She needed specialized support and consistent care. By building trust and offering her individualized attention, we developed a strong and meaningful connection. That relationship showed me the importance of patience, empathy, and the impact a caring adult can have on a child's growth.

My ability to build strong connections with children was recognized by my colleagues, especially the site manager. The site manager at Kai Ming encouraged me to pursue further education in early childhood development. Motivated by this support, I earned my associate degree and later my bachelor's degree. I began working as a substitute teacher, which gave me valuable classroom experience and deepened my commitment to this field. Over time, I moved into a full-time teaching position and ultimately advanced to the role of site manager.

Edna Jean Vargas: A Journey to a New Frontier

In the Philippines, I worked as an HIV/AIDS program officer in one of the nongovernment organizations serving children, adults, and families belonging to the poorest sector of the society. I was also an advocate for social justice transformation at that time. My journey to becoming an early childhood education teacher in the United States began when I came across a volunteer opportunity at a Montessori school during a short stay in the country. This experience encouraged me to make up my mind to pursue a teaching credential in early childhood education. I was very determined, so I started taking early childhood education units and earned a Montessori Certification from the University of California, Irvine. Going back to school while balancing coursework and life was difficult, but eventually, an H1B visa sponsorship allowed me to stay in the United States permanently.

I had to adjust a lot to become familiar with the early childhood education field, such as feeding children and changing diapers. I also needed to adapt to American English conversational styles. I was so discouraged when my former supervisor criticized me for my Filipino accent at my previous job. Within that environment, I had to learn to accept that my fellow new immigrant colleagues and I would never be considered for promotion. It was a difficult period, and so I had to learn to be resilient. Since then, I have gained additional experiences and accumulated more success. Now I am serving as a regional manager at Kai Ming, overseeing multiple sites to support families in need. I overcame my own fear of "not good enough" and became confident to embrace my accent and culture as part of my identity. I have learned to support my multicultural team members with culturally responsive approaches and to be supportive to parents and teachers to advance their education. I know it won't be an easy process for anyone. This is my new path as an advocate for a better society through early childhood education.

Bandi Lim Park: Classroom as Crossroads of Culture

My journey as an early childhood education educator in San Francisco began with a lot of self-doubt. Even though I had teaching experience in South Korea, I questioned whether I could teach in this new country with a class of mostly Caucasian families. I worried that my Korean accent might prevent me from earning trust. This insecurity reflected my broader struggle to reconcile my Korean identity with my new life in the United States. My name, Bandi, means "fireflies in the forest," but I didn't appreciate it when I was young. It stood out to other people because it was unique, and I didn't want people to focus on it. However, when I first moved to America, I felt slightly disappointed that no one seemed to find my name noteworthy. It caused me to start thinking about my name and my Korean heritage, and later I would realize how important my name was to my identity.

I reached a turning point at my first US teaching job when a parent survey showed that families actually valued how I could bring my cultural perspective to the class, which was encouraging. I started to see how I can bring forth my heritage as a strength. I began weaving Korean traditions, like the Seollal (Lunar New Year) and Chuseok (Thanksgiving) celebrations into my curriculum, collaborating with colleagues from Japan and Latin America. My classroom became a vibrant crossroads of cultures. Over time, what I once saw as limitations became my greatest gifts, helping me form unexpected connections with families who shared their own family stories in return. Beyond sharing cultural traditions for a diverse curriculum, I could start sharing the important values underneath them and find common ground with American families on universal values like the importance of gratitude, love, and caring for family. Now I could connect with American children and their families on a deeper level.

Today, as a regional manager at Kai Ming, I continue to embrace and celebrate cultural differences by creating an inclusive atmosphere filled with cultural activities. Since the families and teaching staff here are mostly people of color, I can understand why some may not yet feel confident about their cultural identities in America. I am here to support them and their children to build a brighter future where they can all embrace who they are and, recognizing their shared values, confidently connect with other people from diverse backgrounds.

Yanling Zhao (Angel): Learning as the Most Persuasive Role Model

I immigrated from China 13 years ago to join my husband. I had a background in accounting and a very limited English proficiency. Like many immigrants, I faced significant challenges in daily life. Until I became a mother of two young children, I had not spent much time engaging in the community. Then I found a way to open my door to my new world, attending CCSF noncredit ESL classes. I learned to advance my English conversation there. Gradually, I earned my Associate of Science in child development and family studies, and then later on a Bachelor of Arts in early childhood education.

My path in early childhood education began when my older son attended Kai Ming Head Start Richmond Center. I started as a classroom volunteer and Parent Policy Committee member, eventually becoming the chairperson. This experience opened my eyes to the fact that there are many program activities in health and family support available; it's not just child care. I also learned about the STEP program to become a substitute teacher to earn some income while I received support to get my degree and permit. The opportunity offered the flexibility I needed to balance my three roles: a mom, a student, and a teacher. Now, as a full-time teacher, I actively promote multicultural understanding in my classroom, believing that when I open up to accept others, they do the same.

It was quite a journey. It took mental strength plus a lot of family support to go through it. I am so fortunate that my husband and my kids have become my best supporters. I also found that my kids grew up more empathetic when they saw their mom working with such dedication in difficult situations. It is so touching seeing my elementary-age children complete their homework and help with housekeeping when I had finished my college courses. They are supporting me in the way they could. I am so glad that I can be a good role model for them to care for others. I often tell my children to "never give up" and to love their lives, work, and everyone around them.

Cheng-Ta Yang (Jerry):

I was drawn to early childhood education's philosophical depth while reading Piaget's epistemology, which explained how people learn. As an international student from Taiwan admitted to Arizona State University in 1996, I was fascinated by the affluence and diversity of American society. Blessed with the opportunity to work as the only male classroom assistant at an on-campus preschool for six years, I earned a master's and PhD degree while gaining valuable hands-on experience. This experience allowed me to apply theoretical knowledge in a practical setting and interact with families from diverse socioeconomic and cultural backgrounds. That experience continues to inspire me to develop hands-on learning opportunities that foster an interest in early childhood education to entry-level individuals.

I highly respect frontline early childhood education educators who have come a long way and continue to stay in the field. Having held various roles in early childhood education, from preschool assistant teacher and college assistant professor to non-profit executive director, I have developed a deep respect for the skills, creativity, and compassion that frontline educators need to support the growth of children and parents. I have shared many experiences with many new immigrant early childhood education educators in a wide range, such as learning English for different settings (daily life, classroom, and academic), learning how to fit into the US early childhood education paradigm, keeping their curiosity, sustaining themselves on limited wages, fulfilling more and more program requirements, and eventually, finding a sense of belonging by gaining small wins little by little. I realize that self-discipline and external support are both important in this process. Therefore, I find my purpose in my current job to create various conditions where educators can thrive and reveal the best of themselves to pay it forward.

I now believe that there are many parallels between working with children and working with adults like teachers and parents. Young children focus on what to play and explore different ways to play the same game; adults also are creative and come up with new ideas on the same topic. I enjoy working with people of all ages, whether adults or children.

Switching the Perception: Obstacle as Asset

Repeatedly through these shared stories we read about English as a second language. This is a common challenge for new immigrants. The journey to overcome this barrier often becomes one of self-discovery. It is a process about learning the language, understanding cultural identity, and realizing self-fulfillment. Often, the transformation remains unconscious as we diligently work through it.

For example, Irene initially didn't see her Korean heritage as a barrier in her teaching career, but deeper interactions revealed limitations: "The more I interact with others, the more challenges come up. It's harder when I want to express something deeper." This realization motivated her to improve her English skills. Edna faced direct criticism for her Filipino accent when a supervisor told her, "I really hate Filipino accents." This negative comment hurt her for many years until she ultimately embraced her identity: "I cannot change it because it's part of my culture and my whole self."

Sarah and Angel both felt anxious and isolated in the beginning because of their low English proficiency, until they took English courses to start a journey to step out of the house on their own feet. Jerry struggled a lot to master a second language, especially when he had to get used to daily conversation and learn about academic languages at the same time. "I found I had to learn one English but in three separate settings with distinct context: the academic, the daily life with adults, and teaching kids in the classroom."

English will always be our second language. We will always have accents. In this sense, the language is always a barrier. However, if we look at the rich cultural heritages that Asian teachers bring to society, the minor imperfections become insignificant. Instead, our English as a second language (ESL) background, plus the rich cultural heritages we bring, are an invaluable asset. By broadening our perspective and elevating our viewpoint, what once seemed to be a disadvantage could transform into a unique strength that enriches and empowers our community.

The Secret: Perseverance

Moving to a new country, there is something we usually refer to as "resilience," an innate power to support us in fighting against stress in order to survive. This is the case for all of the contributors of this chapter. Some of us have utilized support from public assistance, such as food programs, subsidy early education and comprehensive services, and teacher pathway programs. Public assistance played a role for our families to cope with the challenging times. However, we refused to rely on it for the long term. Through all the story sharing, one common theme emerged: We want to be self-sufficient, useful, and be able to pay it forward to the next generation of immigrants and to the children we teach. These are ambitious and often unclear goals, but they are strongly expressed in our dialogues. Now our storyline is almost clear: As immigrant Asians, we learned to fit in by dealing with challenges with resilience, picked up life skills, explored opportunities, and wanted to be useful. Now, we have two remaining puzzle pieces to complete our stories: where and what we do, and what is the self-driving force.

First, where, and what do we do? All of us are working for a non-profit organization. This opportunity serves us in two ways: The organization provides us with a lot of opportunities for professional growth. At the same time, this work gives us an opportunity to serve the most vulnerable families (those with low and moderate incomes or receiving public assistance, homeless, foster children, and children with special needs). We all have a good opportunity working for a non-profit; we make a living, and we help people in need.

Second, what is the self-driven force? People have plans driven by their dreams. The execution of plans determines whether the dream has come true. Some plans may always remain as dreams. If our resilience provides us with the internal strength to bounce back, our perseverance offers us the internal force to propel us forward.

Belonging Is Earned, Not Given

In a group session, many of us shared that staying in our home countries would have made our lives significantly easier. Fitting in is a long process of learning how to be accepted. We learned to be able to communicate using the common language in our society and to create opportunities to bridge the language gap and promote interaction. These can be achieved through diligence and hard work. Thinking of the difference here in the United States compared to our home countries, it feels like there is something missing that makes us feel that the United States is our second home.

The final chapter of our story is about "belonging." We want to put it up front; each of us earns the sense of belonging through our own hands; it was not given by someone. Belonging is never just someone saying to us that "you are welcomed, and you are part of us." The external assurance is much appreciated, and indeed, it is the foundation of establishing a sense of belonging.

However, earlier we mentioned that we want to be useful, able to pay it forward. This is probably the simplest way to explain the word "belonging": I want to be accepted, I want to be useful to my team, I want to be able to help people, I want to continue to learn and grow, etc., and most importantly, I am in a place where I have the opportunity to make those wishes happen step-by-step. This is our definition of belonging: I have control of my own life, and the environment provides me with the condition for me to try and accumulate these small yet significant wins.

Conclusion

The authors in this chapter have all navigated unique pathways and finally came across working at the same organization. They are all bumpy roads; we accepted the challenges and found ways to break through and even turn the perception of obstacles into assets. We don't consider ourselves as model minorities. We simply try hard to recover from dramatic life change and exercise our perseverance to make every day count. We can prove to new Asian early childhood educators that even though it was not easy to fit in in the beginning, as long as you keep up your resilience and perseverance, one day you will feel that you belong to this early childhood education community, and you will continue to grow.

CHAPTER 14

Indigenous Home Visiting

A Sustainable Approach to Culture and Language Reclamation for NHPI Families Away from Our ʻĀina

KAMALEI BRANDON

He māmā au. *I am a mom.* ʻO kona māmā au. *I am his mom.* A ʻo kuʻu keiki ʻo ia. *And he is my beloved child.* There was a time in my postpartum where I truly felt like this might not have been possible. A traumatic birth stole away my capacity to do hard things, my brain and body forcing me to spend all my effort on protecting my baby and me during what was supposed to be a beautiful home birth. I was left as a new "mother" trying to unravel the knots while also claiming my new role as makuahine (mother) with my healthy infant boy, Kalaʻikoa. My moʻolelo (story) is not unique, especially in the United States, where 45 percent of birthing people report feeling traumatized during their childbirth (Beck et al. 2018). Thankfully, it was during this time that two concepts entered into my life and helped me heal: Indigenous culture and language reclamation, and early childhood home visiting. These two things helped me prevent the ripples of birth trauma from affecting my keiki kāne (son) and ʻohana (family) more than it already had.

Indigenous Culture and Language Reclamation

I am a huge believer in Culture is Healing; Culture is Prevention. As a Kānaka Maoli (Native Hawaiian) woman, I have seen the power of culture in my own Indigenous community. With culture, we are able to prevent trauma from taking over the brain and body since "[t]rauma is not what happens to you. Trauma is what happens inside you, as a result of what happens to you" (Maté 2021). When culture is present, our inner selves breathe a sense of relief and are able to maneuver the space with more ease and pride. This gives the brain the ability to process through traumatic events using a worldview that is compatible with oneself and the generations that came before one.

In the thick of my own birth trauma processing, I was reminded of this as ʻŌlelo Hawaiʻi (the Hawaiian language) reentered our ʻohana. I do not remember the exact moment, but, one day in my early postpartum, I looked down at my keiki kāne, Kalaʻikoa, and said to him, "I cannot let this language loss go another generation." Language loss had developed in my dad's branch of the ʻohana for two generations: My Grammy Nona was the last known person that could understand ʻŌlelo Hawaiʻi and potentially my Papa, whom she married. This is unfortunately not uncommon for most Kānaka Maoli; very few of our Kānaka Maoli families were able to keep a hold of our language amidst colonization and racism during and after the illegal overthrow of our nation.

At that point, I saw the pathway that my kūpuna (elders/ancestors) were trying to light up for me. Back when I was hāpai (pregnant), my husband and I knew we wanted to raise our son to be a proud Kānaka Maoli keiki (Native Hawaiian child) despite being off of our ʻāina. We decided to put his inoa Hawaiʻi (Hawaiian name) as his legal first name, bought all the Hawaiian culture books we could find, and quickly started logging Hawaiian cultural events here in Washington State. However, that was *not* enough. How can one have culture without language or language without culture? That was the question my kūpuna were trying to get me to ask myself as they forced me to realize you need to have both. Thus, our ʻohana committed to reclaiming ʻŌlelo Hawaiʻi as our kuleana (responsibility). It has been a journey that holds some of my greatest joys in life and parenting as well as the grief of what colonization took away. ʻŌlelo Hawaiʻi was a way for me to carve out a pathway to accept my role as makuahine amidst trauma from our birth and generations past.

Early Childhood Home Visiting

It is incredibly hard to reclaim and sustain your Indigenous language and culture of our ʻāina and in the diaspora. Our language and culture is built from the ʻāina because we are keiki o ka ʻāina (children of the land). Also, culture and language take frequent practice and uplifting in order to truly learn and teach ourselves and our future generations. Upon running into some roadblocks myself as a Kānaka Maoli parent living in Washington State, I went into an intense state of research trying to find a sustainable way to reclaim and sustain our Indigenous culture and language with our kamaliʻi (youngest child) while away from my ʻohana and living in the diaspora. It is important that we support ʻohana in giving these foundations during the critical period of early childhood.

A Very Brief History of ʻŌlelo Hawaiʻi

ʻŌlelo Hawaiʻi is the language that was and is spoken on our ʻāina (land) in Hawaiʻi. ʻŌlelo Hawaiʻi was an oral language pre-European contact, and in 1818, Henry ʻŌpūkahaʻia began to make a written system for it, with the missionaries adapting the speech to the English alphabet in the 1820s. In the 1840s, ʻŌlelo Hawaiʻi was the medium for all public schools in Hawaiʻi, and we had very high literacy rates.

However, in 1893, our Kingdom of Hawaiʻi was illegally overthrown. Colonization did not stop there, because in 1896, Act 57 mandated English-only schools for both public and private education. Act 57 combined with horrific practices by teachers forced most Kānaka Maoli families to give up ʻŌlelo Hawaiʻi for survival.

Thankfully, during the Second Hawaiian Renaissance in the 1970s, many community members, activists, and scholars engaged in ʻŌlelo Hawaiʻi revitalization. In the 1980s, two ʻŌlelo Hawaiʻi immersion programs began: the ʻAha Pūnana Leo preschools and the Hawaiʻi Department of Education's Kula Kaiapuni. Since then, there have been so many beautiful and vital efforts to sustain our language both on and off the islands! (Ng-Osorio & Ledward 2011)

I consumed a limited amount of peer-reviewed research and explored models that worked for culture and language conservation back home in Hawai'i. At one point, inspired by the famous 'Aha Pūnana Leo preschool program for 'Ōlelo Hawai'i immersion, my husband and I were ready for me to open my own 'Ōlelo Hawai'i in-home daycare. However, given the geographic dispersion of Kānaka Maoli across 100 miles of the I-5 corridor here in Washington State, a localized daycare did not make sense at the time. Feeling disheartened, that was when I found it: early childhood home visiting. An early childhood education outlet that takes into account geographic dispersion. Back home in Hawai'i, we have seen several successful models that have done wonders to support 'ohana while also preserving our culture and language: Partners in Development Foundations' *Tūtū and Me* traveling preschool program and INPEACE's *Hi'ilei* home visiting program. I felt hopeful. Early childhood home visiting could be the best way to sustain our NHPI cultures and languages while not on our islands.

What Is Early Childhood Home Visiting?

Early childhood home visiting is an early childhood education service delivery strategy that pairs parents and caregivers of young children with a support professional, such as an early childhood educator, nurse, or social worker. Their home visitor helps them with the early childhood stages of parenting through parent/caregiver coaching, developmentally appropriate activities with the parent and child, and community referrals to meet the family's needs. The services are typically provided in the family's home or another location of the family's choice and are voluntary.

"Diaspora": Living Off-'Āina

In this chapter, I utilize "diaspora" as "the movement, migration, or scattering of a people away from an established or ancestral homeland" (Merriam-Webster). "Diaspora" gives a common vocabulary to the experience of living off of our 'āina and on another Indigenous people's land. It is a saddening experience for many of us, but one that is often driven by economic refugeeism, climate change, and other harrowing factors. Each experience of Native Hawaiian and Pacific Islander (NHPI) families in the diaspora is unique, but all of the NHPI families I have worked with or know personally have expressed a need for more support when they get to the United States continent and enter into the "diaspora."

Did You Know . . .?

Now, due to many of the reasons listed above, 53 percent of Kānaka Maoli/Native Hawaiians live on the mainland United States, according to the 2020 US Census. Only 47 percent of Kānaka Maoli/Native Hawaiians live on our ancestral lands of Hawai'i. The states on the US mainland that have the most Kānaka Maoli/Native Hawaiians are California, Washington, Nevada, Texas, and Oregon.

Additionally, according to the 2020 US Census, the populations of nearly all the 31 NHPI groups increased over the past decade. For example, the Chuukese population was the fastest-growing NHPI group, increasing 296.2 percent to 10,500 people from 2010 to 2020 (Rico et al. 2023).

Hummingbird Indigenous Family Services and the Pilimakua Home Visiting Program

Around the same time, I found a potentially sustainable pathway for my community and my ʻohana/son. Hummingbird Indigenous Family Services was hiring for a program manager to design and launch the organization's own home visiting program. Hummingbird Indigenous Family Services, colloquially called "Hummingbird," gave my ʻohana our birth and postpartum doula, without whom I truly wonder if I would still be a makuahine today. Launched in 2019, Hummingbird is a non-profit with the vision of healthy Indigenous babies being born into healthy Indigenous families being supported by healthy Indigenous communities. It is the first and only Indigenous non-profit agency in King, Pierce, and Snohomish Counties in Washington State to exclusively serve Indigenous babies and families from ages 0 to 3. Hummingbird is also one of the growing number of Indigenous agencies that includes and recognizes NHPI as Indigenous; we serve families who are American Indian, Alaska Native, Native Hawaiian, and Pacific Islander (AIANNHPI).

It seemed like kūpuna intervention that, at the same time I developed this thesis about Indigenous early childhood home visiting, Hummingbird also needed more long-term postpartum support for families and decided on their desire for a home visiting program. After going back to school to get my home visiting certification and some home visiting experience, I applied to Hummingbird's program manager position and was blessed to be hired.

Now, as an official Hummingbird staff member, I was tasked by our urban Indigenous community to develop a home visiting program. With our first Hummingbird home visitor, Charlotte Pfeiffer, and Hummingbird's founding executive director, Camie J. Goldhammer, the three of us set out to do so. We held Indigenous Perinatal Community Listening Sessions and gathered formal and informal feedback around what our fellow AIANNHPI families needed during their early childhood journey with their 0- to 3-year-old Indigenous child. From the community and our own experiences and expertise, the Pilimakua Home Visiting Program was born and launched in July 2023.

The Pilimakua Home Visiting Program is one of four programs under our now-expanded Pilimakua Family Connections Department at Hummingbird. Our Pilimakua Home Visiting Program offers weekly, biweekly, or monthly visits with a Pilimakua home visitor to discuss topics around the family and child, do activities, and hold space. The home visits are cocreated with families and their home visitor based on the unique goals and needs of their Indigenous family and child. Just like all of our programs in the Pilimakua department, the Pilimakua Home Visiting Program is centered on reciprocal knowledge sharing of our three Pilimakua themes:

1. Indigenous Culture and Language Reclamation and Sustainability
2. Caregiver Mindfulness and Self-Compassion
3. Child Development

Like my own ʻohana, many of our Indigenous families in Hummingbird's service area also expressed a need for support in their own culture and language reclamation journeys. Especially from those away from their traditional lands and in diaspora, we heard sentiments of the journey feeling impossible

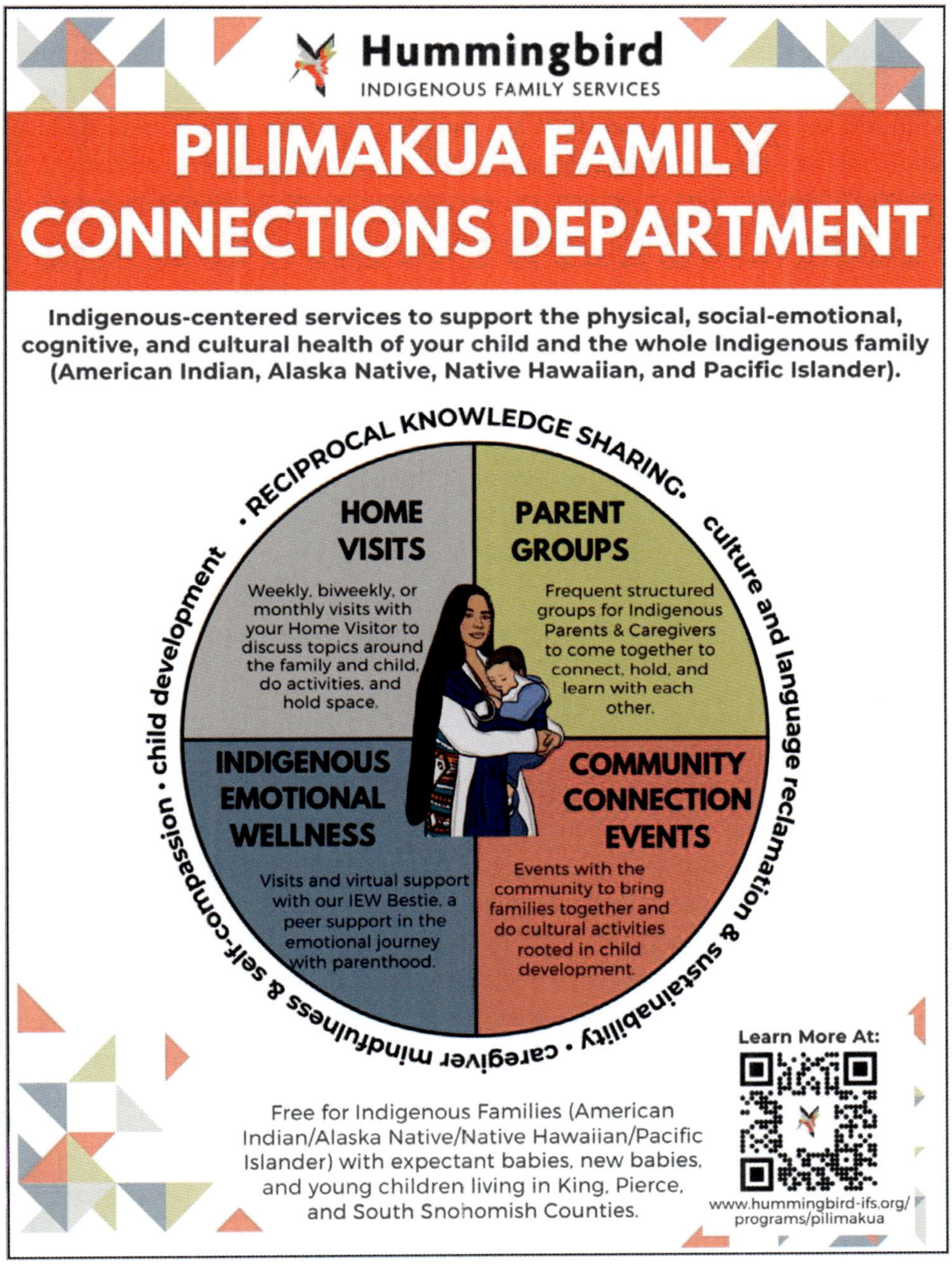

Pilimakua Family Connections Development Poster. (Courtesy of Hummingbird Indigenous Family Services.)

sometimes, which felt traumatizing in itself, since culture and language were so deeply important to how our fellow Indigenous families wanted to raise their children. We even had some families express a similar connection I saw between the healing of historical trauma and birthing trauma and being able to deeply engage their baby and young children in their own Indigenous culture and language. Thus, Indigenous Culture and Language Reclamation and Sustainability was solidified as a theme for our Pilimakua Home Visiting Program.

This Pilimakua theme of Indigenous Culture and Language Reclamation and Sustainability is defined as the act of reconnecting with our ways of being—our ancestral knowledge, unspoken rules, ways of communicating, etc. It is also when we acknowledge and take back what colonization and racism did to our communities collectively and individually. Once we reclaim the culture and language of our past generations, we must then find a way to sustain them for our future generations. Our Pilimakua home visitors and Pilimakua home visiting families (the families we serve) engage in reciprocal knowledge sharing of this theme within each home visit.

Indigenous Home Visiting: Introduction to Best Practices for Indigenous Culture and Language Support

Although we now serve over 38 Indigenous families with our team of five, my own ʻohana was one of our first Pilimakua home visiting families that piloted the program with two other Indigenous families. Charlotte is still our Pilimakua home visitor helping to support our ʻohana with the three Pilimakua themes and especially works to help our ʻohana's kuleana to ʻŌlelo Hawaiʻi. Charlotte is Klamath Tribes and not Kānaka Maoli. However, she is a perfect example of how shared Indigenous identity combined with best practices can support our Indigenous families even when it is not a one-one-one tribal/Indigenous community "match."

Although I am leadership, I like to keep a small caseload as a Pilimakua home visitor to stay connected to the work and continue to directly test out my thesis around Indigenous home visiting being a sustainable approach for culture and language reclamation for NHPI families in the diaspora. Through my work and the supervision of our Pilimakua home visitors, I have seen my thesis actualize, and we have received data to support the impact too. In our winter 2024 survey, over 80 percent of our Pilimakua home visiting families said their family's Indigenous identity was strengthened due to their involvement in our program. There are many concrete ways we support our Indigenous families in explicit Indigenous Culture and Language Reclamation and Sustainability within our program. For the rest of this chapter, I will detail a few of these strategies that I have used within my own home visiting work, especially with NHPI families. Being a former kindergarten/early childhood education classroom teacher, I also tried to include how a classroom-based educator can implement these ideas within their classrooms as well.

Indigenous Home Visiting Practice #1: Indigenous Language Posters

Language fluency takes frequency. We must have a huge amount of input of the target language because that input translates to a smaller amount of what we actually intake and understand, and then that will translate into our own output of the target language (Kumaravadivelu 2006). This is difficult with Indigenous languages, all of which are endangered due to colonization and racism, especially when the family a home visitor is working with is in the diaspora and disconnected from potential immersion schools, books, language programs, and resources. However, even if the home visitor does not speak that family's Indigenous language, they can still support by removing barriers towards increasing that input of the target language and supporting the output.

One way to do so is with Indigenous language posters. These are posters with aesthetically appealing visuals and vocabulary words/phrases translated into the Indigenous language the family is reclaiming. Oftentimes, these posters can be around family rhythms/routines that they already hold to support Family-Guided Routines-Based Intervention (a tried-and-true home visiting best practice) or be posters to support a child development activity the home visitor is bringing for the home visit. If the family is in their language reclamation journey, this supports the Indigenous family's ability to use their own Indigenous language during rhythms and activities without having to constantly consult their language dictionary. If the family is fluent in their Indigenous language already, this supports them by encouraging them to use their language during key childhood development moments as well as provide written text exposure for the Indigenous child.

Me working with a Pilimakua home visiting family using an ʻŌlelo Hawaiʻi language poster during a child development activity.

On a home visit with one of my fellow Kānaka Maoli families, I brought over a mini-poster with key vocabulary translated into ʻŌlelo Hawaiʻi. These key vocabulary were words that I knew the makuahine would need to engage in the child development activity I brought over using our ʻōlelo makuahine (mother tongue). The makuahine was able to use our words for *float*, *tongs*, *sink*, etc. to promote the language with her own keiki (child) and feel uplifted in doing so.

Bringing Practice #1 into the Classroom

Early childhood educators can support NHPI families with their Indigenous language reclamation and sustainability by utilizing Indigenous language posters in a way that hopefully does not require a huge lift for you all either! Some ways to do so are:

- Send home a monthly poster with the key vocabulary you are focusing on this month in the classroom. This can include the vocabulary for your science and social studies lessons as well as commonly used words in math, writing, and reading.
- Send home blank posters that you use in the classroom for NHPI families to translate and send back for use in the classroom. For example, if you are studying about the plant life cycle, instead of just sending home the English version of the poster, send a copy of the poster with the English taken off or in a smaller font, with room for the family to translate.
- Display any translated posters around the classroom or keep it in the NHPI child's cubby to pull out when you work with them one-on-one or in a small group.

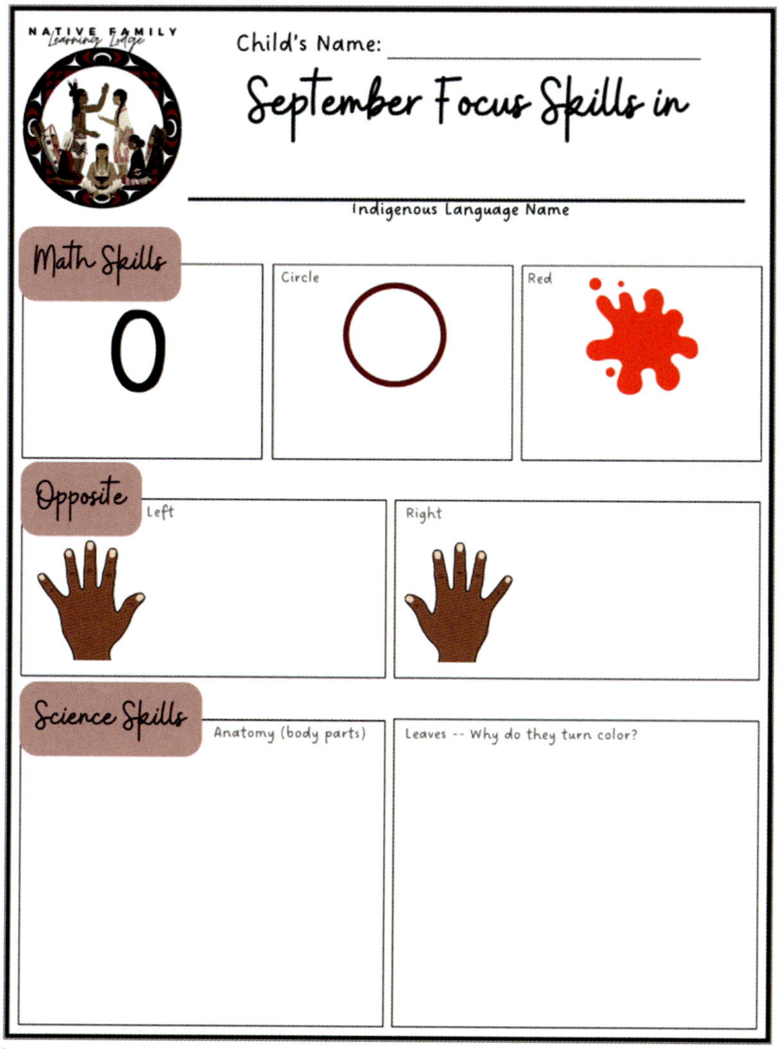

A monthly Indigenous language poster template I made to support the Native Family Learning Lodge (a classroom-based cooperative preschool for Indigenous children in Seattle, Washington) in encouraging families to translate our monthly vocabulary into their Indigenous language to use within our classrooms. Our Lodge teachers have since made this template even better!

Indigenous Home Visiting Practice #2: Board Book and Simple Book Translations

Another way for home visitors to support Indigenous language reclamation and dual language fluency is by providing board books and simple books for translation into the Indigenous language. For a visit, a home visitor can bring over simple books and blank address labels or paper and tape to cover up the English and have the family translate the book into their Indigenous language to the best of their ability. This requires the family to have access to a quality English-to-Indigenous language dictionary, access to a fluent speaker, or some fluency themselves.

A home visitor can provide books that meet the Indigenous home visiting family where they are in terms of fluency and the child's literacy level:

- **Beginner Indigenous Language Fluency:** Try board books with one to three vocabulary words per page with no sentences. An example of these books is *Colors: Early Learning Board Book With Large Font* by Wonder House Books.
- **Intermediate Indigenous Language Fluency:** Try decodable reader or early-level reader books with one sentence per page. Try to pick books where the sentence on each page is a simple sentence structure with just a subject, verb, and maybe an object (i.e., *She runs. He likes the ball. They kick.*).
- **Advanced Indigenous Language Fluency:** Try any early childhood book that has high popularity with children (*The Very Hungry Caterpillar*; *Llama Llama* books, etc.). This will support the Indigenous family in feeling that their language has a place in pop culture and that their children will be encouraged to use the language with their favorite characters.

A family from an HIFS Pilimakua and FOCS Indigenous Parents Group translated a board book into the Marshallese language. Courtesy of Aunty Alice Oligario.

Unless the family requests, please do not just leave these books with the family to do after your home visit. Take a home visit and support them in translating these books by entertaining their child, helping them navigate their dictionary or formulating their translation request to a fluent speaker in their family/community, and holding any feelings of frustration or grief that may come up.

Bringing Practice #2 into the Classroom

Early childhood educators can support NHPI families with their Indigenous language reclamation and sustainability with this practice by providing board books or simple-level readers that align with the classroom content. If you have the resources, send home a copy of the books you are reading in a classroom. Encourage (emphasizing that it is not a requirement of the classroom) your families to translate the books in their NHPI language. Ask if they would be open to sharing their translation to keep in their child's cubby at school. If you have a strong relationship with the family, you can also ask if they would be willing to read the book on audiotape. Then, the child can have access to the book being read verbally within their English-focused classroom using a tape recorder, QR code on a tablet, CD player, or a screen-free audio player (like a Yoto with their "Make Your Own" cards).

Indigenous Home Visiting Practice #3: Deeply Rooted Cultural Child Development Activities

Our Indigenous cultural practices and traditions have grown healthy babies since time immemorial, so why would we feel like we have to do anything different? A home visitor may bring over child development activities that are deeply rooted in the family's specific Indigenous culture. This can help enlighten the ways that our cultural practices develop a child's social/emotional, language/communication, cognitive, and movement/physical skills. A home visitor can even specifically voice these ways for the family to empower them in continuing to use our traditional ways and stories.

Some ways an Indigenous home visitor can deeply root their child development activities in culture include:

- Utilizing traditional stories and songs in activities, such as using them in oral storytelling, felt board activities, books, drawing activities, and/or social-emotional lessons.
- Teaching their music or rhythm activities using Indigenous cultural instruments or using the instruments families have at home.
- Engaging the family in their traditional styles of dancing during movement activities with the children.
- Celebrating traditional times of the year, such as Lonoikamahaiki season for Kānaka Maoli families, with the traditional stories, games, and practices for that specific time.

An example of a cultural activity. My son, Kala'ikoa, is working on an ipu, a traditional musical instrument and ceremonial item.

A home visitor must be cautious while doing this to make sure not to enter into cultural appropriation or make the family feel "less Indigenous" than you. This is why reciprocal knowledge sharing is so important; we all must learn with each other. If you are not from the same Indigenous community/tribe as the family you are working with, lean into verified resources put out by that community/tribe, such as books or curriculum. You can easily utilize a traditional story from a verified community resource to create a respectful child development activity that does not lean into cultural appropriation but instead celebrates and uplifts the story for the family!

Bringing Practice #3 into the Classroom

An early childhood educator can use some of the same strategies listed above in their classroom with two huge caveats: (1) Please make sure to have a strong relationship with your NHPI family that you want to support with this practice; and (2) try to only use curriculum and activities from verified resources from the specific NHPI communities and NHPI authors. Because of the individualized manner of home visiting, when one translates the strategies above into a diverse classroom, they need to be even more wary of cultural appropriation and "exotifying" our NHPI cultures.

Indigenous Home Visiting Practice #4: Emotional Support for 'Ohana Engaged in Culture and Language Reclamation

I always say that Indigenous culture and language reclamation is the most joyful and the most utterly grief-filled process. We are reclaiming (or sustaining) languages and cultural practices that should have been ours since our birth; and, for many of us, they were taken away by colonization, racism, and forced assimilation. With that holds an intense amount of kaumaha (heaviness, sadness). However, reclamation also leads us into fierce joy and healing, as I shared at the beginning of this chapter.

Because of this, a home visitor must be there to hold these emotions with the ʻohana they are working with along this journey of reclamation and sustainability. Support them by engaging them in reflection, problem solving, and (oftentimes the best strategy) bearing witness to their emotions.

Bringing Practice #4 into the Classroom

As a classroom early childhood educator, please note the intense emotions that come with NHPI reclaiming or sustaining their NHPI culture and language on the mainland United States. Some ways you can help hold these emotions, too, include:

- Sharing any time the child uses or talks about their NHPI culture or language.
- Expressing genuine gratitude for the family and child any time they bring in their NHPI culture or language.
- Asking what, if any, support they need to feel like their NHPI culture or language is uplifted in your classroom.

Sustainability Means Pathways for Our Next Generations

Indigenous home visiting gives our NHPI community a chance to heal from trauma: historical trauma brought on by colonization, intergenerational trauma, and even birthing trauma. It can provide us with a sustainable pathway to usher in realistic support for our communities to reclaim and/or keep our languages and cultures despite being off of our islands.

Early childhood home visiting is an established and decently well-supported service delivery. It is so similar to how our own Indigenous communities have uplifted the families in our communities since time immemorial: an aunty coming over to their houses and helping the parents raise strong Indigenous children in our cultural ways and using our mother tongues. This is what I want for my son and his generation. This is what I needed to help me step into my role as makuahine. This is a sustainable approach to culture and language reclamation for NHPI families away from our ʻāina. *Eō, e nā ʻohana Pākīpika!*

CHAPTER 15

Tūtū and Their Moʻopuna

Reimagining Early Childhood Education Through Intergenerational Relationships, Culturally Grounded Pedagogy, and Power Sharing

CHARIS-ANN F. SOLE

Introduction

In late 2013, I returned home to Hawaiʻi after obtaining a master's degree in child development from a school in Chicago, Illinois. I had worked for years with young children and their families, but now armed with this degree, I was ready to work and find my place within my state early childhood system. What I found out through various employment experiences over the following years is that the early childhood field is varied, nuanced, full of joy, complex, confusing, and does not always serve all of our keiki (child/ren) and their ʻohana (family/families) in culturally congruent ways.

By reflecting on my experiences, tracing my own history, and gleaning wisdom from three early childhood education alakaʻi (leader) administrators of Native Hawaiian early learning (EL)–focused programs, this piece explores some ways EL settings might be re-created and reimagined in order that Native Hawaiian, Polynesian, and perhaps more broadly Indigenous children can experience early childhood education in a way that feels congruent within themselves and to their families.

Background

Upon my return to Hawaiʻi, I obtained employment working for a FCIL program (Family Child Interactive Learning program), where family members came to the program with their keiki to teach, learn, and interact with them. The focus of this type of program is to create an intergenerational EL setting in which caregivers are supported in their role as their child's first and most important teacher. This particular program was one that focused on Hawaiian culture-based curriculum and instruction, where the program provided child-appropriate, culturally focused learning opportunities for the caregiver and child to participate and learn together (lei making, which promoted patterning and practicing fine motor skills; pounding taro root into poi (a traditional dish), which promoted hand–eye coordination through fine and large motor movements; integration of senses through tasting, etc.).

Often, tūtū (grandparent/s) came with their moʻopuna (grandchild/ren) to the program, and I was fascinated by how the tūtū took an active role in teaching and caregiving for their grandchild/ren. This experience felt more congruent to me than the more typical classroom-based programs where I worked previously in which parents dropped off their children and left them in my care. The programs that focused on intergenerational interactions were more in line with my own childhood and background. The learning was set up to occur between family members and children instead of teacher and child. It was a great joy for me to see Tūtū and their moʻopuna playing and learning together. It reminded me of my own tūtū and upbringing.

My tūtū took an active part in our lives, once her moʻopuna started arriving. She did not live with us, but she would sleep over at our house some nights and in the morning make the ʻohana breakfast before we children went off to school. She would take me, her only granddaughter, with her for weekends, and we would go holoholo (to go around) to whatever activities she had planned: church, mahjong with friends, shopping, meetings, movies, any activity that filled her day. By then she had already retired from having a career in our state library system and had the time and space to help my parents with child-rearing tasks. My tūtū was a part of my life for as long as I can remember; I cannot picture my childhood without her. She passed away in the late 1990s. It is from her, my mother, and these early experiences which then built upon themselves, that I was taught and learned what it means to be a Native Hawaiian woman—with all its strength, resilience, complexities, and intricacies.

Much later, my brothers and their wives began having their own children, which brought changes to the dynamics of my family of origin and the roles each of us were endowed. Watching my brothers turn into fathers was, in itself, fascinating, but even more interesting for me was watching the process of my parents transform from "my parents" into "tūtū" and in the way they decided to develop and progress into that role.

When the grandchildren came along, both my parents were incredibly proud. My mom chose the title of "tūtū", my dad, "grandpa." As grandparents, they also took an active part in the lives of their moʻopuna. With the birth of the first moʻopuna, my parents became her babysitters. When she turned two, they attended a FCIL program with her.

I have many favorite memories which reflect a generational pattern in our ʻohana. This is one: Growing up, reading was always emphasized in our house as my tūtū spent her career around books. When I was a child, we would often go to the library to visit my tūtū at her workplace, then borrow and return books—as I still do today. My mom emphasized reading with us from a young age and with her moʻopuna as well. Whenever my mom babysat any of the grandchildren, she brought a pink bag full of books to read with them. It was such a routine that when a moʻopuna decided it was time to read, unprompted, they would go to the pink bag, pick out a book, and take it to their tūtū for some "reading time."

Historically and presently, tūtū hold an important place in Native Hawaiian families and society. In traditional and modern-day Hawaiʻi, they hold vital roles in the family, including caring for young children and the passing on of knowledge and cultural practices to the next generation.

Remembering my tūtū and her role in my upbringing, seeing my parents become tūtū, and thinking about the relationships of the tūtū and moʻopuna I saw in the FCIL program where I worked, I began to wonder and ask questions of myself, of the programs I worked previously, and of the wider sociocultural and sociohistorical contexts in which I live—in which we all live and participate. Questions surfaced about the role grandparents play in the lives of their grandchildren. However, there is little to no research on how such tūtū, or for that matter, other family members beside parents who are also tasked with caring for and acculturating young children, interact with early care and learning programs. I began to ask myself, "Why is this?"

After working in the EL field in Hawai'i, I decided to go back to school and pursue a second master's, this time in early childhood education. As part of my coursework, I enrolled in a class entitled Indigenous and Post-Colonial Perspectives in Education, which questioned how power structures (theoretical, societal, and belief) came into being and why these structures remain in the educational world. A new lens of looking at the world of education began to form within myself. This lens is influenced by a critique of settler-colonialism, a framework which "destroys to replace" (Wolfe 2006, 388). The goal of settler-colonialism is the "elimination of the native and the erasure of Indigenous sovereignty so that the settlers can take over the land as their own" (Wolfe 2006, 388). This happened in Hawai'i with the overthrow of the Hawaiian monarchy in 1893. Subsequently, settlers and a newly formed government took over the land for their own purposes. Ripples of settler-colonialism still affect Native Hawaiians and Hawai'i today, including in the area of early education.

I began to think about and question the historical way in which Western early care and education settings were constructed. Educational practices were historically based on the factory model wherein parents separate from their home environments and go to work. Therefore, children were also separated from their home environments and sent to (class)rooms where they were taught, with emphasis placed on production, memorization, repetition, and following instructions of authority figures (Cramer 2010). I see ways in which the above themes echo in our early learning settings across the nation: Children are still being separated and sent outside the home to be cared for and taught in order for parents to work. I began to question how we might teach children in more culturally congruent ways that incorporate kūpuna and Native Hawaiian ways of being. When thinking of these things, other questions surfaced, such as:

What is the value of learning from our kūpuna, and why is this multigenerational relationship absent from the body of knowledge in family engagement in early childhood education?

How can early learning programs support the lessons children can learn of themselves from the knowledge that their kūpuna, 'ohana, and culture possess and pass down?

Then, quickly, the questions widened into questioning the very structure of early childhood education as we currently know it:

What is the value of learning lessons from home versus a school environment?

Why, for some children, are school systems separate from the knowledge gained at home?

What is the value of learning, discovering, and critically evaluating educational structures for the purpose of an education system that works for all children?

These questions serve as an underpinning to begin to examine how and why some early care and education structures are in place, who they benefit, and do not benefit. Asking questions is an important first step in thinking about who the current structures serve and do not serve. The stance of this piece privileges Native Hawaiian narratives and perspectives by questioning the assumptions which inform our current early childhood education system, some of which are mentioned above and addressed below.

Review of Pertinent Literature

Traditional Western educational systems have historically educated children away from knowledge gained through traditional Indigenous methods; this can be seen particularly with Native and Indigenous children. Indeed, the Western educational systems, schools, and classrooms have been historically used to culturally assimilate ways of thinking and being rather than teach ancestral language, traditions, practices, and cultural value systems (Kanaʻiaupuni et al. 2017). The practice of educating away from, rather than towards, Indigenous knowledge systems can be confusing for children, as it may contradict what they experience, know, and live in their daily lives outside of formal places of learning (Goodyear-Kaʻōpua et al. 2008).

On the other hand, a number of Indigenous parents and EL educators want to pass on ways of learning and being that are congruent and rooted in Indigeneity and Indigenous identity. In EL settings, this may look like learning about and getting to know the land they originate from; learning histories of the people, including their relatives and ancestors that have come before them; learning Native language(s); and developing a spiritual identity (Ball 2012).

This creates an inherent value conflict between the practices of Western educational systems, which seek to educate away from Indigenous knowledge, and Indigenous families, who want their children raised in ways compatible with and immersed in traditional thinking and practices. The United Nations General Assembly (2007) has recognized that children have, as one of their fundamental human rights, an inherent right to their cultural identity, language, and values (Battiste 2013). In line with this, there are efforts to (re)create and (re)construct Indigenous education models lost through colonization or occupation. These efforts are being made in order to revitalize languages, knowledge, practices, and beliefs, and build upon the linguistic, cultural, and cognitive strengths held within Native cultures (Demmert & Towner 2003), which reflect the unique cultural knowledge and values of Indigenous populations (Smith-Gilman 2015). An essential component to this (re)education model is the integration of elders, families, and communities into everyday educational settings (Bang et al. 2019).

Likewise, in Hawaiʻi, the approach of centering Native Hawaiian culture and language is becoming a part of early childhood education practices (Kaomea 2005) as more and more early childhood education programs are embracing Native Hawaiian practices and ways of living (Lees & Bang 2023). As more educational programs in Hawaiʻi create environments that allow children a connection to their Indigeneity, revitalization of languages, knowledge, and practices are being renewed and forging connections between elders, families, and community voices.

Recommendations for Early Childhood Education Programs and Native Hawaiian Children and Families

The following recommendations were garnered through interviewing and gathering moʻolelo (stories or narratives) from Native Hawaiian alakaʻi, who are administrators of culturally focused programs for young children. The recommendations first published in 2024 by Sole, Primacio-Maddox, and Han are presented for those working with families of Native Hawaiian young children, or possibly more broadly, also for children of Polynesian ancestry and/or cultural ties. These recommendations may be relevant to early childhood educators and administrators, curriculum developers, and policymakers when thinking about how to serve Indigenous or Native children in their charge. The quotes used below are taken directly from the interviewed Native Hawaiian alakaʻi.

First and foremost, a fundamental tenet of early childhood education is the idea of "relationships." It is repeated here—the significance of building strong, caring, reciprocal relationships between families, staff, and community cannot be understated. When thinking about this in relation to Native families and communities, this often goes beyond frequently used "family engagement" strategies—beyond family nights, emailing of classroom schedules and activities, picture sharing through an app, or Open House "Meet & Greets." This relationship building is about developing trust with your families and communities; this is no easy task and may take years, even generations, of work to actualize. Indeed, the specifics of this can mean various things in the many different places Native people exist. But the underlying value of building strong and caring relationships between places of learning/schools (places of power), educators (people in power), and families (made up of people that are historically disempowered) that feel reciprocal to both parties and is built on the element of trust is the foundation upon which all other work is built and will go forward.

Lena, one of the alakaʻi and early childhood education administrators I spoke to, said it this way:

> "Relationships are very important here. Relationships are extremely important to me; they mean everything. They're gold." *Lani, another alakaʻi and early childhood education administrator, said this:* "It really is not going to be a complete cycle [of learning] until you have relationships with people who are there with you. . . . The people who mentor you, they notice things in you and they try and help you move forward. The people I have learned from have always said, "Come, sit down, bring a glass of water for me, and then we talk story. The older kūpuna, they knew that it was about a relationship." (Sole et al. 2024)

Second, the pedagogy used in EL spaces should be culturally grounded, which includes introducing and using Native languages or words. When educating toward Indigeneity or when working in places where Native populations are high, having pedagogy that is culturally grounded in the EL environment and introducing or using Native language(s) is especially important due to the historic erasure of language, culture, and cultural ways of being. Normalizing and encouraging the use of cultural practices and Native language(s), or even the use of Native words in the early learning setting, can go a long way in helping a young child build a sense of continuity, belonging, and connection from their daily life experiences into the school environment.

Kaleilehua, the third alakaʻi and early childhood education administrator, said this:

> "One thing that ties . . . connections [together] is language. Three of my grandparents were Native Hawaiian, and they were punished for speaking their own language. When trauma like this happens, part of that language dies. Language then diminishes between the generations. In the last 30 to 40 years, people have worked hard to bring our language back. I've seen the joy that it brings when parents are able to communicate with their own children in their native tongue. . . . Language connects us to our culture. If we don't tell our own stories, someone will tell them for us. We need to share them with others and with our keiki (child/ren)." (Sole et al. 2024)

If educators are uneasy or do not know how to bring these constructs into the EL setting, the third and fourth recommendations will help.

Third, it is a necessity to embed within EL programs multigenerational relationships to connect children to the broader contexts in which they are from and live within. These connections include their ʻohana, their moʻokūʻauhau (genealogy or generational line), and a connection to the ʻāina (land) which they live upon. This recommendation is built upon the understanding of a shared lens—that the children in your program or classroom are not "yours" but a part of a wider whole. It is also built upon the understanding that EL programs do not hold all the knowledge that children need to know and indeed values the knowledge that others who are connected to children also have. This includes the children's ʻohana, including tūtū. It also recognizes that in Indigenous or Native communities, usually kupuna are the keepers of knowledge and are the ones that might have the time, space, and resources to share this knowledge. Kūpuna are more likely to be aware that passing down this knowledge is important and worth the effort of pouring it into others, particularly the younger generations.

Lani says it this way:

> "In family engagement, people add to the program in different ways. In early childhood in an American system, they don't see elders as being part of the family. They're like, "They've had their time." But if you go to Africa, Mexico, the Caribbean, South Pacific, or Indonesia, you'll see the elders are all included. . . . The rights of children to have access to the elders in their family—for parents or early childhood systems to separate them from their grandparents is a real concern. ECE underestimates the power of elders in a program. I am talking about family engagement and the different ways different people add to the program. I think that's what early childhood should look like—not like a mini third-grade classroom." (Sole et al. 2024)

This understanding naturally leads to family or community engagement opportunities within EL settings. Kaleilehua, Lena, and Lani all give illustrations of how they accomplished this in their specific programs below.

Fourth, power and influence in the EL setting needs to be a space that is shared. The sharing of power should include asking for community and ʻohana input in the ways that education happens for young keiki. Power (time, subject matter, pedagogy, etc.) in EL programs can be a shared construct to teach what is important to the broader community, which can include ways of being, ways of interacting with others, and with the environment/land, etc. This knowledge can be passed down by asking others to share through family or community engagement opportunities, either by them coming into EL spaces or children going into community spaces. However, EL educators or administrators cannot dictate time, learning outcomes, pedagogy, etc. These things need to be coconstructed with those you are partnering with, as power should be viewed as shared for as long as the engagement continues forward.

Integration into Early Learning Settings

Keleilehua shares how she integrated kūpuna into her program:

> "I started to think about how our kūpuna are incredible resources, full of knowledge, talents, and experiences. I thought about integrating the talent and resources they bring into my class. I decided I would invite them to share their knowledge in my classroom. The first kupuna was a grandfather who was a retired firefighter, pig farmer, and beekeeper. He was excited to share all of his experiences with the children in our classroom. He taught us about taking care of the land and what happens when we do not. He also taught us the importance of bees and the role they play in our ecosystem. He taught us how to be safe and protect ourselves. He brought bees to the classroom, showed us how to extract the honey from the comb, and families were able to taste honey from the native lehua (flower), coconut, and kiawe trees. . . . It was the most amazing curriculum that we've ever had. We started to invite more kūpuna to participate in our classroom. Not only did the kūpuna enlighten the classroom, but they, in turn, were enlightened. They were so grateful to be asked to participate. I learned the importance of including kūpuna in our work; different people have different things to teach to you. Again, if we don't share the stories; if they don't share their stories, the stories die with them." (Sole et al. 2024)

Lena also shared her experience of inviting kūpuna into the EL space:

> "We invite the kūpuna to come and join us in the learning environment. For example, last year, we had a Tūtū come and talk about fishing and the techniques that he uses for fishing. He's a lawaiʻa (fisherman) that uses traditional ways of fishing. For example, he throws the ʻupena style net. He brought in different kinds of fish and talked about the fish with the kids. He made poke (cubed food, mostly fish), and the keiki ate the poke. We had another kupuna come in and did lei (garland) making, who

talked about the different kinds of plants involved in lei. We have kūpuna that have some of these skills; we utilize them to come in and share with the keiki. We had another one that talked about medicinal kinds of plants. We obviously have kūpuna that know how to grow kalo (taro), tend to the lo'i (taro patch), ku'i kalo (to strike or pound the kalo) and how to pound the poi (food made out of taro). They come in and they demonstrate the kinds of things that have been passed down to them. They're part of our class and they're part of the activities we do here. We found with our kūpuna, they hold different types of knowledge and are cultural practitioners." (Sole et al. 2024)

Lastly, Lani speaks about inviting parents and other important people into the EL setting:

> *"How did we include families in our program? We would ask for their ideas. At the end of the day, we would ask the parents, "Can you go home and see if your child asks anything new?" We would also send activity ideas home with them on weekends or holidays for families to become involved in the teaching of their keiki. "Just try this one thing: go to the beach and look at the kinds of sand on the beach. See if your child can use words to identify it." We tried to arrange the instructions so that anybody in the family could do the activity and have the child experience it. We really encouraged it. In class, we would try it, sure, but then we would always send them home—either with something to do or something to achieve. This included having the elders take the kids to their favorite place and talk about it, no matter where it was. That encouraged some interaction. And of course, when they came back, we would hear all kinds of really neat stories, "Oh, there's Tutu-man's favorite beach!" We also encouraged parents to bring other members of their family with the child. If they had grandparents available, then bring the grandparents with them to the program. A grandparent, a father, an aunt, or an uncle who just happened to be hanging out for the day."* (Sole et al. 2024)

All three chose to share space within their classrooms, but what does it require of staff? Keleilehua answers in this way:

> "I have learned that we, as teaching staff, have to be quiet. That is the hardest thing—because we're bound by time, we're bound by a lesson plan, but we have to understand that Hawaiian culture was an oral culture. We have to be the facilitators. We have to know when to listen and when to ask questions. We need to understand that just as important as any college class, the richness and the values that kūpuna bring with them to the classroom are priceless." (Sole et al. 2024)

Conclusion

My journey of discovery that I've written about in this piece intertwined my scholarly studies, as well as my personal and professional experiences, and the richness and knowledge that my grandparents brought to all three of those worlds. This was done in an effort first, to affirm the preservation of cultural identity and values, and second, to emphasize and support the EL programs which engage in this work as they partner with young children and their families.

By tracing my own story, influences, and work done on this topic, this piece offers some ways that might be helpful for others when working with those from Native Hawaiian, Polynesian, or other Pacific Islander cultural backgrounds and communities in EL spaces and settings. Perhaps the ideas herein can be extrapolated and applied to other Indigenous groups as well.

The work of how to educate our youngest Indigenous children toward their Indigeneity is especially important due to the history of settler-colonialism and historical trauma. As a result of this exploration and other similar work, it is my hope EL settings and spaces will continue to be (re)imagined and (re)created in order for children and their families to be supported in who they are culturally, generationally, geographically, and linguistically.

In a broader sense, and in a similar vein to my own experience, this piece is also meant to encourage early childhood professionals to reflect on the sociocultural and sociohistorical contexts they come from as individuals, to reflect on the sociocultural and sociohistorical contexts of the children and families they serve, and to reflect on current early childhood education practices and norms. Where dissonance exists between the three, it is my hope that they will take on the exploration and work that needs to be done in those spaces.

So Many More Voices . . .

> **My Vietnamese-Cambodian identity reminds me that education is never neutral. I want young people to inherit pride, not silence, and see their families, cultures, and brilliance celebrated in classrooms and decisions.**

Jenn Nguyễn
Doctoral student
UW, Seattle Education Policy, Organizations and Leadership
Seattle, Washington

CHAPTER 16

Dual Language Learners in Early Childhood

XYZLORA BROWNELL

Growing up hearing "What are you?" was confusing. I'm a person, what do you mean? My light black skin, somewhat kinky hair, and eye shape always made people curious. I was always explaining my ethnic heritage to strangers. The spelling or sound of my name doesn't help, thinking it had some ethnic background. It doesn't. Having to explain "what" you are is exhausting. Asian was not the go-to. African American wasn't the go-to. I was seen as ethnically ambiguous, maybe a mix of Asian, maybe Filipino? Black, Korean American. That's how I identify, and that's how I was raised.

Born in Tong du Chon, South Korea, to a Korean mother and an American Army soldier, I was brought to the United States as a baby. My mother spoke no English, and my father spoke very broken Korean, but somehow they found each other. In our military family, we brought in kin that were not blood related. We had many aunts, uncles, and grandparents that became a permanent fixture in our lives. Our biological relatives were miles away, and my parents grew an extended family for us to have growing up. We call our family by Korean titles "imo" (aunt), "samchon" (uncle), "halmeoni" (grandmother). In my upbringing, you did not call those older than you by their names. Even my aunts would not use my mother's name if they were younger than her. It was "Lora's mom" or "big sister." My younger sister, to this day, will not use my name; she calls me "eonni," or big sister.

I was raised to know both sides of my family, even though they did not live nearby. My dad settled us in Washington State. His family lived in Fresno, California, while my mom's family was still in Korea. We spent many summers visiting family. We alternated our summer visits between California and Korea. By the time I was 10 years old, we stopped our visits to Korea; my dad's work became more demanding as he moved up in rank. I missed my cousins.

The importance of education was instilled in me early. They wanted my sister and I to have an education beyond their own experiences. Before I started kindergarten, my parents were told that I needed to stop speaking Korean or I would be confused and not do well in school. My mom began English lessons when I was 3 years old. From then on, I only heard Korean spoken between my mother and my "imos." My mother made this decision as a way to exist in this new world. I lost my first language so I could be "successful," but the consequence is losing a piece of myself. I sat with her at the kitchen table with her tutor doing the lessons at her side. As my mom worked hard to assimilate, things got lost. She did not teach us how to make traditional foods. We didn't celebrate Korean holidays. We learned through the media and what society believed about us. Bias of society is something we absorb; it crept in subtly and early, so I don't really know if I am who I am because of how I was raised or because it is what I am supposed to be. I did well in school; I could read by the time I entered kindergarten. I was great at spelling and math. I'm polite (to a fault) and have a good work ethic. I got A's, I was the teacher's pet, and my parents expected nothing less and were disappointed if I didn't meet their goals. That's when the pressure to perform, to always be good, to never fall short began.

I am wearing a hanbok at age 8.

Mr. Oas, my fifth-grade teacher, was the only Asian American teacher I ever had. He had a level of expectation for me that no other teacher did; my behavior, my schoolwork needed to be perfect. I didn't see that he had the same standards for others in my class. At the time, I didn't fully understand it, but looking back I can see how I was being held to a standard shaped by the "model minority" myth. Because I was doing well in school, I was expected to continue excelling without struggling, making mistakes, or needing support. There was an unspoken kind of pressure to be a certain kind of student: quiet, high achieving, and always in control. That expectation didn't always feel like encouragement and made it harder to ask for help, show vulnerability, or just be a kid.

Adult Life

I married a White man. We raised our mixed-race babies to be proud of their different identities. Our children identify with all their different backgrounds and ethnicities. At first glance, my children do not look like me but still have an ambiguous look about them. Their race is always mistaken by others. I have little related to their Korean ancestry to hand down. I wanted my mother to speak Korean to my children, but she refused, saying they didn't need to know it here. That was still my mother's belief about being bilingual.

Career

I have always worked in early childhood. When my daughter was 4 years old, she attended the local Head Start program in town. It was a great opportunity for her to gain skills she would need in kindergarten as well as giving my husband and I some tools to use at home to engage in her development. It was my first experience with early childhood, and I loved it! Besides the academic pieces to being ready for kindergarten, Head Start also helped her to develop self-help skills. When my mother learned that she was going to school, she was horrified. "She's just a baby," she would tell me. She believed that she needed to be at home with me, and it was my job to educate her. I wanted her to socialize before kindergarten; that was really the goal. We had worked with her, she was reading short books, knew simple math, but had not had interactions with children her own age, which I believed was important.

After taking our children to Korea for a visit while my daughter was still in Head Start, we had the opportunity to share about the experience with her class. We brought in a traditional dress (hanbok) and chopsticks for all the children. She was able to share her experience with her friends. They asked curious questions, and you could tell she was proud to share.

This experience led me to begin my career in early childhood education at my daughter's Head Start program as a classroom aide. I eventually became a Head Start therapeutic lead teacher. I worked for 15 years in direct service, supporting children and families. It was in my fourth year of teaching that I was in a room with another teacher of color. She was Black, she looked more like me, and there was comfort there.

I did not have many Asian children in my classroom in all of my years of teaching. I remember one little girl: Her parents were Japanese and only spoke to her in Japanese as they were learning English. I remember my coteachers being worried by her quiet, "clingy" behavior and were concerned that she did not interact with the other children in a way that seemed normal to them. She came to us using only Japanese to communicate. Educators worried that she would not be efficient in English as she entered kindergarten.

My coteachers lacked knowledge and training about how to engage with dual language learners. They did not understand that the phases of dual language learning are much like learning your first language. Children begin by listening; they are mainly silent and taking in all the information around them. Experiences support learning another language, finding things that seem familiar in objects and actions. Without ample experience, there is no context for knowledge (Kavak & Deterala Gül 2020).

I learned everyday words and phrases in Japanese to help her become independent and feel welcomed in the classroom, such as "hello," "thank you," "coat," "wash your hands," and "time to eat." I posted Japanese words around the room for her parents to engage with. I became her person. I took the initiative to connect with her and create a sense of belonging in the classroom for the family. I did not push her to speak in English. I supported her in playing with peers, giving prompts on interactions. I repeated instructions in English and narrated her play. She began saying one or two words in English to identify an object or need. Eventually, she became more confident and used her new English skills to engage with peers. She did not rely much on other adults in the room and continued to seek me out when she had a problem or need. None of the other teachers learned any Japanese words to interact with her. Her sense of safety belonged with me. Once she began speaking English, the other educators saw her intelligence. At times she would code switch, which concerned my coteachers, who thought that she would only learn English when her parents could speak it. She knew her colors and shapes, did simple math, and had enormous empathy. They could not see this when she only spoke Japanese; they did not see her potential. Their bias stood in the way.

Even during mealtimes, they did not understand why she had a hard time. I had to give them context to her behaviors, assuring them that she was learning and on track for her development. The food was unusual to her; she ate very traditionally at home. There were no chopsticks, no rice. Not only was she learning English, but she was also learning about another culture and way of being. Many Asian children spend most of their time with their mothers when they are young. Mothers keep close to their children and spend most of their early years instilling respect, kindness, and learning (Lee 1997).

Even though I only had a handful of Asian children during my career, I had other dual language learners throughout the years. I worked as an educator in a bilingual classroom where half of the children did not speak English. I implemented a 50/50 model. Instruction in English was twice a week, and two other days were in Spanish. It wasn't very long before children could understand both languages, English-speaking children picked up Spanish, and Spanish-speaking children picked up English. This was more than learning a language. The interactions in the classroom changed. Before, the children only played with the children that knew their language. Once we began teaching in both languages, we saw children interacting with each other. Even the English-speaking children began to code switch. When learning two languages, it's common to bounce from one language to another.

Children learning two languages can be a benefit. Children coming into early learning environments with a home language other than English need support to learn English while keeping their home language. Bilingualism continues to grow around the world and in America. Before the 1960s it was a popular belief that children who were bilingual had lesser vocabulary and were seen as disadvantaged. But having multiple words to identify or describe something gives children different perspectives of seeing the world. It involves flexible and creative problem-solving skills (Kavak & Deterala Gül 2020). I encourage parents to continue to speak with their children in their home language, assuring them that they will learn English as they get more exposure.

From my experiences, home language is important. It connects children to their heritage and supports their sense of self. Keeping a home language benefits not only the child but the family as a whole. Educators can support this with intentional engagement with children and understanding the benefits for lifelong learning.

CHAPTER 17

Grief, Growth, and a New Life in Education

MANJU KUMARI

The first portion of this story examines familial and communal support in the development of emotional maturity during early childhood. It underscores the vital role these networks play in enabling individuals to navigate experiences of grief and loss, thereby fostering their capacity for healthy child development. Subsequently, the narrative offers a personal account of the immigrant experience, highlighting insights and challenges gained in a new landscape and a path to a new life.

The Roots My Father Planted

I was born into a loving middle-class family in India, the eldest of five siblings. Despite limited resources, our home was filled with love, joy, and life. My grandfather's family occupation was farming, and my grandmother was a strong and brave woman whose influence still shapes us today. My father was the first person in our family to earn a college degree and attended law school. His dedication to helping others and his ability to navigate complex situations with wisdom and empathy set him apart. He established a public school in our grandparents' village, providing underprivileged children with access to quality education, which made a real difference in many lives. He began his career as an attorney and later moved to the city to start his first job. As life got busier for him, my mom did her best to keep the family in order.

In my early childhood, I experienced my first profound sense of loss. At the time, we lived in a small city in a kind and welcoming neighborhood. Next to our home lived a family that, despite speaking a different language and having a different culture, felt like an extension of our own. Their presence was a constant in my life. I affectionately called my neighbor "Auntie," and she treated me like her own daughter. Her family was an integral part of our lives. We had a good life, not knowing anything beyond what we had.

One morning, I woke up to see a large truck being loaded with Auntie's belongings. The process took hours, and I was in shock. Neighbors had gathered and watched silently. I felt utterly helpless and couldn't understand what was happening. I sat in a corner, crying, with only the loud shouts and the sound of heavy furniture filling my ears. I wondered why no one else seemed bothered by what was happening, and I feared something terrible had happened to Auntie's family. I don't recall seeing any familiar faces—my parents and Auntie were nowhere to be seen. I only remember hiding, watching the back of the truck, and crying.

I realize now that I may have been reacting out of fear of change—a situation I wasn't ready for. It was the first time I experienced something like this, and it left me feeling broken, empty, and isolated. At some point, Auntie came and hugged me, but I don't remember what she said. However, I can still vividly recall the big green truck, my Auntie, and the back of the truck moving away, fading into the distance until it disappeared. I thought someone had come to take Auntie away, and I kept waiting to see her again. At that age, I didn't understand that they had moved to another city, far from us, and that I would never see her again. The sudden departure left a deep void in my heart. I don't remember anyone explaining what was happening; all I recall is waiting for Auntie to call me from somewhere.

My parents, my brother, and me.

In my distress, my parents tried to comfort me. Although I can't recall my father's exact words, I was in a state where nothing seemed to make sense. My father did his best to reassure me, promising that he would take me to the city where they had moved. He encouraged me to express my feelings in my own words and helped me put my thoughts together in a letter, ensuring it was sent. This reflects the Indian family structure, where elders often play a crucial role in supporting individuals during painful experiences. Although this gesture brought some comfort, the pain of their absence continued to linger. In that moment, the act of writing became a way to process my overwhelming emotions, even if it couldn't fully mend the emptiness I felt.

Looking back, I am amazed that 50 years ago my father understood my emotions in a way that is now considered an essential part of helping children develop, both socially and emotionally, by helping them process their emotions. His support helped me heal from the deep sorrow of losing Auntie. Over time, I slowly began to grow, and when I eventually moved past the pain, I didn't even realize it had happened. Without my father's involvement in the situation, I may have developed a disorganized or insecure attachment style, which would have greatly influenced future relationships with partners, parents, and my own kids. This experience taught me the importance of acknowledging and validating children's feelings, a lesson that has profoundly influenced my approach as an educator. As an educator, I strive to create a safe space where children feel heard and understood, knowing that their emotional experiences are real and significant.

My father's guidance in expressing my grief through writing taught me the value of providing children with various outlets for communication, whether it's through art, storytelling, or play. As an educator, I create opportunities for children to express themselves freely and develop healthy coping mechanisms. I empathize with the children in my child care facility who are entering a new program, which can be daunting and unfamiliar. As early childhood educators, it's our job to make them feel comfortable. Caregivers and parents in our early lives have profound and lasting effects on our psychology and the subconscious. Being aware of this as an early childhood educator can help us be more mindful of how we care for the children.

A few years later, my family relocated to a new city. Instead of feeling excitement, I was overwhelmed by detachment and pain—feelings that reminded me of my earlier loss. The move was marred by tragedy when my father's elder brother died under unnatural circumstances. Shortly after, another uncle passed away. During this tumultuous period, I learned how to cope with sorrow; the painful memories of my early childhood never truly faded.

I observed that in India, grief was often a shared experience, with rituals and community practices providing a framework for processing loss. This contrasts with the more individualistic approach I've often seen in the United States, and it has made me more aware of the importance of cultural sensitivity in supporting grieving children and families.

When I was pregnant, I faced another devastating blow: My younger brother, who was in the eighth grade, tragically drowned during a special family occasion. The incident was sudden and almost unbelievable. This loss brought back the deep sorrow I had felt before, intensifying the grief I carried within me. Two months later, I gave birth to my son. His arrival brought a small glimmer of hope, offering our grieving family a new direction and a promise of renewal amid the overwhelming pain.

These collective experiences, witnessing death up close, enduring profound losses, then finding hope and joy return again, have made me stronger and more resilient. Navigating these life-altering challenges took a long time, but every painful event—and every joyful one as well—has helped shape the person I am today. These experiences have instilled in me a deep empathy for the human experience and the challenges we face and helped me become a more well-rounded educator.

Witnessing my family's resilience in the face of tragedy has shown me the power of community and support. In my classroom, I foster a sense of belonging and encourage children to support one another, knowing that this collective strength can help them navigate challenges.

My sister and brother.

Navigating a New World

In 2000, after years of relative stability, my husband and I made the decision to relocate to the United States with our two children. This move marked a new chapter in our lives, filled with challenges and opportunities as we adapted to a new culture and environment. A year into our new life, I recognized that my 2-year-old daughter needed social interaction with peers her age. I enrolled her in a local preschool and simultaneously began attending English classes to improve my language skills. After one semester, I discovered a passion for child development and decided to pursue a career in this field, aiming to better understand and support my children's growth.

Raising children in America without family support was daunting. My husband worked as a software engineer, and I felt the responsibility to assist our family back in India—a common sentiment among immigrants deeply connected to their roots. To balance family and education, I attended evening classes for early childhood education at a local college while my husband cared for the kids. Despite the challenges of managing household duties, child care, and academics, I completed 16 units over two quarters and was hired at a reputable school in November 2001. My initial days at the school were challenging. As an immigrant among predominantly English-speaking colleagues, I felt out of place. Some educators were unwelcoming, and I often questioned my ability to thrive in this environment. Three weeks into the job, a coeducator accused me of taking extended restroom breaks without informing her. Despite my attempts to explain in my limited English, the administration asked me to sign a termination paper. Upon reaching home after an hour-long bus ride, tears streaming down my face, I noticed a "Now Hiring" sign at a newly opened Target store near our apartment. I applied immediately and was hired as a cashier. Shortly after, I secured a position at another well-respected preschool that offered a 70 percent discount for my daughter's enrollment and better pay. Life had its ups and downs, but I remained focused on raising my children in a manner that would make my family proud, even in a foreign culture.

Years later, tragedy struck again when my father passed away. I flew to Delhi and held his hand as he took his last breath—a profoundly painful experience. The loss took a toll on my well-being, and I felt like I needed a break from work to deal with my own emotions. During this time, I realized how my father always worked for himself, and that gave me the push to start my own family child care. Bringing my mother to live with us provided some solace, and life gradually regained its rhythm.

I have been an early childhood educator for 23 years, 10 years in schools and 13 years running my own family child care business. I have dedicated my career to supporting families and children. My facility primarily serves underprivileged families, including children of domestic violence survivors, ensuring they receive the care and support they need. To amplify my impact, I joined a union to advocate for our community and better understand societal needs.

Growing up, my father modeled empathy and service, and when I experienced my first significant loss with my Auntie's sudden departure, he intuitively validated my feelings and encouraged me to express myself. This early experience, and his supportive response, deeply influenced my understanding of childhood emotional needs and has shaped my approach as an educator, emphasizing the importance of acknowledging and providing outlets for children's feelings. Moving to the United States presented many challenges in adapting to a new culture and building a support system. Experiencing unfair treatment early on underscored the difficulties immigrants can encounter, which inspired me to establish my own child care business to better serve my community. Ultimately, my journey reflects my resilience in navigating a new world and my deep commitment to supporting vulnerable children and families.

The Indian culture's emphasis on education as a means of social mobility and personal growth has instilled in me a deep commitment to providing high-quality learning experiences for all children. I also strive to foster a sense of respect and responsibility in my classroom, drawing on the values I learned growing up. One of the ways I help the children take responsibility is during class projects. I encourage the older kids to help the younger ones. This develops camaraderie and a sense of belonging. Helping kids process their emotions in a healthy way is really important. A big factor is being able to recognize the onset of these emotions as it starts and recognizing which type of emotion it is. Is it sad, hurt, angry, or something else? Two of the most common emotions are being angry or sad. When I recognize this, I immediately go sit next to the child and calmly ask questions that allow them to express themselves. Helping one talk through emotions helps them calm down. Next is helping them solve the problem. I discuss how to deal with similar situations in the future and offer ways and techniques to manage the situations appropriately.

My AANHPI identity, shaped by my Indian cultural background, has deeply influenced my professional practice. The emphasis on family support and community, as well as the understanding that grief is a shared experience, has informed my approach to creating a caring and equitable learning environment. I believe we need passionate early educators focused on creating a caring, equitable community of engaged learners, emphasizing the social and emotional aspects of early childhood education

So Many More Voices . . .

I am Hawaiian, Chinese, German, and Norwegian. I've learned the value of showing up and offering what skills I have to my communities, even when I don't have my own identity fully mapped out. Being mixed comes with many points of connection—drinking boba and eating poke before they were trendy, surprising people by speaking Chinese, a love for Hawaiian and island music. It also can be fraught with impostor syndrome, feeling not quite Hawaiian enough or Asian enough when walking into a room of unfamiliar people. Seeing reflections of myself in both mentors and younger colleagues has helped me to claim these identities and to step up to the kuleana (responsibility) of giving back with the skills I've been fortunate enough to cultivate.

Max A. Halvorson
Research Scientist, University of Washington School of Social Work
Seattle, Washington

CHAPTER 18

Fitting In and Standing Out

Why We Are Pairing Our Stories Together

MISA OKAYAMA AND YUJI UCHIDA

For the past two decades, our paths have intertwined at Nihonmachi Little Friends, a community-based, Japanese bilingual and multicultural program founded in 1975 in the heart of Japantown, San Francisco. We have worked side by side in the same preschool classroom, forging a partnership built on trust, respect, and an unwavering love and passion for our collaborative learning journey with our young citizens.

At the center of where we work, we have five core values: omoiyari 思いやり (thoughtfulness), nintai 忍耐 (resilience), kansha 感謝 (gratitude), souzousei 創造性 (creativity), and gakumon 学問 (inquiry). These principles have fostered an environment of collaboration and reflection, allowing us to learn from one another and grow together as educators. Differences in perspective have become opportunities for dialogue, mutual understanding, and professional growth.

We believe in the transformative power of teamwork. It is the collective dedication of a caring, courageous, and cohesive team that truly allows a school community to flourish—one that honors social justice roots and embraces a love of learning that transcends language, culture, and time. By celebrating successes, navigating challenges together, and embracing moments of introspection, a community grows stronger and more connected.

Our involvement in this writing project stems from our reflections on this shared journey and heartfelt desire to share the significance of collaboration, connection, and harmony. Moreover, it is in our realization that our perspective has been profoundly rooted in our upbringing in Japan while interwoven with our varied experiences building a life in the United States.

First Days in the United States

Misa

I came from Tokyo as an international college student after graduating from high school. Arriving in the San Francisco Bay Area, I met so many people of different ethnic or racial backgrounds and heritages. My host family was an immigrant family from the Philippines. My first impression of the country was that anyone could be "an American" in this rich, diverse society! On the contrary, in mainstream narratives, I began to realize that this multiracial, multiethnic societal reality is either rarely represented or portrayed in narrow, devalued ways. Beneath the surface, I learned that dominant cultural norms shaped who truly belonged and who were diminished, considered to be out of the picture. Amidst all this rich diversity, for example, it felt strange to be grouped simply as "Asian," with all its implications and stereotypes—as if we were all the same. There are countless ways to be Asian, yet here I was collapsed into one broad category.

Having started a new life in a completely new place with a different language, it was as if I was a baby all over again. Learning everything from the ground up, I was on a journey to seek and reencounter my identity and my sense of self. I started asking, "Who am I?," "Where do I belong?," "How do I answer those questions?"

In my early adolescence back in Japan, I went through my own phase of rebellion. There was a time when I was in denial about Japanese society. For example, learning extensively about the Japanese role in World War II through schools and travels to other Asian countries made me resentful about our society and history.

I have always had an adventurous spirit, and I wanted to explore something different, something else, something more in this wider world rather than being contained in a small island country called Japan.

Yuji

I was born in Tokyo, Japan, in 1974 and moved to the United States in 1993 at the age of 19. I am both a martial artist and an educator. As the second child in a family of four, I grew up immersed in Japanese culture before transitioning to life in the United States. Now, having lived in the United States for 32 years, my time here has surpassed the years I spent in Japan.

When I first arrived, I was deeply influenced by Hollywood's portrayal of American life. I especially had a fascination with the movie *Top Gun*. I thought that being American meant playing volleyball on the beach and riding motorcycles. I believed that by living in the United States, I could fully assimilate and become "American" in the way I had seen in movies. Fascinated by these media depictions, I consciously distanced myself from my Japanese heritage, attempting to reshape my identity to fit my idealized vision of American life.

But when I arrived in Oregon as a young adult to attend a small college, I was placed in a dormitory where I was the only foreigner. America was not the place I imagined. I was scared to go out, even to eat at the cafeteria. For three weeks I hid in my room. It was my resident assistant and the other guys in the dorm that came and pulled me out. "Who is living here?" they asked. They were my bridge. Without their kind invitation I wouldn't have made it.

Misa

It didn't take long for me to realize that America also has its own pros and cons—probably true for anywhere else in the world. Every place has its own beauty and challenges. Experiencing life outside of Japan, I came to appreciate my own roots and country in a new way. Living abroad allowed me to see my native country from a different perspective, making me recognize and appreciate its unique values and customs that shaped my identity. It's common for people to ask me, "Which country do you like better?" For me, this is an impossible comparison. It's not an either-or question. Both places feel like a significant part of me. My experience living and working in the United States has been eye-opening, and I have expanded my perspective of who I am. I have experienced that identity shifts and evolves based on how society perceives you or "labels you" too—along with all the implications and complexities that come with it.

If asked to identify myself now, here's what comes to my mind: Japanese, Japanese person living in the United States, woman, woman/person of color, "Asian," non-native English speaker/dual language speaker, early childhood professional, "Misa-sensei," colleague, team leader, advocate, aunt, sister, (grand)daughter, partner, violin player in quartet, and simply "me!" Regardless of all the hats I might be wearing, I am simply who I am.

When I return to Japan, I find myself looking at my own home country with new eyes. I become conscious about mannerisms, behaviors, and even become aware of my gaze towards others. Sometimes I catch myself using more traditional Japanese language, making sure to be proper. It feels like a way to reconnect with where I come from and something within myself, from a sense of gratitude for the culture woven into my being. It's a quiet reminder that no matter where I live, that part of me is still alive.

Yuji

As the years passed living in the United States, I came to realize that the country was not the one I had once envisioned in my dreams. While there is much to admire, I could not overlook the challenges related to racial inequity, subtle cultural preferences shaped by historically dominant identities, economic disparities, substance abuse, an emphasis on individualism, and the influence of long-standing religious traditions on societal norms. The idealized image I had formed through Hollywood films gradually crumbled, and I found myself confronting the stark contrast between my aspirations and reality. Perhaps rather than saying that my idealized image of America has crumbled, I see it as a process of shedding the layers of admiration and illusion—like sculpted clay peeling away—to reveal my true self. In doing so, I have been able to shift my awareness back to the essence of who I truly am. With the passage of time, my perspective has evolved, leading me to a profound appreciation of my Japanese heritage, which I now recognize as an integral part of my identity. Instead of seeking to erase my cultural background, I now embrace it with a renewed sense of appreciation. Living in a different country and culture, I have come to realize that had I not left Japan and come to the United States, I likely would never have gained this awareness. This has led me to explore and reconnect with my heritage, fostering a greater understanding of my own identity and the richness of Japanese culture.

I used to view identity not through the lens of race but rather as a reflection of who I am and what I stand for. My perspective was more philosophical and centered on questions about human origin, my purpose in being born in this era, and how I could contribute meaningfully to society. I often contemplated what kind of life I should lead and what my role in the world ought to be.

Growing up in Japan, a largely homogeneous society, I never gave much thought to racial identity. It was not something I was consciously aware of, nor did I feel the need to consider it, as everyone around me looked similar—predominantly East Asian. Interestingly though, I still distinguished myself from other Asians, such as Chinese, Koreans, Thai, or Vietnamese. This distinction was not rooted in negativity; in fact, I deeply admired aspects of other Asian cultures, particularly Hong Kong cinema, and was greatly influenced by figures like Jackie Chan, Bruce Lee, and Chow Yun-fat.

My family comes from a traditional lineage, and a strong sense of national pride runs deep, especially on my paternal side. My grandfather, who served as a high-ranking officer in the Japanese military during World War II and was entrusted with guarding the emperor's quarters, embodied this pride. I recall that during family gatherings, even joking about the emperor was strictly off-limits, emphasizing the reverence my family held for tradition and national identity.

It was only after moving to the United States that I became more acutely aware of identity—particularly racial identity. Living in a multicultural society, I observed how people from various backgrounds coexisted yet remained largely segregated along racial and socioeconomic lines. This experience forced me to reflect on identity in a new way.

Ultimately, I believe identity is shaped by self-worth, understanding, and lived experiences. It is fluid, evolving in response to life's events and personal growth. However, as one continues the journey of self-discovery, there is often a natural inclination to reconnect with one's roots. To truly understand who we are, we must look back to our origins—our bloodline, our family.

Reflections in the Field of Early Childhood

Misa

At one time, I was a teaching assistant and the only foreign teacher in the school. Up until then, I had been trying to assimilate into the environment, almost erasing or downplaying my Japanese background to blend in. But one day, a new child joined the classroom, and I soon learned that his mother was Japanese. When I met the mother for the first time, I cannot forget how we both instinctively greeted each other with a bow. In that moment, I was surprised at how the gesture naturally came to me—something I hadn't consciously thought about, yet it emerged effortlessly. It felt like a deep, internal, instinctive reflex. That small, yet profound exchange reminded me how culture is woven into our being. I remember speaking in my native language and seeing the look in both the child's eyes and the mother's eyes. It validated at that moment that my cultural background and connection could be meaningful and empowering.

Sometime later, I began working in the program where I've been for the last 20 years—one rooted in Japanese language and cultural inheritance. Being part of this community became a process of personal rediscovery. As someone who had newly come from Japan to the United States, it was an eye-opening education to learn deeply about Japanese American people—their history, resilience, roots, and identity—things I had rarely encountered while growing up in Japan. Through the stories of their lived experiences, I found myself undergoing an internal awakening: a rediscovery of my own cultural identity, alongside a growing collective understanding and appreciation of how culture lives, adapts, and evolves through layers of experience, relationships, and memory.

Yuji

As someone deeply rooted in Japanese culture, I hold great respect for the values of etiquette, sincerity, and omotenashi (おもてなし)—the spirit of wholehearted hospitality. These principles are not just social customs; they reflect a way of life that emphasizes mindfulness, harmony, and gratitude. Whether in my interactions with colleagues or in my role as an educator, I strive to embody these values, treating those around me with thoughtfulness and care. Living outside Japan has only deepened my appreciation for these cultural ideals, reinforcing my belief that they are essential in shaping a meaningful and respectful way of engaging with the world.

There was a moment one day during circle time with the children when I realized that I could bring my cultural experiences, a deep part of who I am, to the children. I could teach them that everything has a feeling and soul. I helped the children think about the connections between the air, the trees, and the people. In these grounding exercises with children, they can become more aware and grow, internalizing these experiences together. The parents of these children deeply appreciate my work with their children and will often thank me. It is deeply rewarding to me, and I can feel my purpose and gifts that I bring from my lived experiences.

Messages and Implications

Misa

I have come to believe that our work in early childhood education and our everyday life with children is, at its core, an act of social justice. It is about cultivating the *joy of living together*, recognizing and honoring the many forms of diversity that exist in our world and creating spaces where every child, family, and member of staff feels seen, valued, and empowered.

My Japanese cultural roots and language serve as both *mirrors* and *windows* (LeeKeenan 2019). As mirrors, my heritage and experiences reflect and validate children's own stories, affirming their identities—not only for those with Japanese backgrounds but also for children and families from other "nondominant" cultural or linguistic communities. At the same time, they act as *windows* for all children—opening the door to the richness of human diversity, broadening their idea about the world and its vast, colorful ways of being. Through curiosity and deep appreciation, we learn together, as members of a community, not only to see ourselves but to recognize and welcome one another.

We have the responsibility to stand together—across all kinds of differences—not just as allies but as coconspirators (Love 2019) in creating a more equitable world. Each of us indeed carries histories and unique stories. Whether those stories serve as mirrors or windows for others, they hold the power for us as a vehicle to move forward collectively.

Yuji

One of the most important lessons I hope to pass on to children is a traditional Japanese perspective on life: the belief that everything—people, objects, and even nature itself—possesses a spirit. This idea, deeply rooted in Shinto and Japanese folklore, teaches us to treat everything with reverence and gratitude. If a child learns to see the world this way, they naturally develop kindness, humility, and a sense of respect toward others and their surroundings. This is at the heart of my approach to early childhood education.

I believe that children learn not just through instruction but through the example set by the adults around them. I believe that, on a more instinctual level, other living creatures on Earth share the same concept as humans—that children are a reflection of their caregivers. Children observe the actions of the adults around them, empathize with them, imitate them, and perhaps grow and develop within the environment they are given. By living these values myself—by showing respect for objects, speaking with sincerity, and approaching daily life with care and love—I hope to provide an unspoken lesson that children will internalize and carry with them. Japanese culture is not just something to be taught; it is something to be lived and experienced, shaping one's spirit and worldview. In today's world, early childhood education often prioritizes academic skills—such as knowing letters and numbers for kindergarten entrance exams—but I believe that fostering a child's heart and spirit is far more important at this stage.

People often ask me why a man like me works in early childhood education, and my answer is always the same: I do this work for world peace. I truly believe that we, early childhood educators, have the power to unite the world and create a future filled with peace and love. As activists entrusted with this incredible mission, we have the privilege of planting seeds of love, kindness, and courage in the hearts of children—nurturing the next generation to build a more compassionate and harmonious world.

True education begins with cultivating a sense of compassion, gratitude, and harmony with the world. This belief guides me every day as I share moments of joy, curiosity, and wonder with the children in my care, hoping that they will grow into individuals who embody the kindness and mindfulness so deeply woven into Japanese culture. I believe that kindness and mindfulness are the essential sources from which the next generation can build a strong foundation as social justice advocates and allies against bias and injustice in the world.

In closing, I would like to share a revered Japanese proverb that I hold in the highest regard:

> Japan's national flower, the cherry blossom, carries profound significance. Its fleeting bloom, followed by a swift and graceful descent, serves as a poignant reminder of life's transience. This impermanence symbolizes the beauty and fragility of existence, inspiring us to cherish each moment and embrace life with wholehearted dedication.

CHAPTER 19

Beyond the Single Story

Writing Curriculum as a Freedom Practice

SARAH ELAHI

It was 2009. I was an undergraduate, assisting in an early childhood classroom in a small town in Western Massachusetts. Our activity for the day had introduced the 4-year-olds in the classroom to the idea of there being different scripts for different languages, and they all wanted me to write their names in Urdu. A little girl leaned over my shoulder as I wrote, her brow furrowed. "Your language is wrong, it's backwards," she said. The White teacher jumped in, embarrassed, and said, "That's not a nice thing to say!" I explained to her that Urdu, and many other languages, are written from right to left. The boy next to her asked, "But where do they write this way?" I told him I'm from Pakistan. I saw his mouth fall into an "O" shape. "Did you live in a cave there?" he asked.

I can't remember precisely what I said to those children all those years ago, but I do remember I wasn't surprised or offended. Pakistan, along with "all the other *-istans*," according to a colleague, was vaguely associated by adults, not 4-year-olds, with terror, barbarism, backwardness, and little else. By then, eight years after the war on terror had brought chaos and destruction to my part of the world, I was accustomed to the assumptions and stereotypes that followed me around. I did not yet have the vocabulary to address it adequately, but the need for community took me to an Asian affinity group, composed of people whose origins ranged from Hawai'i to Afghanistan. We had a dedicated cultural house on campus, and I had a part-time job as a coordinator for the five cultural houses. There was a lot of talk in those days about the importance of finding spaces for people who looked like one another. We needed space to feel comfortable and secure about our identity as we struggled to understand our marginalization. The AANHPI house was unlike many others because of the sheer number of identity groups who frequented it. Through intergroup dialogue, meetings over tea and dinner, and deep friendships, we unraveled the threads that were common to us all as Asians and Pacific Islanders, but also the tapestry that made our community so varied. It was there, as a trainee teacher, a student of history, and writer, that I began to consider what it would mean for education to truly serve all children.

Introduction

I am a Pakistani American educator. I was raised in many cultural contexts, having lived in two countries and six cities. I describe myself as bilingual and bicultural in the United States, where "Asian" is the broad census box I am allocated. I describe myself by my various ethnicities: North Indian, Punjabi, and Kashmiri when I am among South Asians. The boxes of my identity grow smaller and more specific the more intimately I am acquainted with anyone. As a result of my grandparents coming from three different ethnic groups, I am racially ambiguous to most Americans. Different people have told me I look Puerto Rican, Nepalese, Turkish, Afghan, and Indian. As a light-skinned person with a common name, I know I have the privilege of being White passing in many spaces, but only until people begin to pick apart the various strands that make me, me.

I've been a teacher for 17 years now. In the last decade, I've moved into curriculum work—researching, evaluating, designing. But even back when I was just starting out, I knew that the stories we put in front of children mattered. The idea of "mirrors and windows"—where kids see themselves reflected and also learn to understand others—stuck with me. These days, my work centers on decolonizing curriculum. It's not just a passion; it's the reason I do this work.

I know that to many people, my background as Muslim, immigrant, and Asian is a professional liability, although I see it as my greatest asset. It gives me a deeper lens to look at how knowledge is created and how education can either shrink or expand a child's sense of the world. Education is often framed as politically neutral, especially in public discourse, but I believe everything is political—especially curriculum. Curriculum choices shape not just what students learn but who gets to belong and who doesn't. In many postcolonial countries, and South Asia, where I am from, schools became ground zero for defining national identity. What language should we teach in? What role does religion play? What is a good citizen supposed to look like? I may not have realized it when I first arrived in the United States, but I had been wrestling with the intricacies of curriculum design for many years.

In Pakistan, the education system has been deeply influenced by both colonial legacies and Cold War politics. After independence in 1947, the country struggled to define what it meant to be Pakistani. Islam became central but not in the way many imagine—it was shaped by political agendas, foreign funding, and military interests. Under General Zia-ul-Haq, a Saudi-influenced version of Islam reshaped schools, narrowed opportunities for girls, and pushed boys toward jihadist ideologies—part of a larger geopolitical game with the United States and the Soviets.

These histories aren't abstract or purely academic to me. They live in the experiences of my family, my students, and my community. They shape how I think about resilience, identity, and what education should actually do. As a scholar of history, sociology, and child development, I am shaped by thinkers like Freire, Said, and Ungar—not just as academics but as guides for how to imagine something better.

The actual lives of children and families, which we can only know by talking with them, are far more important than stereotypical beliefs about youth from South Asian and Muslim backgrounds. The push to engage children, particularly through curriculum, took on new urgency in the post–War on Terror era, and that urgency has only continued to build in the decades since. This often fuels widespread narratives that frame Muslim children as being especially "at risk" for religious radicalization—a theme echoed in mainstream media coverage, such as a *New York Times* series that portrayed Muslim youth through the lens of heightened suspicion and moral concern. These realities operate within a framework of hegemonic power, in which Eurocentric beliefs about youth from South Asian and Muslim backgrounds are afforded greater power than the lived experiences of children and families.

The Western gaze is perhaps nowhere more evident than in early childhood education, where the trials experienced by children and youth are framed by a racialized form of deficit thinking. In my own experience, I have noticed many tired stereotypes at play. We are all accustomed to the idea that Asians are *naturally* better at math, but I have also heard colleagues say that Asian students are less creative, more likely to plagiarize or cheat, and have less aptitude for language arts. Speaking "good" English, or speaking English with a mid-Atlantic American accent, is associated with intelligence and competence. Many times over the course of my career, I have returned to the moment when I was asked why I write "backwards" and imagined teaching the child who asked me how rich the world is, how many ways there are to tell a story. Of course, as a 19-year-old, I didn't do that—but today, I know I would. Today, I have my pre-K classroom wall decorated with the alphabet in different languages. I ask parents how their children say important words at home, and I make sure the teachers I train learn to pronounce each precious syllable with the love and respect each child's language deserves.

As educators, we know stories shape understanding, and when those stories are one-dimensional, they can do real harm. That's why I've turned to postcolonial scholarship: to push back against the narrow, Eurocentric narratives that often dominate how the global South is portrayed. Too often, children in places like Pakistan, India, or Bangladesh are framed only through the lens of race and poverty. Since the War on Terror, gender has also become a key part of this narrative—especially when it comes to Muslim girls. One of the clearest examples of this was the global response to Malala Yousafzai winning the Nobel Peace Prize. The way Western media and politicians reacted told its own story. Former Australian Prime Minister Julia Gillard talked about the "tears in our eyes," and how dangerous it is for girls to get an education in countries like Pakistan. Journalists like Nicholas Kristof and Gordon Brown used the moment to spotlight violence against women, not just in Pakistan but in a sweeping list of countries across the global South in Latin America, Africa, and Asia. The message was clear: Asian Muslim girls are victims, and the men in their lives are violent and backward.

This kind of oversimplification does real damage. It pulls complex issues out of their political, historical, and economic context and flattens them into a single, familiar script. As scholar Shenila Khoja-Moolji puts it, these portrayals collapse all Brown and Black girls into one universal victimhood, and all Brown men into one universal threat. If we've seen one, we've seen them all. Even my fairly sophisticated colleagues in early childhood education are often shocked by the fact that my South Asian Muslim family invested heavily in my education, from birth through graduate school; that all the women in my family are highly educated working professionals; that the men in my life are deeply engaged fathers and loving, equitable partners.

I've seen how this plays out in the classroom. Back in 2009, my pre-K students had only one story about people like me, and it was shaped by these same stereotypes. In early childhood education—and across the system—those narrow stories are still the ones most kids hear. Where are the mirrors for children who look like me? Where are the windows that help others understand our lives in all their complexity?

If we're serious about equity, we have to go beyond performative sympathy. That means questioning the narratives we've inherited and expanding the ones we offer in our classrooms. It's not just about representation—it's about dignity, truth, and justice.

That single story about me was not accurate. We need to go beyond the single stereotypical story (Adichie 2009) by offering multiple lived stories from children and families of our community. According to critical race theory, "racism is often well disguised as the rhetoric of shared 'normative' values and 'neutral' social scientific principles and practices" (Yosso 2005, 8). Every academic field today has been affected by gatekeeping, which has prevented disenfranchised peoples from being active participants in creating the knowledge which comes to define the normative culture. Paulo Freire wrote about this phenomenon decades ago, emphatically asserting that "the educator has the duty of not being neutral" (Freire 1968). Where do education programs, child policymakers, and teacher-educators fall into this paradigm, then? It can be argued that a thoughtful interrogation of the values guiding children's education in the developing world can only be achieved through the recruitment of teachers from diverse contexts. However, merely involving communities of color or Indigenous peoples cannot correct what is essentially an institutional problem. There will always be questions of bias and possibly silencing. The only answer then is to empower educators to cocreate curriculum in community with one another, with the families they work with, and with the voices of the children they serve. In my journey as an educator, administrator, and curriculum developer, the voices of children, their families, and their community leaders are critical to determining the content as well as tone of what I teach.

As early childhood educators, we often talk about helping children build resilience, but too often, we treat resilience as an individual trait instead of something nurtured through relationships, identity, and community. In many classrooms, the inherited curriculum and teaching style work against the sacred bond of nurturing, which early childhood education can promote, particularly in postcolonial or marginalized communities.

I've seen this in practice. In some early childhood education spaces, children are rewarded for quiet compliance and penalized for curiosity that doesn't fit neatly into a scripted lesson. I remember a 4-year-old in my child's class—full of questions, storytelling, and joy. But when they shifted to a rigid literacy block, she stopped improvising during play and started asking "Is this right?" before drawing. It was heartbreaking. The very system that claimed to be preparing her for "success" was flattening her voice.

This is what author and artist adrienne maree brown calls the violence of "imposed order"—the way dominant systems teach us to shrink ourselves to fit structures that were never made for us. In her book *Emergent Strategy*, she writes that change doesn't come from control but from adaptability, relationships, and trust in collective wisdom. That idea has transformed the way I approach my classroom. When I invite students to bring in stories from home or cocreate the classroom calendar based on cultural holidays they celebrate, I'm not just checking a "diversity" box; I'm giving them power, visibility, and a sense of belonging.

Resilience in education isn't just about surviving; it's about creating the conditions that allow us to thrive. In early learning, this means moving away from control-based pedagogy and toward liberation-based practices. It's the difference between managing behavior and cultivating agency. I've had success shifting circle time into a morning where kids pass around a talking piece and share what's on their mind–joys, fears, questions. We teach each other how to listen deeply and respond with care. That's community-building. That's liberatory pedagogy in action.

The Reggio Emilia philosophy offers a powerful model for this kind of transformative education. It views children not as empty vessels to be filled but as full citizens of the classroom: curious, capable, and deeply connected to their environment. In my own practice, incorporating Reggio-inspired elements has meant creating spaces where children's questions guide the curriculum, where materials are chosen for their capacity to spark wonder, and where documentation honors their thinking as real and valuable. When we treat the classroom as a place of shared inquiry, where the teacher is a colearner, not a gatekeeper, we're not just teaching content. We're practicing democracy. We're building resilience by showing children that their voice matters, that their ideas shape the world around them. That, too, is liberatory pedagogy in action.

As Chimamanda Ngozi Adichie powerfully said in *The Danger of a Single Story*, when one narrative dominates, it robs people of dignity and flattens their humanity. This is especially true in early education where too often children are only exposed to single stories about people of color—either as victims or as "exceptions." For me, that realization began the day I was asked if I lived in a cave. That moment forced me to reckon with what we weren't teaching. So now, I promote reading books that show everyday Black, Brown, and Asian joy—stories about children cooking with grandparents, playing soccer, losing teeth, celebrating Eid, Lunar New Year, or Diwali—not just surviving poverty or escaping conflict.

As a South Asian educator, my goal isn't just about helping kids bounce back from adversity; it's about creating learning spaces that affirm their full humanity. That's liberation. And it starts in the earliest years.

So Many More Voices . . .

> As a transracial Chinese adoptee, I spent much of my childhood feeling isolated and misunderstood by others. Therefore, I always make it my goal that every child under my care feels seen and loved for who they are.

Olivia Hobert
Lead Teacher and Summer Program Director
Henry Frost Children's Program
Boston, Massachusetts

CHAPTER 20

Filipino Storytime

Reclaiming My Identity by Building Community

CLARE JUICO

My Filipino Identity

I am a Filipino, born and raised in the Philippines. I take pride and gratitude knowing that my roots are intact. I know my values, my religion, my language, and most importantly, the plight of my people brought on by centuries of colonialism and imperialism. I left the Philippines to break a cycle of poverty, the story of millions of Filipinos. But after I moved to the United States in 1998, I started to imagine my roots getting undug, as if going over the soil and finding a different way to go I lost a part of myself. I was raised to be heavily, culturally assimilated in the United States.

Yet, some of the strengths my Filipino identity and culture have instilled in me are resourcefulness and industriousness. Growing up in almost poverty-level conditions without any governmental support, my family experienced natural disasters like floods, earthquakes, and extreme heat, and became resourceful in order to survive. It was something we had to learn, which my parents and family modeled in their everyday lives. We would build, reuse, and repurpose different materials for general living conditions. Trash was transformed into treasure and toys. We played in trees damaged by storms. We prepared meals of very few ingredients that could feed the whole family.

Moving to the United States

When I came to the United States in 1998, Seattle was my port of entry. I first lived in Beacon Hill, which is historically a neighborhood where a lot of Asian communities laid down their roots. After I arrived, I wanted to blend into my community. I tried my best to speak the way native English speakers do, pronouncing their words carefully because I wanted so deeply to be understood. I experienced firsthand the biases that my mother experienced from others when she spoke because she has a really thick accent. I felt robbed of my identity as a Filipino. The way I spoke, the sound of my voice, the way I pronounced certain words so that I could mask my way of saying them just to blend in, all left me feeling invisible.

When I married a Canadian man and started my family, I relocated to a neighborhood a few miles north of Seattle. There was not a big Filipino community in the new neighborhood, or a lot of Filipinos in the church I went to, nor in the schools that my two daughters attended. All of my mom's side of the family lives south of Seattle, and my husband spoke English, so our daughters were not exposed to hearing the Filipino language. Our daughters come from a bilingual/biracial household where my Filipino language is not the primary language spoken at home. They did not grow up learning my language.

My older daughter is now learning our language. She visited the Philippines not too long ago on an outreach mission to understand the conditions in farming and fishing communities in the provinces. She is a community organizer and works towards addressing the migrant worker problems, especially Filipino migrant workers in the country. My other daughter is also interested in learning Filipino and is beginning to think about volunteering just like her sister did this year. I think it's wonderful that they are reestablishing and getting to know their Filipino roots on their own time. It's more authentic that way. It's also honoring their identities as individuals who inherited two sets of cultures growing up in the United States. They have their own experiences outside of ours where they form their own identities in their own time.

My siblings and I growing up together in the Philippines. My sister, Monica, still lives in the Philippines. One of the hardest parts of emigrating was spending most of my adult life separated from her and her family.

Experiencing Bias

My first professional role was as a receptionist at a medical clinic. That was the first time I became conscious of experiencing microaggressions. I worked at the front desk and was highly visible on the front line. I was often told to speak louder when others were not comfortable with the way I pronounced things. I gravitated towards completing non-public-facing tasks such as filing charts or stuffing envelopes because I did not want to speak at all. I felt like I lost my voice.

Eventually, I was designated to work in the phone room, where I had to answer calls. It was a relief because I could mask who I was since people could not see me. They did not see my lack of confidence. That was how I learned to speak in a way that is more acceptable for others. I tried to mimic how other colleagues spoke and learned certain lines over and over that I used as templates for frequently asked questions.

I remember times on public transportation where, for safety purposes as a young woman, I made it a point to sit closer to the driver. There were multiple times when people would just tell me to move to the back of the bus. Others would even say, "Go back to your country."

These are things that stick with me, though I learned to shrug them off and ask for no trouble. I did not want to put myself in harm's way by trying to defend myself. I constantly wanted to avoid conflict and confrontation.

Becoming a Filipino American Professional

It took a long time to overcome my experiences of isolation and bias when I first moved to the United States. To become a professional, I had to set aside my lack of confidence and push through. It has been over two decades since I set foot in this country. I am now more comfortable and rooted here. Now I recognize myself and can empathize with others who just moved to Seattle from a different country, or even from a different state. I recognize the importance of creating a welcoming environment in the workplace and in the classroom that fosters a sense of belonging. I recognize that there are some who are not yet comfortable in the environment that they're in. I know how it feels to not be seen or to feel out of place. I have a strong desire to create a space where people can grow their roots at their own pace and in their own time. I have learned through my education that one of my crucial roles as an educator is to advocate for children and families, especially those who have been marginalized. I need to be able to raise concerns and share their stories, which will help improve conditions for the children and their families.

One of my strongest traits from my Filipino identity is the desire to create a sense of community and foster unity. We have a word, "bayanihan," that means a group of people, usually neighbors and relatives, which work together to address someone's needs. One concrete example of this is in agricultural towns in the Philippines where the whole town (bayan) will come together to help a farming family relocate a house by carrying it on their shoulders together. This collective and unified effort is made without any expectation of payment. Filipinos bond together to alleviate the suffering of others. We want to include everybody in our daily lives, and we especially rally to be of service to others during times of need. I have learned to tap on my resources and professional network to explore groups that help me find my sense of community.

Building Community

I am one of the organizers of Filipino Story Time–Seattle, a volunteer group serving families and caregivers in the Seattle area. We are a small but mighty group of Filipina women who have regular children's book readings in different locations—libraries, museums, community halls, Filipino restaurants, and even the aquarium! Most of the books are written in Filipino, the official national language of the Philippines, but we also try to find books in other languages used in the Philippines. Based on the National Commission for Culture and the Arts, there are 80 major languages and about 500 regional dialects spoken in the country (Philippine National Commission for Culture and the Arts, 2025). We are in constant search of books that reflect the linguistic diversity of the Philippines. We choose books by Filipino authors and illustrators who share stories about our heritage, history, and daily lives.

The original intent in establishing this group was to support children's Filipino language acquisition through book reading and engaging them in activities that support their vocabulary growth. Occasionally, we have guest readers who enthusiastically spend their time with us. In every event, we introduce new Filipino words from the book. The children listen for those words during the reading, and then we practice saying those words out loud. The postreading activities are designed to help them learn about the Filipino culture as well as strengthening their skills in other areas. We read *Lolo's Sari-Sari Store* by Sophia N. Lee, about a child's experiences helping in her grandfather's corner store. We set up a makeshift store with Filipino snacks, and the children used replicas of Philippine pesos to purchase their snacks. They used new Filipino words to buy what they wanted and practiced math skills using their pesos, getting a glimpse of buying from a corner store, which is a staple in most neighborhoods in the Philippines.

Five years after its founding, Filipino Story Time–Seattle is serving as a vehicle not only for book reading but also as a way to connect Filipino families together. Some have come from the Philippines or were raised by parents who migrated here and are now raising their own children. Some of them lost the language and want to relearn it, but all of those who join us desire to expose their children to their roots and cultivate a deeper understanding of Filipino culture.

Filipino Story Time is a demonstration of the bayanihan spirit; it builds a community that raises a generation who are in touch with their roots even if they are miles away from home.

Strategies for Creating a Sense of Belonging: Supporting New Immigrants to the United States

- *Remember that families who have just moved to our country may not be comfortable speaking the language.* Environments that foster a sense of belonging help everyone feel brave to express what they want to say. One of the best ways to encourage children and adult speakers to communicate with others is making sure that they are given time and grace to process what they want to say. Practice patience; pause and wait until they can express what they want to say. Be open to silence as they try to come up with the words they want to say. Try not to jump in and give them the words or ask them clarifying questions about what they want to express. Keep in mind that most non-native English speakers have a deep-seated fear of being dismissed, ridiculed, or rejected. In adult classrooms, try to conduct group discussions where there is a balance of non-native English speakers and native English speakers if possible. Encourage a space that maximizes participation where everyone has a turn to talk and listen to with openness.
- *Talk about commonalities.* Food is always a good place to start. Certain dishes have different variations in other cultures. For example, the counterpart of Chinese dumplings in the Philippines is called siopao, in Korea it is mandu, and in Afghan cooking, it is mantu. Then go deeper and apply it in other aspects of our culture. How are our values and beliefs the same, and how are we different? Open conversations with curiosity about how and where caregivers and colleagues grew up, how they play, what they eat, what holidays are food related, what holidays are faith or religion based. Ask questions that can lead to them opening up, questions they may not have heard before, that are about things they might like to share.
- *Learn greetings in others' home languages.* When I was working for the clinic, we had patients who did not speak English. Fortunately, we had a lot of translators available who spoke common greetings in different languages to help the patients feel welcome. I asked the interpreters to write syllabically how to say different greetings. Later, I took

this idea into our family child care classroom, where we had families speaking many languages; some children were brought to school by grandparents who spoke no English. I had to get creative on how to pick up different phrases, especially when a child was new to the environment and would only cry or say nothing at all. I had parents record in their home language typical greetings and words we needed to help children understand what is going on or provide words of comfort and reassurance. We had voice memos for words like "outside time," "naptime," "eat," and "How are you feeling?" In adult classrooms, consider doing the same for students who speak a language in addition to English. Have them record common social greetings or affirmations that can help them throughout the course.

› *Incorporate assignments that encourage students to connect with other cultural or language affinity groups in college coursework.* Find ways to encourage students to research about cultural and language affinity groups that they are most interested in. Sponsor a club for those who want to start a language group or book club that helps students connect with others within the program or the school who have the same background or are interested in learning more about their heritage.

So Many More Voices . . .

> **In understanding and valuing your own identity, you can value other people for who they are and what they bring to the table, to the classroom, or to the group.**
>
> Donna Elizabeth Kaleiokalani Reid-Hayes
> Chapter Author

CHAPTER 21

Suda [수다] on Korean American Teacher-Educators' Lived Experiences

SOHYUN MEACHAM, JINHEE KIM, SU-JEONG WEE, AND SOPHIA HAN

Prologue: What Is Suda?

Our journey as Korean American teacher-educators in early childhood education has been shaped by the power of suda—which we reclaim and redefine as the act of deep, ongoing conversation rooted in Korean culture. In a field where relationships and dialogue are central to children's learning, suda has been our anchor—a space where we, as first-generation Korean American immigrant teacher-educators and mothers of children born and raised in the United States, exchange ideas, refine our scholarship, and navigate the complexities of preparing future educators.

Suda, often dismissed in the past as futile chatting among women, is in fact a powerful practice of meaning-making and knowledge production (Han et al. 2023; Meacham et al. 2019, 2022, 2025). More than mere casual talk, suda is an intentional and relational act of engaging in dialogue to construct understanding, share lived experiences, and challenge dominant narratives. It has long been a way for Korean women to resist silence and marginalization, using conversation to sustain and empower one another. Today, as educators and scholars, we reclaim suda as an emancipatory research method—one that values relational knowledge-building and the voices of those often left unheard in traditional academia.

Suda is not just a method of conversation; it is deeply rooted in our Korean cultural heritage. In our families and communities, we have always gathered around tables, floors, and cafés, engaging in suda as a way of making sense of the world. It is how our mothers and grandmothers processed life's challenges, how generations before us sustained each other through war, migration, and resilience. This tradition of storytelling, questioning, and collective meaning-making lives on in our scholarly and professional lives. It is through suda that we bridge our past and present, weaving our cultural identities into our work as early childhood educators.

As an emancipatory research method, suda is particularly significant in early childhood education. Just as we, as educators, use dialogue to reflect and transform our pedagogies, young children also engage in their own forms of suda—through storytelling, play, and interaction. By recognizing and valuing these conversational exchanges, we affirm the importance of relational, communal, and culturally sustaining ways of knowing. In our research and teaching practice, suda allows us to listen deeply to the voices of children and educators alike, coconstructing knowledge in ways that challenge hierarchical and Eurocentric models of learning.

Through suda, we create spaces where both children and adults can speak, be heard, and engage in collective meaning-making. What was once dismissed as trivial talk is now central to how we understand and transform our work in early childhood education. It is through suda that we empower ourselves, our students, and the young children we teach, ensuring that dialogue remains at the heart of education and research.

Suda Amongst Ourselves

In the following section, we present conversations between coauthors to illustrate how suda works. Each coauthor will share their story, and another coauthor will respond to her. Suda, being an oral form of communication, is inherently more open-ended and nonlinear compared to the written form presented here, so this form may not fully capture the spontaneous and dynamic nature of our original oral exchanges. Through this process, we aim to still preserve the essence of our conversations and the rich, fluid nature of suda in our scholarly work.

Planting Seeds and Creating Synergy Through Suda: Soh and Jinhee's Suda

Soh: One night, after an emotionally exhausting day of teaching and meetings, I joined a Zoom call with my suda sisters for suda. Each of us came with stories—concerns about threats to diversity, equity, inclusion, and justice; challenges in advocating for young children of color; and moments of joy in seeing preservice teachers' growth. As we spoke, our voices overlapped, creating a shared understanding of what it means to influence the field of early childhood education as Korean American educators.

I remember Jinhee sharing a moment of doubt. "I sometimes wonder if all this effort is making any difference," she confessed. Immediately, Sophia responded with heartfelt reassurance, "Jinhee, your work is planting seeds. We may not see the full bloom, but the impact is there." This exchange reminded me of the importance of our collective support. Another time, Su-Jeong recounted a small victory. "One of my students finally opened up about her struggles at home," she said, her voice filled with emotion. We all celebrated with genuine delight, knowing how significant that breakthrough was. These moments of connection, of shared knowing, are what sustain me.

These conversations are not just about support; they have transformed my work. As a scholar of dialogic pedagogy (Matusov 2009) inspired by the Reggio Emilia approach, which emphasizes the importance of discursive culture in early childhood classrooms to promote democracy (Dýrfjörð 2006), delving into suda from my inherited Korean culture felt so natural. Through suda, I have sharpened my scholarship, refined my pedagogical approaches, and deepened my sense of purpose. When I bring our discussions into my teaching, I see my early childhood education students engaging in their own forms of suda, although they do not necessarily call it suda, discovering their voices through dialogue, collaboration, and reflection.

Jinhee: I cannot forget the several meaningful moments we spent engaging in suda. Through suda with my suda sisters, including you, Soh, we built a safe space to share and listen to each other genuinely without judging others. Our suda on various topics in early childhood education has helped us recognize the power of collective storytelling and its benefits for us as teacher-educators. In particular, reflecting on our observations of our children's experiences in preschools and primary grades in elementary schools deepens our understanding of how even children within the same ethnic or racial groups have diverse experiences. For example, we shared different experiences and strategies on various topics, such as maintaining heritage language and culture, in relation to our own children. We noticed that our approaches to preserving heritage language and culture vary among our families. Through suda, these differences allowed us to discuss how early childhood educators can create more welcoming and inclusive classroom environments. Suda also led us to discuss how our teacher candidates can be more open and critically aware of the practices taken for granted, such as playtime and snack time, in classroom settings. Additionally, through suda—a space where we share our diverse experiences and stories—we realized that storytelling is more than just recounting experiences; it requires active listening and the development of trust among those involved. Sharing stories with suda sisters through suda can create synergy by fostering support and facilitating the exchange of best practices for young children. I believe suda is valuable for early childhood educators, providing a platform to share their experiences, including challenges, rewards, joys, and laughter, much like what we experienced. Creating such spaces can lead to meaningful reflections on teaching practices and offer emotional support for educators in this field.

Navigating Validity and Building Solidarity: Jinhee and Su-Jeong's Suda

Jinhee: It is reported that non-Hispanic White individuals predominantly make up the early childhood education workforce, with 63 percent working in center-based early childhood education, while a relatively small percentage of AANHPI individuals, only 5 percent, have served in this field (Paschall et al. 2020). Likewise, early childhood teacher education programs, including the one where I have worked, are not an exception. I was often placed in situations that led to persistent self-doubt about my teaching, forcing me to justify my knowledge with questions like, "Is my knowledge valid?" and "How do I prove that my knowledge is valid?" Rather than fostering an acknowledgment of differences as assets that enrich diverse and critical perspectives, I felt pressured to provide evidence to justify my knowledge of teaching. While continuous reflection on teaching is generally encouraged for teacher-educators, my reflections are often intertwined with the need to find evidence to justify my knowledge of teaching. Sharing different practices and perspectives related to teaching and understanding children is sometimes well received by students but often met with initial resistance or an automatic default to view me as merely a symbolic representation of AANHPI. One day, I introduced practices in some Asian cultures, such as cosleeping as a parenting approach or valuing silence during conversation as a form of active listening, to help students better understand children from diverse backgrounds. While some students welcomed the discussion, others defaulted to viewing me as a spokesperson for all AANHPI experiences and perceived the practices as a deficit parenting practice, rather than engaging with it from a critical and culturally responsive perspective. In addition, the current political climate, which restricts teacher-educators from freely addressing diversity, makes me feel even more vulnerable and needing to justify my teaching.

Su-Jeong: I feel like I've been in a very similar situation with you, Jinhee. At my previous university, I was the only East Asian faculty member in my department for almost 10 years. The same year I was hired, a Southeast Asian female professor also joined, but she left after a year. I never found out if she moved to another institution. As the sole East Asian faculty member, I naturally ended up teaching multicultural education. When external evaluators came for NAEYC accreditation, they treated me as if I were a "living example" of diversity. In the late 2000s and 2010s, there seemed to be a trend in early childhood education departments where hiring one non-White faculty member was seen as a way to enhance diversity, which educators in higher education often referred to as having a "multicultural faculty." It was a perfect example of tokenism. I remember asking myself, *Would I have been hired if I weren't Asian?*

I completely understand how frustrating it is to be in a position where you can't openly discuss diversity or Critical Race Theory. My research and publications have centered on immigrant children and families, racism, and cultural diversity, yet in the current climate, some institutions' faculty can't even mention these topics in class, and research grants for such work are being cut. It's an incredibly stifling situation.

Trying to overcome this kind of challenge alone must be incredibly difficult. It's understandable to feel frustrated and even want to give up at times. But we are not alone. We need to come together, raise our voices collectively, and resist these injustices together. There is strength in solidarity, and by supporting one another, we can push back against these barriers more effectively than any of us could on our own.

From Solitary Islands to a Sea of Shared Wisdom: Su-Jeong and Sophia's Suda

Su-Jeong: While working in higher education, I often felt like a solitary island—adrift in the middle of the sea, disconnected from any land. Although I believed I was collaborating with colleagues, they often felt like birds that would briefly land before flying away, never to return once their needs were met. Even within the workplace, professional relationships remained temporary, and over time, I found myself becoming increasingly isolated.

I struggled to keep myself from drifting too far, to prevent complete disconnection from solid ground. Preparing lectures in a language that was not my own required me to invest several times more effort than my peers. When teaching early childhood music, I had to tirelessly practice unfamiliar chants and songs—melodies that were second nature to my students but foreign to me. To bridge this gap, I bought CDs and listened to them repeatedly, striving to make these cultural elements my own. Yet, despite my efforts, I often found myself asking, *What am I doing here?* The sense of isolation lingered.

Then, I met my suda sisters. When I shared my thoughts, they didn't narrow their eyes in confusion as if to say, *What are you talking about?* Instead, they nodded in understanding, smiled, and shared their own similar experiences. They didn't offer empty, generic responses but rather thoughtful advice and guidance rooted in their lived experiences. It felt like islands coming together to form a cluster.

Through these suda conversations, my life became richer, and the research topics I had agonized over alone for years suddenly expanded into exciting possibilities for collaborative inquiry. With the four of us together, there were so many research projects we wanted to explore.

Sophia: Your analogy of feeling like a solitary island drifting in the middle of the sea is so perfect, Su-Jeong! I am deeply sorry that you felt so isolated and uncertain in your professional relationship with your colleagues as well as students. At the same time, I am relieved that I was not alone because that is exactly how I have been feeling about myself for so long until I was able to get united with this group of suda sisters.

Just like you, I remember learning about not only all those children's songs, nursery rhymes, and fingerplays but also popular children's TV shows or books to better connect with my students and to rebut them whenever anyone complains, "Oh, you don't know, that's not how we do it," about my professional expertise or experience. Perhaps one of the ways I benefited from having my own kids was that I had opportunities to experience US early childhood classrooms firsthand. Although it was extremely hard to give birth and raise two kids during my tenure-earning years at a research-intensive university, this exposure and insights helped me tremendously to stay more relevant with early childhood teacher candidates I teach.

Lately, I began to develop more confidence to expose my students to more diverse resources and strategies for teaching young children. Once I introduced global versions of children's play or folktales, such as how the "days of the week" chants (i.e., English starts with a Sunday, when Korean starts with a Monday) or "rock paper scissors" game (i.e., English order is rock-paper-scissors, when Korean order is scissors-rock-paper) differ in different cultural contexts in hopes to expand their perspectives. Moreover, I am also grateful that we are making efforts to expand the research paradigm by embracing our suda theory. I know a lot of new ideas and possibilities are awaiting us, and together nothing is impossible!

From Whispers of Doubt to Echoes of Assurance: Sophia and Soh's Suda

Sophia: When I first started a faculty career in the United States and walked into the college classroom full of early childhood teacher candidates, I still vividly remember the puzzling looks of my students. They looked around the classroom with unspoken words: "Are we in the right room? Is she going to be our professor?" Although I had all the necessary qualifications to become a faculty member, and I was so excited and prepared to be their internship supervisor, it was pretty evident that my students had more doubts than trust in me. For instance, whenever there was any misunderstanding in their internship or issues with their assignment, they didn't hesitate to ask, "Did you clarify that with my teacher? Can you explain again?" as if I failed to communicate something or I did not know what I was supposed to do. I tried to self-assure myself with thoughts like, perhaps it was their first time, and they did not have any teachers throughout their schooling experiences who looked like me or spoke with an accent like me. I also thought things would improve if I built better relationships with my students, which proved to take so much longer than I had hoped.

As an early childhood researcher, I am interested in teacher education and the roles of internship experiences. Similar to my teaching, I ran into many visible and invisible barriers whenever I approached US school districts and/or teachers for research collaboration. It was disheartening and discouraging not to have a role model or mentor who I could look up to. In fact, once an Asian American colleague who is my senior shared her experience that US educational institutions are incredibly conservative organizations to outsiders like us. While I have become much more confident in navigating US colleges and schools after over 20 years, I am still not free from feeling the burden of proving that I belong. I am so grateful to have my suda sisters as peer mentors as I continue to find my place.

Soh: Sophia onni [언니: Onni is a Korean term used by females to refer to an older sister. However, it is not limited to biological sisters; it can also be used for close female friends who are older. (Male individuals do not use this term; instead, they use noona to refer to an older sister or older female friend.) Your story really hits home for me. When I first started my faculty career, I remember those puzzled looks from my students too. They seemed to be silently asking, "Is she really our professor?" I remember one of my students wrote, "Soh is Korean and teaching English literacy," in the points for improvement section of my teaching evaluation. They did not elaborate on it at all, making it seem as though my Korean American identity was problematic, regardless of my PhD degree in literacy education from an accredited research university in the United States. Since then, I have introduced my Korean American identity more openly to students at the beginning of each semester, explaining that I use a Midwest accent because Seoul is located in the Korean Midwest region. I like to tell them, "Yes, you heard that right! Seoul is basically the Iowa of Korea!"

I resonate with you regarding the lack of role models or mentors who look and speak like me. This is especially true for me as an associate dean, as I aspire to become a higher education leader. Asian American women deans in colleges and schools of education, particularly those who speak with a heavy Korean accent like mine, are incredibly rare. However, having my suda sisters as peer mentors has been a lifeline. They help me find my place and remind me that I am not alone in this journey. Thank you for sharing your experience—it makes me feel seen and understood. It even gives me the courage to continue my journey, despite not having role models.

Embracing Suda as Scholarship and Resistance

The act of suda—deep, intentional conversation—has been central to our lives as Korean American teacher-educators. Through our dialogues, we have created a space where we can share our lived experiences, navigate professional challenges, and support one another in the face of systemic barriers. This chapter has illuminated how suda is not only a cultural practice but also a method of resistance, knowledge production, and professional sustenance.

Suda as a Counter-Narrative

In a field where dominant narratives often marginalize the voices and perspectives of faculty of color, suda allows us to reclaim our agency. Our experiences as Korean American teacher-educators in early childhood education are shaped by our identities; our accents, cultural knowledge, and ways of engaging with students are sometimes questioned or undervalued. Through suda, we resist these marginalizations by validating our lived realities and asserting the legitimacy of our knowledge. We have collectively reflected on how suda helps us push back against tokenization, implicit biases, and institutional pressures that often demand we justify our presence in the academy. By naming and analyzing these experiences together, we create counter-narratives that resist the silencing and erasure of AANHPI voices in teacher education.

Suda as a Method of Knowledge Production

Our discussions reveal that suda is not simply an informal exchange of words but a generative process that shapes our research and pedagogy. We have explored how suda mirrors the relational and dialogic nature of early childhood education, where children can coconstruct knowledge through storytelling, play, and social interactions. Just as young children learn by engaging in meaningful dialogue, we, as educators and scholars, engage in suda to develop new understandings of our field. The process of dialogically sharing and responding to one another's stories has deepened our insights into issues such as the racialized experiences of AANHPI teacher-educators, the significance of cultural perspectives in early childhood classrooms, and the political challenges of teaching about diversity and equity.

Suda has also allowed us to bridge the gap between personal and professional knowledge. Our discussions have helped us make sense of the struggles we face as mothers, daughters, and educators, and how these roles intersect in our work. From navigating heritage language maintenance with our own children to advocating for culturally sustaining pedagogies in our classrooms, suda has provided a space to critically examine the tensions and possibilities within our work. This process of meaning-making aligns with feminist and decolonial methodologies that center relationality, storytelling, and collective knowledge-building as legitimate forms of scholarship.

The Emotional Labor of Being Korean American Teacher-Educators

One of the most powerful themes that emerged from our suda was the emotional labor required of us as Korean American teacher-educators. Many of us have felt isolated, doubted, or pressured to assimilate into dominant norms of academia and the field of early childhood teacher education. Whether it was having to repeatedly prove our expertise, navigating student resistance to diverse perspectives, or struggling with the lack of mentorship and role models, we have carried emotional burdens that are rarely acknowledged in formal academic spaces.

Yet, through suda, we have found solidarity and affirmation. We have shared our frustrations, fears, and small victories, realizing that our struggles are not individual failings but reflections of larger systemic inequities. This recognition has strengthened our resolve to push forward—not just for ourselves but for the next generation of educators and scholars who will walk similar paths.

Moving Forward: Suda as a Sustaining Practice

As we conclude this chapter, we recognize that our journey with suda is ongoing. We have found strength in each other's voices, and we envision this practice continuing to shape our scholarship, teaching, and leadership. Beyond our own experiences, we hope that suda can serve as a model for other educators—especially those who feel isolated or marginalized in their institutions. Whether through formal research collaborations, informal mentoring, or community-building efforts, the principles of suda—deep listening, relational meaning-making, and mutual support—can create transformative spaces for faculty and students alike.

For us, suda is not just a method; it is a way of being. It affirms our identities, sustains us through challenges, and empowers us to create knowledge that is deeply rooted in our lived experiences. In reclaiming suda as a scholarly practice, we affirm the value of our voices in the academy and commit to continuing this work—not just for ourselves but for the collective good of our field.

PART 4

Advocacy and Leading for Change

The contributions in Part 4 show that as the authors understood more about their own identities, they were encouraged to set goals and do work to move the field forward and create change. These chapters follow early childhood education leaders' experiences abroad and in the United States as they bring their own lived experiences across Native Hawaiian, Korean, Samoan, Chinese, Punjabi, and Vietnamese cultures into their professional roles. Their chapters point to the need for having a more diverse workforce that would make the profession more attractive to future Asian American and Native Hawaiian, Pacific Islander (AANHPI) educators. Allowing students to see and experience teachers who reflect their culture, language, family structure, or gender could inspire more students to become educators. Adjusting curriculum to be responsive to all cultures also would make the education profession more appealing to today's increasingly diverse student body and help address the long-standing underrepresentation of Black, Indigenous, and People of Color (BIPOC) teachers in our schools and universities. This outcry also points to the need for more advocacy and policy change, which can only happen when AANHPI educators can make their voices heard and build coalitions across our different constituencies to benefit all students, families, and educators.

These are stories of reclamation, intersectionality, resilience, and hope. All of these chapters echo the sentiment that there is hope that the next generation of AANHPI educators won't have to choose between authenticity and acceptance. They can walk into any room, speak in any accent, carry any name—and still be seen as leaders.

Reflection Questions

As you read the chapters in Part 4, we encourage you to reflect on the following questions:

- Each generation has a role to play, their choices and experiences impacted by both culture and social political contexts. How do the lives of your ancestors shape your journey? How do your lives intersect?
- What is your theory of change? In other words, how do you think positive changes come about, and what are the necessary conditions and actions needed to create change? What did you read in the chapters in this section that might inform your theory of change?
- Growing up, what messages were you taught about leaders and changemakers? What do you think today's young people need to learn that will empower them to see themselves as leaders and changemakers?
- What examples of leadership and advocacy did you connect with most deeply in this volume? What examples do you draw inspiration from in your own life?

- What change/advocacy work do you think you can bring to early childhood education? Looking at your own spheres of influence, what concrete steps might you take to expand your capacity as a changemaker?
- What are the most pressing issues and problems that impact your local community, and how might you broach these topics with young children in ways that help foster their sense of justice, agency, voice, and empowerment?

CHAPTER 22

Bringing Your Whole Self to the Classroom

A Native Hawaiian Perspective on Identity in Early Childhood Education

NICOL RUSSELL

Opening Reflection

It was during my second year as a teacher that I first felt the sharp contrast between who I was and who I was expected to be. I was preparing for a class cultural celebration—an opportunity, I was told, to "highlight diversity" with the students and families. As a Native Hawaiian teacher in a school in Maryland that had students and families from many different racial and ethnic backgrounds, I was excited to have an opportunity to share my culture with students and families. I planned a lesson centered around moʻolelo, sharing a story my grandmother used to tell us about the night marchers, the restless spirits of our ancestors. It was a story that had been passed down to me with reverence and awe, one that spoke to the living presence of our kūpuna (grandparents), and I knew it would help the children connect to the idea that stories carry more than entertainment—they carry identity.

But just before the lesson, my supervisor pulled me aside. "Maybe choose something a little more . . . accessible," she said gently. "Something the parents can relate to." I nodded, but my stomach sank. What she meant, of course, was something less Hawaiian. Less spiritual. Less me.

That moment wasn't isolated. I learned to wear my identity carefully—visible enough to seem "authentic," but not so visible that it might disrupt the carefully curated expectations of what a professional early childhood educator should be. I was allowed to speak of community, but not in ways that challenged individualistic approaches. I could mention culture, but not critique colonial legacies. I could bring parts of myself, but not the whole. This chapter is my answer to that tension.

This chapter is written from a place of deep love—for the children and families we serve, for the educators walking this path, and for the culture that raised me. It is also written from a place of deep frustration—born of the many times I've felt invisible, underestimated, or asked to leave parts of myself at the door to "fit" into early childhood education spaces that were not built with people like me in mind.

I am Kanaka ʻŌiwi, a Native Hawaiian woman shaped by the stories of my ancestors and the values of my culture. I have spent my life navigating the spaces in between—between Indigeneity and professionalism, between reverence for ancestral knowledge and pressure to conform to dominant paradigms, between deep pride in who I am and the constant calculation of how much of that I am allowed to show. These tensions do not go away when you become an educator. If anything, they become sharper.

This chapter is an offering to all who are trying to bring their full selves into the classroom, especially those whose identities have been historically marginalized, misunderstood, or erased. It focuses on what it means to be a Native Hawaiian educator in a field shaped by Eurocentric norms—where the language of equity is often present, but the practices of true inclusion are still catching up.

I write specifically through the lens of AANHPI identity, and even more specifically through the lens of my experience as Kanaka ʻŌiwi. While I cannot speak for every AANHPI educator, I can speak to the erasure and flattening that often occurs when our communities are grouped together, without regard for the unique cultural, historical, and political experiences we carry. I hope this chapter helps to illuminate those nuances—and the powerful contributions we bring to early childhood education when we are seen, heard, and valued.

More than anything, this chapter is a challenge to the field: to expand its imagination of who educators are, and what we are allowed to bring into our practice. It is a call to create spaces where children and adults alike are embraced as whole beings—where no one must fragment themselves to belong.

My AANHPI Identity

I am Kanaka ʻŌiwi. My identity is not a demographic checkbox. It is an inheritance, a way of seeing, a rhythm that moves through me. It is the sound of the ocean at sunrise, the scent of gardenia in my grandmother's yard, the cadence of a language that holds stories older than memory. It is kuleana—responsibility—to care for the land, for each other, and for the wisdom passed down by our kūpuna. It is aloha—not the watered-down version that decorates tourist shops but the fierce, abiding love that roots us to each other and this ʻāina (land).

Growing up in rural Hawaiʻi, I didn't always have the language to describe the tension I felt between the world inside my home and the world outside of it. Inside, we were loud, tender, loving. We danced hula, sang together, and "talked story" over long dinners. Outside, there were rules. Speak "properly." Don't be too emotional. Don't say "I am Kanaka" too loudly. Our ways were often seen as quaint, or worse, unprofessional (I entered the workforce at 14 years old).

In my first Hawaiian Studies course at the University of Hawaiʻi, I learned this tension wasn't unique to me. Other Kanaka felt like me, and, in fact, Kanaka scholars and writers were talking and writing about this experience in ways that were making our internal struggles visible and known. I read *From a Native Daughter*, and it changed my life. In it, Hawaiian activist Haunani-Kay Trask said, "When I was young the story of my people was told twice: once by my parents, then again by my school teachers" (1993). Yes, it was like two stories always at odds. I learned early that my way of knowing and being didn't always match the dominant norms of school or work, and that storied Indigenous mismatch has followed me into the field of early childhood education.

When I became an educator, I brought with me the values that shaped me—relationships over routines, collective care over competition, spirituality and story as essential parts of learning. I brought with me the belief that children are not empty vessels to be filled but deeply connected beings with mana, with spirit, with knowing of their own. And I also brought with me the fear: Will I be taken seriously? Will I be seen as "too much" or "not enough"? Will my culture be honored or merely tolerated?

These questions still linger, especially in professional settings where cultural diversity is celebrated in theory but often avoided in practice. Still, I return to my roots. I remember that I come from a long line of teachers, healers, warriors, and storytellers. I remember that my identity is not something I leave at the door; it's the compass that guides my work.

Knowing and Being in Early Childhood Education

Our identities shape everything—how we speak to children, what we notice, what we celebrate, what we challenge, what we believe is possible. As a Native Hawaiian educator, my identity influences every part of how I teach, lead, and show up in community. My teaching philosophy is rooted in relationships. In Hawaiian culture, learning happens in the context of aloha (love) and pilina (relationships)—deep connections. You cannot teach a child you do not know. You cannot know a child without knowing their family, their history, their gifts. Hawaiian scholar Dr. Manulani Aluli Meyer, in her article "Our Own Liberation: Reflections on Hawaiian Epistemology" (2001), helped me understand the depth of this view of children as learners and me as an educator. My knowing and being is in their knowing and being. So my classrooms were always built around those relationships, around the belief that learning flows from connection, not compliance.

My relationships with families are guided by the value of *hoʻokipa*—welcoming with generosity and care. I see families not as clients but as partners, carriers of cultural knowledge, and coteachers in the lives of their children. My own experience growing up in a multigenerational household taught me that learning doesn't begin or end in the classroom. It's everywhere.

My approach to equity is informed by the understanding that many of our systems were never designed with Indigenous children in mind. Equity, for me, isn't about treating everyone the same—it's about restoring what was taken, making room for voices long silenced, and challenging practices that perpetuate harm, even when they are labeled as "best practices."

There is so much that Native Hawaiian traditions offer the field of early childhood education. We bring an understanding of communal responsibility, of the sacredness of childhood, of learning that is embodied, intergenerational, and land based. We understand the power of ritual, of chant, of story. We know that to teach is to lead with aloha, and that to lead with aloha is to be in relationship—with people, with place, with spirit. Our identities are not distractions from professionalism. They are the foundation of authentic, effective, and just teaching. When we honor who we are, we create space for children to do the same.

My multigenerational, multiracial family in my hometown of Wai'anae, Hawai'i, where people and place—Kanaka and 'aina—are one.

The Disconnect: Whole Children Versus Fragmented Educators

We talk often, and rightly so, about the importance of seeing children as whole beings. We affirm that children are capable, curious, complex. We speak of honoring their cultures, families, and lived experiences. We celebrate their languages, their emotions, their stories. But what happens when the people teaching those children are not offered the same wholeness? What happens when the very educators tasked with nurturing the brilliance of diverse children are asked—explicitly or implicitly—to shrink themselves?

There is a painful paradox in our field. Early childhood education claims to honor identity, yet it so often makes little room for the identities of the adults doing the work. We are expected to leave our accents, our grief, our spiritual practices, our political consciousness, our ancestral wisdom at the door. We are allowed to teach diversity but not embody it. We are asked to show up fully for our students but only partially for ourselves.

When I was a classroom teacher, I was not neutral. I carried passion, memory, resistance. I brought my ancestors into the classroom with me. I spoke with conviction and cultural fluency. And I learned that this makes some people uncomfortable. The truth is, when we talk about "professionalism" in early childhood education, we are often talking about assimilation. We are talking about codes of conduct, dress, and demeanor that prioritize White, Eurocentric norms. We rarely ask, *Who gets to be seen as professional? Who decides what professionalism looks like?*

Cultural Implications for Native Hawaiian Educators

As a Kanaka ʻŌiwi educator, navigating these expectations has meant constantly translating—my language, my values, my intentions. It means watching cultural practices be misunderstood or dismissed as "inappropriate" or "irrelevant." Even worse, it is seeing and having to participate in events that dishonor your culture (like "luau"-themed staff lunches) or the awkwardness of explaining why a child calling me Aunty isn't disrespect—it's love.

I have been told more than once that I'm "too passionate," that I "take things too personally," that I "care too much." But what others don't see is that in my culture, to teach is to care with your whole being. To lead is to be in a relationship. To educate is a spiritual act.

There have been moments when I've felt deeply disconnected—sitting in staff meetings where equity is discussed in abstract terms, but my lived experiences are invisible. Walking into professional learning spaces and knowing I am the only Native Hawaiian in the room, again. Being asked to explain my culture as though it's a footnote in someone else's narrative rather than the center of my own.

And yet, I remain. I remain because I believe our children deserve to see themselves reflected in those who teach them. I remain because our stories matter. I remain because every time I bring a Hawaiian chant into the classroom, or speak the names of my ancestors, or make space for a child's tears without trying to fix them, I am reclaiming something sacred. The disconnect between how we see children and how we see educators is not a small thing. It is a rupture. And if we are serious about equity, about justice, about truly honoring identity, then we must begin by extending the same wholeness to teachers that we extend to children. Because we are worthy of being seen.

What Is Intersectionality?

The word intersectionality may feel academic, but the experience it names is deeply personal. Coined by legal scholar Kimberlé Crenshaw (1991), intersectionality describes how systems of oppression—like racism, sexism, and classism—don't act independently of one another. They intersect, overlap, and compound, creating layered experiences of discrimination or privilege depending on who we are and how we move through the world. For those of us in early childhood education, intersectionality helps explain what many of us already know in our bones: that the field is not neutral. That how we are seen, heard, and valued is shaped by our race, gender, class, our language, and so much more. And that those of us living at the intersections—especially Indigenous, Black, and Brown women—often carry invisible burdens while doing visible labor. Intersectionality gives us a framework to name what we've experienced. But long before I had the word, I had the feeling.

How Intersecting Identities Shape My Experience

There are days when I walk into early childhood spaces and feel like I'm carrying a hundred names: Native Hawaiian. Woman. Educator. Leader. Daughter. Caregiver. Scholar. Advocate. And beneath those names are the deeper layers—stories, struggles, responsibilities, expectations, dreams. As a Native Hawaiian woman working in a system built on Western values, I constantly navigate the tension between honoring my culture and meeting the expectations of a profession that often does not see me. My leadership style is grounded in pilina—relationship and reciprocity. But in many early childhood education circles, leadership is still defined by hierarchy, individualism, and detachment. I prefer consensus over control. I speak in story. I pause when others rush. These are not deficits—they are my strengths. And yet, they are not always recognized as such.

There are moments when I feel the power of holding multiple truths. I can speak the language of policy and the language of the ancestors. I can sit in a boardroom and see the child in the data. I can teach a workshop on assessment while naming the cultural violence of certain measures. These are gifts, born of lived experience. But carrying them often feels like walking a tightrope—careful not to say too much, to come across as too radical, too soft, too ethnic, too angry, too . . . me. Still, I continue to hold my ground. Because my presence in these spaces is not a gift the system gave me—it is one I bring with purpose.

Challenging Misconceptions and Stereotypes

There are persistent stereotypes about Native Hawaiians that shape how we are seen in education and beyond. We are often portrayed as laid-back, simple, or spiritual in a way that is palatable but disconnected from the political realities we live with. These stereotypes erase our complexity and our resistance. They flatten our identities into something ornamental. I've experienced this firsthand. I've been expected to bring a "cultural touch" to events but discouraged from challenging structural inequities. I've been asked to bless a room but not to question the policies being implemented inside it. I've been positioned as a bridge but not as a builder.

There are also stereotypes about AANHPI educators more broadly—that we are agreeable, quiet, diligent, apolitical. These assumptions are not only inaccurate, they are dangerous. They obscure the real and ongoing struggles our communities face, and they silence the deep wells of strength and leadership we carry. I do not exist to make people comfortable. I exist to create change. And I believe that when we challenge these narrow narratives, we make space for something more honest, more expansive, and more human.

Cultural Mismatch in Early Childhood Education Leadership Spaces

Early childhood education leadership spaces are often grounded in Eurocentric systems of power—hierarchy, efficiency, individualism, competition. But these are not the values I was raised with. To me, leadership looks like service. It looks like consensus-building, humility, and taking time to listen before making decisions. It looks like kuleana—knowing that leadership is not a title but a responsibility to others. And it looks like making space for laughter, prayer, and tears—not only strategic plans. So when I bring those values into a room shaped by dominance, they are sometimes seen as weakness. My desire to cocreate a vision can be mistaken for indecisiveness. My pauses for reflection can be labeled as inefficiency. My relationship-based leadership style can be viewed as "too soft."

But I'm not soft. I am rooted. And roots, when deep and nurtured, hold strong—even when the winds of dominant culture try to bend them. My leadership is grounded not in performance but in ancestral knowledge. I feel most empowered when I lead from this place, guided by the stories and wisdom passed down to me. As Dr. Kuʻualoha Hoʻomanawanui (2014) writes, "Moʻolelo are not merely stories. They are our maps, our ancestors' voices, and our guideposts for future generations" (p. 2). These stories shape not only how I teach but how I navigate and lead, reminding me that every decision, every relationship, every act of care is connected to something larger than myself.

Stereotypes About Leadership

The dominant narrative of leadership—especially in early childhood—still carries narrow expectations. Leadership is often equated with being assertive, polished, confident in a way that demands space without first listening. And when you don't fit that mold, you're either invisible or misunderstood. There's a subtle but persistent idea that a strong leader looks a certain way—sharp blazer, business speak, a tone that says, "Trust me, I have the answers." My leadership doesn't always look like that. I lead from a place of humility. I ask questions. I center relationships. I share power. I make decisions by listening first.

I've been told that my style isn't "professional enough," that it's too emotional, too collaborative. I've seen my approach dismissed as not "data-driven," even when it's deeply informed by observation, listening, and lived experience. These judgments don't just hurt; they reinforce the belief that leadership must conform to dominant ways of being to be taken seriously. But I know that the kind of leadership our children, our teachers, and our communities need cannot come from rigidity. It must come from heart. And heart, as it turns out, is radical.

There is a constant push and pull to my existence in this field. One foot in dominant early childhood education culture, the other rooted in my Native Hawaiian worldview. One hand advocating in systems built by others, the other tending to relationships and values that were handed down by my ancestors. There are moments when I feel disconnected from colleagues who don't share these tensions. But there are also moments when connection emerges—when someone leans in with curiosity instead of assumptions. When someone says, "Tell me more." When someone asks, "What do you need?" And in those moments, the pull becomes a possibility. A place where two worlds can meet—not in compromise but in cocreation.

The Strength of Navigating Multiple Worlds

When you exist in more than one world, you learn to see things others might miss. As a Native Hawaiian woman in early childhood leadership, I move between perspectives—carrying the strength of my ancestors while navigating systems that weren't built with me in mind. And because I move between these worlds, I see the gaps. I notice what's missing, what's unspoken, what's being left out of the conversation. I notice the children whose stories aren't reflected in the books, the teachers who feel unseen in their staff meetings, the families who are treated as visitors rather than cocreators. This in-between space can feel heavy. But it's also where my leadership is forged.

When you lead from the margins, you develop vision. You learn how to hold complexity, how to build bridges, how to listen deeply and speak with care. You learn how to lead without replicating the very systems you're trying to change. By honoring my Native Hawaiian identity, I do more than represent my community; I disrupt the idea that leadership must look and sound a certain way. I lead with pilina, with mālama, with the unwavering belief that leadership is not about power over others but about responsibility to each other. When I bring my full self into leadership, it creates space for others to do the same.

Leading from the Margins: The Power of Identity-Rooted Leadership

Leadership has often felt like standing at the edge—present but not fully included; valued for what I do, not always for who I am. I'm invited to the table but not to shape its purpose. There's a quiet loneliness in being both seen and unseen, in carrying bold vision while making daily compromises, knowing your voice is needed but may be too much for some to hear. There's also the double-bind: Leading with cultural values—consensus, reflection, compassion—can be dismissed as weak. But adopting dominant traits—assertiveness, quick decisions—can be seen as inauthentic or aggressive. It's a constant negotiation that demands courage, clarity, and community. Still, leading from the margins is not a deficit. It's a form of resistance, a reminder that we're still here—teaching, rising, and reshaping the field.

Transformational leadership begins when we bring our full, intersectional selves into the work. It's not about having all the answers but asking better questions. It's about widening the lens, challenging norms, and creating space for truth, healing, and joy. My presence in leadership is intentional. Ancestral. Revolutionary. Every time I speak Hawaiian values into forgotten spaces, I offer a different path forward. Every time I name injustice and still choose joy, I model what it means to lead with integrity. This is the future of early childhood education: leadership that is relational, restorative, and rooted in identity.

Reimagining Professional Identities

If we are serious about equity in early childhood education, we must begin by reimagining what it means to be a professional. For too long, professionalism has been narrowly defined, and this limited definition excludes the richness of identity that so many educators bring into the classroom. We cannot continue to ask educators to bring their whole selves to work—and then punish them for doing so. It's time to broaden our collective imagination. What if professionalism included cultural fluency? Emotional vulnerability? The ability to teach, sing, or tell stories in your own language? What if we stopped asking educators to fit a mold and started asking how we can shape the system to reflect the people within it?

Educators of color, especially Indigenous educators, should not have to choose between authenticity and advancement. We should not have to tone down our identities to be taken seriously. Our presence is not performative—it's powerful. And when we're allowed to be whole, we create environments where children learn wholeness too. In this way, identity is not seen as an add-on to the work of equity—it becomes the heart of it.

In my own classroom, my identity as a Native Hawaiian wasn't something I occasionally brought out for "cultural days." It was embedded in everything I did—from the way I greeted families, to the stories I told, to the way I built community. That cultural grounding gave children permission to bring more of themselves into the space. It created openings for families to feel known and honored. It created opportunities for colleagues to reflect on their own identities too. When educator identity is valued, classrooms become more than places of learning. They become places of healing. Places where equity is not a set of strategies but a shared way of being.

Recommendations for Practice and Policy

To truly support educators in bringing their whole selves to the classroom, we must make structural changes—both in mindset and in policy.

Here are a few places to begin:

- **Recruitment of diverse educators:** Prioritize intentional outreach to Indigenous communities, AANHPI educators, and others historically underrepresented in early childhood education. Go beyond pipelines and into pathways; support retention, mentorship, and leadership development.
- **Culturally responsive professional development:** Move away from one-size-fits-all training. Offer opportunities for educators to explore their own identities, learn from each other's worldviews, and reflect on how culture shapes practice. Make space for Indigenous knowledge systems, not only as content but as frameworks for teaching and learning.
- **Anti-bias training for educators and leadership:** Ensure that training goes beyond awareness into action. Focus on disrupting systemic bias in hiring, evaluation, classroom practice, and leadership expectations. Encourage collective accountability, not only individual growth.
- **Redefining professionalism:** Engage the field in dialogue around what we consider "professional." Challenge norms that reward conformity over cultural integrity. Create policies that protect educators' rights to express and practice their cultural identities at work.

These changes are not small—but they are necessary. And they are possible.

We cannot ask educators to guide children toward freedom while they themselves are expected to operate in constraint. Freedom must be modeled. It must be lived.

Reflections and Hopes for the Future

Bringing my full self to this work hasn't always been easy. There were times I questioned whether I belonged in early childhood education—not because I lacked skill but because the system didn't seem to value what I brought. My language, my ways of leading, my cultural lens—they were often treated as add-ons, not foundations. I once believed I had to be more like "them" to succeed. But I know now my power lies not in conforming but in being rooted. Rooted in my ʻohana. Rooted in my Kanaka ʻŌiwi identity. Rooted in ancestral stories and future dreams. This path—of reclaiming voice, resisting fragmentation, and leading from the margins—has shown me that authenticity isn't optional. It's essential. It's how we build systems that truly liberate children, families, and ourselves.

My hopes are simple but not small. I hope for classrooms where children see themselves in the adults who care for them. For staff rooms where educators feel safe to cry, laugh, speak their truths, and bring their cultures fully into the day. I hope for leadership spaces where consensus matters more than control, and where the wisdom of Indigenous, Black, Brown, immigrant, and multilingual educators isn't tokenized but trusted. I hope for systems that don't just invite us in but evolve to hold us. That honor wholeness over performance. And I hope—deeply—that we are brave enough to build that future. Together. Because the children are watching. And the future they inherit depends on the choices we make now.

Conclusion

I began this chapter with a moment—one of many—where I felt the subtle pressure to quiet parts of myself to be more "acceptable" in early childhood education spaces. To choose comfort over culture. To dilute my identity in service of fitting in. But I don't want to fit in anymore. I want to belong. And there's a difference. Fitting in is about performance—belonging is about truth. Fitting in asks, *Who do I need to be so that others will accept me?* Belonging asks, *Who am I, and how do I build spaces where I am welcome as I am?* That is the work I've committed my life to. And that is the future I imagine for this field. The story I shared at the beginning—the one where I was told to make my culture more "accessible"—wasn't just about one lesson plan. It was about the ongoing tension so many educators face: being called to nurture children's full humanity while being asked to hide their own. That moment hurt. But it also clarified something for me. I cannot teach children to be whole if I am asked to be fragmented. And neither can you.

We must reimagine early childhood education as a space where wholeness is not only for children but for everyone. Where joy, identity, ancestry, and resistance are seen as vital to our professionalism—not in spite of it. If we want to raise children who are confident, curious, culturally rooted, and compassionate, then we must create conditions where the people guiding them can show up the same way.

This chapter is not a blueprint. It's a story. One story from one Native Hawaiian educator who has spent her life walking between worlds, reclaiming voice, and finding her way home. But I believe there are many of us, and I believe that when we come together—when we bring our whole selves—we become a force for transformation.

So here is my call to you: Honor your story. Make space for others' stories. Question what you've been taught about what it means to be "professional," "qualified," "neutral," or "appropriate." Above all, protect your joy. Because joy, as I've learned, is what makes us resilient. It is what makes us whole. And it is what binds us together in this work we've been called to do. Let us build a field that is as expansive as the identities we carry. Let us lead with aloha. And let us never again ask anyone—child or teacher—to leave pieces of themselves behind.

CHAPTER 23

Empowering Early Childhood Educators

My Journey as a Korean Migrant Teacher-Educator in the Pacific

SHIN AE HAN

Life moves, and we move with it. Sometimes that movement is physical, like leaving home, crossing borders, or starting over in a new place. Other times, it happens inside us as we grow and begin to see the world differently. In both ways, we move through life. We move from childhood into adolescence, from uncertainty into understanding, from general schooling into higher education. These movements, both outer and inner, shape who we become and how we continue to grow. Either way, movement leaves traces.

In this essay, I share my story of moving from the Korean peninsula to the southern United States and then to Hawai'i and the Pacific Islands. These journeys are not just about moving from one place to another but about how each environment, community, and culture has influenced how I understand myself and the work I do. This path also traces my growth from a child who spent her days observing and playing with young children in her mother's preschool to a professor of early childhood education, still observing, learning, and growing.

From the Korean Peninsula: Where My Story Begins

I was born and raised in Seoul, South Korea, a vibrant capital city on a peninsula. My home was near the Han River and Namsan Tower, two landmarks that still define the heart of the city. From the hillside near our house, I could see the river flowing through the city. The Han River holds a special place in my memory because it was where my family spent our weekends, enjoying the breeze and taking a break from the busy city.

Yet the Han River carries meaning that goes far beyond my childhood memories. People often speak of the "Miracle on the Han River" to describe South Korea's rapid growth from the 1960s to the 1990s, after the hardships of the Korean War (1950–1953). During those years, the country transformed from poverty to one of the world's major economies. Much of that development began along the Han River, which came to symbolize resilience and transformation. That transformation was not only a national achievement but also a reflection of the hard work and perseverance of ordinary people like my parents. For me, the river represents both the story of my country's rebuilding and the quiet strength of my parents' generation. My parents were part of that generation who believed in working hard, moving forward, and creating something better for their children. Both of them worked tirelessly and were always busy. My mother, Hyunsook Kang, was a preschool teacher and director, and I often spent time with her at the preschool. I remember falling asleep in her lap while she worked late into the night. The preschool classroom felt like my second home. Growing up in that environment, surrounded by young children and the warmth of learning, early childhood education became more than just something I observed; it became a part of who I am.

As a child, I loved being around younger children. I felt the most joy when I was watching and playing with babies and preschoolers. I loved seeing how curious they were, how happy they became when discovering new things, and how they explored the world around them. I would follow them, take care of them, and simply enjoy being in their company. Even though I loved young children, I never imagined becoming a teacher. I saw how hard my mom worked as a preschool director, how long her days were, how much responsibility she carried even when she did not show it. I admired her deeply but told myself, "That's not the life for me."

However, life often leads us where we are meant to be, even when we do not expect it. When it came time to choose my major, I decided to study early childhood education and was accepted into Chung-Ang University, the same university my brother attended. Chung-Ang University has a rich history that dates back to 1916, when it was founded as Chung-Ang Kindergarten. During the Japanese colonial period from 1910 to 1945, this kindergarten played a crucial role in nurturing Korean identity among young children (Chung-Ang University College of Education Kindergarten, 2016). Unlike other kindergartens at the time, which were often established by Western missionaries, Chung-Ang Kindergarten was founded by Koreans, making it a distinct and meaningful institution. Despite many challenges, it became a model for early childhood education in Korea, developing and applying a Korean-centered curriculum. The impact of Chung-Ang Kindergarten extends far beyond its early years, continuing to shape early childhood education in Korea and celebrated in 2015 at its 100th anniversary.

Studying early childhood education at Chung-Ang University made me proud to be part of a strong legacy. I was joining a tradition that helped resist Western influences and strengthen Korean identity through our own approach to early childhood education. Our professors often reminded us of the university's historic role in shaping Korea's education system, particularly in standing for culturally grounded teaching practices. This history inspired me to view early childhood education as a way to honor cultural identity and who we are and where we come from. As I continued my studies, I became more interested in how early childhood education looked in different parts of the world. In my 20s, I traveled to more than 30 countries, visiting early childhood centers whenever I could. I spent time observing how children learned, interacted, and played in their everyday environment. These experiences broadened my understanding of how culture shapes education and deepened my appreciation for the many ways children learn across contexts. They also sparked my desire to move beyond Korea and pursue new opportunities abroad, where I could continue exploring this field from a global perspective.

A turning point came in graduate school when I read *Preschool in Three Cultures Revisited* (Tobin et al. 2009). The book deeply moved me and clarified the direction I wanted to take in my work. The authors' approach to early childhood education, which situated teaching and learning within each country's unique cultural, social, and historical context, expanded my understanding of what it means to study education comparatively. It helped me see that no single model of early childhood education can fit all societies, and that meaningful teaching must always be rooted in the culture and community it serves. This realization encouraged me to step outside my own familiar world and experience education in new cultural and social contexts.

Across the Southern United States: Opening New Paths

In 2016, I moved to the southern United States to pursue my doctorate at the University of Georgia, leaving behind life in Korea, where I had never experienced being a minority. In the United States, I was suddenly an outsider, navigating language barriers and cultural differences. Despite these challenges, this experience became a crucial period in shaping both my professional identity and my perspectives on early childhood education.

Working closely with my advisor, Joseph Tobin (yes, the same Tobin whose book had inspired me earlier), I came to understand that being an early childhood educator is about far more than just teaching. It is about questioning, reflecting, and advocating for what is best for young children, especially while considering the diverse cultural and societal contexts in which they grow. In my research, I used video-cued ethnography (Adair & Kurban 2019; Tobin 2019), a method that uses video recordings to prompt discussion and reflection, bringing in multiple voices and perspectives on children's lives. This approach brings together the voices of children, families, and teachers, and provides a more layered and meaningful understanding of how young children learn, relate, and make sense of their world.

In the middle of my doctoral studies, the world changed. The COVID-19 pandemic struck, turning the world upside down. On top of that, the 2021 Atlanta-area shootings targeting Asian women affected me in ways I could not ignore. As an Asian woman living in the South, I was heartbroken and began to question my place in this country and what it means to live as a minority. In the midst of that fear and uncertainty, one question stayed with me: *What am I really here for?*

It was not an easy question to answer, but I eventually came back to what had always kept me steady. The reason I came to the United States to study early childhood education still mattered. I wanted to support young children and the teachers who care for them, and to keep learning how education can make a difference in their lives. In an uncertain time, that purpose helped me stay grounded and keep moving forward.

In the final year of my doctoral studies, I felt the uncertainty return. The job market was tough, and the future seemed unclear. Each day brought both hope and doubt, but I tried to focus on my work and stay open to whatever might come next. That openness carried me into my interview for a faculty position at the University of Hawaiʻi at Mānoa. During the interview, I picked up a ukulele and played a short tune. It was my way of showing respect for Hawaiʻi and the people I hoped to learn from. Looking back, that small moment became the quiet beginning of something much bigger than I realized.

A few months later, I left Georgia for Hawaiʻi, an island in the middle of the Pacific. When I told friends and colleagues, many were surprised. "Are you sure you want to move all the way out there?" They asked if I was sure about moving so far away. I did not feel nervous or uncertain. It simply felt right, the next step in my journey.

Arriving in Hawai'i: Learning Place, Culture, and Self

Moving to Hawai'i was not just about starting a new job; it was the beginning of a new chapter in my life. I wanted to learn about this place and understand what it means to live and teach here. Teaching early childhood teacher candidates has been both humbling and inspiring. My students come from across the continental United States, the Pacific Islands, and countries as far away as Norway and as close as Japan. Each brings their own stories and cultural backgrounds, which influence how they see the world and how they work with children.

In my first class, I introduced myself as a Korean migrant. The students followed by sharing where they were from, often naming the towns in Hawai'i where they grew up and even the high schools they attended. Many spoke about their mixed heritage, including Native Hawaiian, Filipino, Japanese, Chinese, Portuguese, Korean, Vietnamese, or other ethnic groups, sharing not only their familial heritage but also the stories of their families' migration histories. Their stories revealed how categories such as "Asian American" or "Caucasian" cannot fully capture the complexity of who they are. Listening to them made me think about my own upbringing in South Korea, where society was mostly homogeneous and people rarely talked about race. Their introductions encouraged me to rethink identity itself, seeing it not as a fixed label but as something formed through heritage, history, and lived experience. Living and teaching in Hawai'i has deepened my understanding of identity as something fluid rather than fixed. Unlike the rigid racial classifications I encountered on the mainland United States, Hawai'i has shown me that identity is not about fitting neatly into a single category but about embracing the intersections of heritage, history, and community. Through my students, I have come to see that identity cannot always be clearly defined, especially in the Pacific, where it is often tied to land, language, and genealogy. Instead, identity is something to be understood, negotiated, and claimed on one's own terms. As my curiosity about the Pacific grew, I had an opportunity to deepen my understanding of Hawai'i and to look beyond it to the Pacific Islands.

Into the Pacific Islands: American Samoa

The Pacific Islands stretch north and south of the equator and are often grouped into three regions: Polynesia, Melanesia, and Micronesia. These islands were originally settled by Polynesian, Melanesian, and Micronesian peoples, and over time, other groups including Indians, French, Chinese, Japanese, Americans, and other Asian communities have also settled in the region. Some are affiliated with the United States, such as Hawai'i, the Federated States of Micronesia, Palau, the Northern Marianas, Guam, the Marshall Islands, and American Samoa, while others are affiliated with France, including New Caledonia, Wallis and Futuna, and French Polynesia. Many islands are now independent or self-governing, though they were once administrated by countries such as the United Kingdom, Australia, or New Zealand. This has made the Pacific Islands ethnically, culturally, and linguistically diverse. Each island has its own history, traditions, and educational systems influenced by Indigenous knowledge, colonial legacies, and contemporary challenges. While the term *Pacific Islander* often refers to the Indigenous peoples of these regions, their identities and experiences are varied and complex. This diversity also extends to education, particularly in early childhood teacher preparation.

In 2025, I taught early childhood education students in American Samoa, an unincorporated US territory in the South Pacific. Unlike Hawaiʻi, where early childhood teacher education certification programs are well established, American Samoa does not yet have a dedicated early childhood education major. As a result, students interested in this field must take courses through the University of Hawaiʻi at Mānoa or other far-off institutions outside the territory. Teaching these students helped me understand how educational pathways in the Pacific are shaped by both local traditions and global influences. The opportunity to work with them has allowed me to see their diverse backgrounds and the ways in which they navigate their educational journeys.

Education in American Samoa is deeply shaped by faʻa Samoa, or the Samoan way of life, which emphasizes communal responsibility, respect for elders, and strong familial ties. These values influence not only family and social structures but also education and teaching approaches. Schools in American Samoa often integrate both Samoan traditions and US educational frameworks, creating a hybrid system that balances Indigenous knowledge with Western curricula (Henward et al. 2019a;b).

Teaching my American Samoa class online gave me insight into the diverse experiences of Pacific Islanders. When I first met my students on Zoom, I noticed how many were balancing full-time work in early childhood education while pursuing their studies. Many of them worked as assistant teachers in Head Start centers, and several were nontraditional students. Some were changing careers, others just beginning their path as educators. What stood out to me most was their deep pride and sense of responsibility toward their culture. They clearly understood the importance of bringing their cultural heritage into their teaching, showing a strong commitment to their communities even as they worked hard to complete their studies for licensure. Teaching these students has been both an honor and a learning experience. Listening to their stories and understanding their daily realities has challenged me to think more deeply about what it means to teach across cultures and to stay grounded in the values of place, community, and care.

Going to Pago Pago: Seeing Community Through Early Childhood

After several weeks of teaching my students online, I began to feel that I was missing an important part of their experience. Even with our weekly online classes, I had not fully understood what it meant to teach young children in their communities. To see their classrooms and daily lives more clearly, I decided to visit Pago Pago in person. After a five-hour flight from Honolulu, I arrived at Pago Pago Airport.

With the support of local early childhood education partners, I was able to visit several Head Start programs that serve as the foundation of early learning in American Samoa. During my trip, I met eight of my students and visited six Head Start centers Although the classrooms shared similar environments, each visit offered unique insights into the educators' experiences and practices. Hearing their stories, seeing their commitment, and feeling their care for the children reminded me of the heart of early childhood education.

One of the most memorable visits was to Aunuʻu Island Elementary School, located on a neighboring island nearly two hours from downtown Pago Pago. The lead teacher there commuted by boat every day to reach her students. Her dedication, like that of many others I met, reminded me why teaching matters. Across every classroom, I saw the same sense of purpose, a shared belief that early education is not only about children's learning but also about caring for the whole community.

Many of my students were teaching in the same neighborhoods where they had grown up. They spoke about wanting to give back by helping the next generation of children learn and thrive. Their strong connection to place and community showed me that early childhood education in American Samoa is not just about the present; it is about building a better future for everyone. This belief is reflected in the vision of the American Samoa Early Childhood Education/Head Start program, displayed in every classroom: *TAGA'I MAMAO, E pa'i atu i olaga o tatou fanau i le taimi nei, e mautu ai tatou tagata mo a taeao—Vision, touching our children's lives today, impacting our community tomorrow*. These words were a reflection of the deeply held belief that early childhood education goes beyond the classroom; it shapes the future of children, families, and communities.

Through this visit, I came to see my role as a teacher educator differently. My work is not only about helping future teachers develop knowledge and skills but also about guiding them to reflect on the deeper purpose of their teaching. When educators understand why they teach and who they teach for, they create meaningful, culturally grounded learning environments that reflect and sustain their communities.

The impact of teaching might not always be immediately measurable, but it creates a foundation for a life of lasting purpose. As my students grow in their sense of purpose, they nurture spaces where children can learn and belong.

Planting Seeds: A Reflection on Early Childhood Education

As our class discussions deepened, I wanted to hear in my students' own words what teaching meant to them. When I asked my students, "What does it mean to you to be a teacher in your own community?," their answers were filled with love and a deep sense of responsibility. Some of them drew pictures, others wrote poems, and a few shared beautiful reflections on childhood and teaching. For them, being an early childhood educator was not just a job. It was a *calling*, a way to support their families, neighbors, and communities. Many shared how they felt a close connection to the children in their classrooms because they were from the same cultural background. They expressed a strong desire to give back to their communities, ensuring a bright future for the next generation. One response that stood out was from the oldest student in the class. She shared a song, and as she began to sing, the rest of the students joined in.

Sa ou galue i se faatoaga

Sa 'ou galue i se fa'atoaga tele lava
Ma 'ou totoina ai se fatu la'au
Mana'oga 'o lou nei loto,
'la aoga 'i se aso a sau
'Ua tino mai nei a'u galuega 'uma
'Ae 'ou te le iloa sona taunu'uga
'Oi, 'aue! lo'u pologa,
'a nei 'a fa'atafuna

La'au e o le fa'ato'aga, ua fepulafi mai,
Aue! lo'u nei fatu 'o fea 'ea 'o i ai?
Na 'ou toto ma lo'u faamaoni,
'Ina 'ia fua mai

I have worked in a large garden
And I have planted a seed
The desire of my heart
'To be useful in the future
All my work is now in full swing
But I do not know its outcome
Oh, alas! My suffering,
now it will be destroyed.

The trees of the garden are shining,
Oh! where is my seed?
I planted it with my faithfulness,
So that it may bear fruit.

At first, I could not fully understand the meaning of the song. When the students translated the lyrics into English, I was moved by what they shared. The song itself was not about teaching, but my students explained that to them, it symbolized the work of educators. It serves as a powerful reminder of the journey that comes with being an early childhood educator. The song captures the dedication, challenges, and hopes that define the profession. The metaphor of the garden reminds us that teaching requires patience, resilience, and faith in the transformative power of education. Educators must believe that every seed they plant has the potential to grow into something meaningful and impactful. My wonderful students already understand this and are putting it into practice in their classrooms.

Towards the end of my time in American Samoa, we had a cultural gathering where we sang songs, shared food, and celebrated our shared passion for teaching young children. We also expressed our commitment to our communities. It was a joyful evening filled with warmth and community. In those moments, I came to understand my students' teaching in a fuller way and felt even more committed to supporting them as they continue their work in early childhood education. The experience reminded me of the importance of listening to and learning from educators in American Samoa, who are the true experts in their communities.

Meeting early childhood educators in American Samoa.

Returning to Hawai'i: Continuing the Journey Forward

Each island I have come to know carries its own philosophy and practice of caring for children. Through these experiences, my understanding of early childhood education has become more contextually grounded and relational. In Hawai'i, education is closely tied to place and belonging, where learning emerges from connections with people and the environment. In American Samoa, education is deeply rooted in community, tradition, and family. Teaching there is a collective effort that helps children stay connected to their culture and history.

Looking back on my journey, from a curious child observing young children in my mother's preschool to becoming a teacher-educator, I see how every place and experience has shaped who I am today. My path has taken me from South Korea to the southern United States and then across the Pacific to Hawai'i. Along the way, each new environment, community, and culture has influenced how I understand children, culture, and the purpose of education.

The "Miracle on the Han River" often comes to mind when I think about my journey. Korea's recovery and growth after hardship showed the strength that comes from resilience and continuous effort. I see that same spirit in my own path. Living and teaching across different cultures and communities has not always been easy, but each challenge has brought new lessons and connections. I remember the moments of wonder and challenge along the way, the small discoveries that still guide my work today. Life keeps moving, and so do I—continuing to empower early childhood educators as we learn and grow together.

CHAPTER 24

Diversity Will Sustain the Education Profession

Reflections of a Biethnic Preschool Teacher

IRIS CHIN PONTE

> She was frantically digging. I approached the school sandbox to find out what was going on. There was Molly with a shovel in hand, and Gabriel standing nearby. Tears were pouring down Molly's face. "What's happening?" I asked. Molly looked up at me and said, "Gabe said if I dig a hole deep enough in the sandbox, I can get to China and find my birth mother."

There are moments in every teacher's career that render us speechless. This was that kind of moment for me. I was stunned. Frozen. Incapable of finding the right words. One of my adopted Chinese preschool students was looking to me for support. There was no amount of training, experience, or degree to prepare me for this moment. All I could do was scoop Molly into my arms and hold her while she cried.

I knew from a young age that I wanted to work with young children. As the oldest of 14 grandchildren on my Chinese side, I was tasked daily at my grandmother's house to care for all the children in the basement playroom while she cooked for all of us. I was able to keep everyone busy, happy, and most importantly, playing together. On my Portuguese side, I was one of the younger cousins, always looking up to my older cousins and trying to keep up. They always seemed to catch the bigger fish and swim faster than me. My upbringing was a combination of both of my parents' cultures. I had opportunities to attend cultural events on both sides, travel to both China and Portugal, and be exposed to the foods and languages. There were many times that I felt like I didn't really belong to one side or the other. Phenotypically I present much more Chinese, but personality-wise, I am very similar to my Portuguese relatives. Being biethnic has served me very well as a classroom teacher because navigating cultures has always been my lived experience.

In college, Joseph Tobin's book *Preschool in Three Cultures* was placed into my hands, and there was no turning back. I loved thinking about preschool as the first step out of the home into society. What could possibly be more important than understanding how different cultures train their youngest citizens. Being culturally sensitive—understanding the perspectives of different families and children—has been a critical part of my teaching experience. Taking time to understand and consider all perspectives has enriched my work in the classroom and helped me be a better educator to many children, especially children that are Chinese or biethnic like me.

When I think back to my early years in school, I remember the isolation and loneliness of being the only biethnic child in my class. No one looked like me. In fact, classmates made a point to ask me frequently, "What are you?" All the way through college I never had a biethnic educator that looked like me or shared my lived experience. My closest Chinese role models were my family members. Even my college Chinese language teacher was an energetic, White, Jewish woman from the Bronx! My closest Portuguese role models were also my family members, and to date I have never had a teacher of Portuguese descent.

I raise my hand in kindergarten.

Throughout my experience as a preschool teacher and now a preschool director, I have felt the critical impact of my ethnicity on my students in the classroom. Many families visit my school and are thrilled to select a program for their child where the school leader looks like them. More importantly, my Chinese preschool children find comfort in watching me switch between English and Chinese, model being proud of my heritage, and use chopsticks at lunch. I am so proud to represent my Chinese heritage in an early childhood setting with authenticity and pride. It is sometimes odd that people only assume I am Chinese because of the way I look; many are often surprised when I tell them I am only half Chinese.

There have been a few examples of how critical being a Chinese educator has been in the classroom. First, when a family is more fluent in Chinese than English, I can help them navigate the American preschool experience. I can code switch and help unpackage some of the Western practices Chinese families might not understand. I can help Chinese children that are learning English slowly to comfortably transition into preschool without the stress of a new language. With authenticity, I can share experiences like Chinese Lunar New Year and August Moon Festival. Finally, and most importantly, I am a phenotypic match. While I am half Chinese and half Portuguese, I present much more Chinese in the way I look. Children look up to me, and my Chinese students are proud that we share the same black silky hair and brown almond eyes.

While most of my experiences of being a Chinese educator have been positive, there have been some challenging moments as well. Often, the assumption is that I will align with all their Chinese values and expectations, like an unspoken code when we meet each other. Some parents have assumed that I will be too strict, that I will expect too much seated work, and that I will lack empathy in the classroom. These types of questions would emerge during school tours with parents and sometimes in parent-teacher conferences. There have been parent expectations that I would be a "tiger mom/ tiger teacher" (i.e., I will demand perfection and set the bar very high for my students). Sometimes I would even experience Chinese families feeling ashamed if I needed to report a child behavioral issue in the classroom. In multiple situations, parents have felt more comfortable talking about parenting challenges with my non-Chinese coteacher as opposed to speaking about it with me. In one situation, a Chinese mother was frustrated because her child kept having potty accidents. Often when she spoke with me at drop-off, she would casually say, "Oh she must have been tired; that's why she keeps wetting her bed." If my non-Chinese coteacher greeted the same mother, she would confide in her,

"I am so frustrated! Why does she keep wetting the bed!?!?" In these situations, my ethnic match can create tension between Chinese parents because they internally feel that I might be judgmental or disappointed. Over time, I have learned to be more open with my Chinese families about my own parenting challenges to reduce these feelings and open more genuine channels of communication.

As for my Portuguese side, I have had opportunities to connect with families from Portugal or Brazil. There is an immediate affinity when we talk about different family holidays, recipes, and traditions. Sadly, because I live in an area where there is not a high population of Portuguese speakers, I don't often get to use this skill consistently.

I teach in my classroom.

My own reflection has made me curious about AANHPI educators in the United States. How many other educators are experiencing similar moments in their classrooms? What are their experiences like with their coworkers and directors? What stories do they have to share from their classrooms? Do they have similar interactions with children and parents? What does research say about AANHPI presence in the classroom?

How Many Asians Are in the United States Today? How Many Asians Are Working in Early Education?

The US Asian population is projected to reach 46 million by 2060. Unfortunately, these numbers do not even include Native Hawaiian and Pacific Islander individuals. During the writing of this chapter, it was frustrating how many national organizations do not recognize both Native Hawaiians and Pacific Islanders as a critical part of the "Asian" data set. We hope that work such as this underscores the importance of creating research and policies that recognize their diversity.

In the 1870 census, roughly 63,000 individuals were classified as Asian by the US Census Bureau enumerators. By 1960, the first-time census respondents could choose their own race, 980,000 individuals self-identified as Asian. The nation's Asian population rose to 11.9 million by 2000 and then nearly doubled to 22.4 million by 2019—an 88 percent increase within two decades. Asians now make up about 7 percent of the nation's overall population, and their numbers are projected to reach 46 million by 2060, nearly four times their current total. These numbers indicate that Asian Americans are projected to be the nation's largest immigrant group by the middle of the century, surpassing Hispanics in 2055. At this point, Asians are expected to make up 36 percent of all US immigrants (Pew Research 2021). These numbers are astounding and deeply impactful to the demographic of the United States. With the rising Asian population, one would think that we would observe a similar elevation in our early education workforce. Sadly, this is not the case.

At the preschool and kindergarten level, only 5.7 percent of teachers report to be Asian, compared with 15.5 percent reporting to be Black and 12 percent reporting to be Latine (USBLS 2023). In addition, teacher education programs lack diversity when compared with other college and university disciplines (Constantine et al. 2009). These numbers are shockingly low considering how many Asian children live in the United States. These numbers lead us to consider why Asians prefer other career choices. Growing up, I remember my own family asking me to consider a career in law, medicine, engineering, or business.

Chinese families traditionally put a great emphasis on education and continuous gathering of knowledge, and Chinese American teenagers are strongly influenced by their families in career choices (Harrison 1992; Salili & Hoosain 2003; Sandhu 1999). In many Chinese cultures, students are not viewed as autonomous; rather, the students should live up to their role of being "students" and obeying their parents' requests. Students are expected to adjust to the school environment and maintain a high achievement level, improve their skills, and not embarrass their families. Students are pressured to perform well academically and meet the school's standard for success (Salili & Hoosain 2003; Walker-Moffat 1995). Careers in law, medicine, and engineering are often considered the most lucrative and therefore the best symbols of academic success by Asian parents (Gibson 2000). Even as a university professor in child development, Chinese parents would email me requesting that I help their child choose a different major in college. I was always shocked since it was my area of chosen study. These cultural preferences contribute to the low numbers of Asians in the early childhood profession.

In addition to the challenge of recruiting AANHPI to education, a recent study has found that AANHPI educators in the field experience racial discrimination from parents and coworkers. In fact, more AANHPI educators reported that people assumed that they were foreigners because of their racial or ethnic identity than Hispanic, Latine, Black, or African American educators (Steiner et al. 2022). For this reason, we will need to work even harder to recruit AANHPI individuals into the field of early education.

Again, it is important to reiterate that research with and on AANHPI populations is lacking, which hinders our understanding and ability to support these populations. While AANHPI families have rich, unique experiences that should be represented in research to inform better, more targeted, and supportive policies, data on these populations are often combined, concealing differences and inequities among the groups.

What Impact Do AANHPI Educators Have on Children?

Nationally, nearly 3.7 million (5 percent) of children under age 18 are AANHPI, ranging from just 0.6 percent of children in Wyoming and Mississippi to 34.3 percent of children in Hawai'i (Sun et al. 2023). AANHPI are, collectively, the fastest-growing racial group in the United States. For this reason, it is critical to consider the impact that having an AANHPI teacher can have on both AANHPI children and on non-AANHPI children.

AANHPI Teachers and AANHPI Children

Evidence exists that children benefit when they see their own social identities, including race, culture, and gender, in the individuals who educate and care for them (Dee 2005; Egalite & Kisida 2018; Rasheed et al. 2020). A 2020 research study demonstrated that adults generally underestimate how early children start to notice and process race (Wilton & Apfelbaum 2021). On average, their estimates are off by about four and a half years. This research shows that children can distinguish faces by race early in infancy and that racial biases are often formed by the preschool and kindergarten years (Kelly et al. 2005, 2007). In addition, the age at which adults think children are capable of processing race influences when adults are willing to engage children in conversations about race. For this reason, adults should begin conversations about race much earlier than they think.

In 2004, another study of elementary school students in Tennessee (The Race Connection 2004) found that when students were randomly assigned to classrooms led by a same-race teacher, their math and reading achievement improved by three to four percentile points. A more recent study by David Blazar also employs an experimental approach to study how race-matching affects student outcomes. His 2021 analysis looks at test scores as well as behavior and indicators of social-emotional development for 1,283 students in fourth and fifth grade in four US districts on the East Coast. He finds even larger effects on test scores of about 20 percent of a standard deviation when students are taught by same-race teachers.

Blazar also follows these students for up to six years, finding that the positive test score impacts he observes in elementary school persist when the students attend high school. There are many other studies that find the same pattern, that race-matching student to educator leads to not only higher academic achievement but also increases in higher ed/college enrollment, reduction in suspension, increases in high school graduation, reduction in absenteeism, and increases in special education identification.

Research indicates that there are also social-emotional gains from race-matching student to educator. For example, Egalite and Kisida (2018) looked at data from six school districts across the country and found that students assigned to a same-race teacher are happier in class, more likely to report feeling cared for by their teacher, and more likely to consider going to college. Diversity matters to students. When working with a diverse student population, it makes sense to have teacher demographics reflect the students they serve. Students are best positioned to learn in a diverse school.

AANHPI Teachers and Non-AANHPI Children and Other Children of Color

In addition, non-Asian students can also benefit from more diverse educators. Children can gain knowledge through the lenses of teachers from different cultures, while Asian children also benefit from the presence of educators who reflect their own identities, giving them a safe space to grow.

For example, every year in my classroom, we recognize the Lunar New Year. During this celebration, I will give my students a lesson on how to accept and give a lucky red envelope. My students learn that it is customary to accept the envelope with two hands, demonstrating to the giver your gratitude and respect. It is also customary to offer the red envelope with two hands, with the emblem (or decoration) directed to the receiver. Years later, students have reported to me that the simple lesson of "how to receive and give a red envelope" has been critical to interactions with Chinese friends and work colleagues. Knowledge of these types of customs early on can create friendships and acceptance between groups of people. One alumni student explained, "I remember vividly learning about Chinese customs in preschool. I felt curious and invested even though I am not Chinese. I wanted to learn more and when I got to middle school, I started to learn Chinese. Now I am a Chinese major in college. The seed of learning about China was planted so early in me, and I am so thankful."

Diversity Will Sustain the Education Profession

Having a more diverse workforce would make the profession more attractive to future educators. Allowing students to see and experience teachers who reflect their culture or gender could inspire more students to become educators. Adjusting curriculum to be responsive to all cultures also would make the education profession more appealing to today's increasingly diverse student body and help address the long-standing underrepresentation of non-White teachers in our schools.

The National Association for the Education of Young Children (NAEYC) offers our profession the Professional Standards and Competencies for Early Childhood Educators. The fourth standard calls for "Developmentally, Culturally, and Linguistically Appropriate Teaching Practices" in which teachers need to use "a broad repertoire of developmentally appropriate and culturally and linguistically relevant, anti-bias, and evidence-based teaching approaches." As educators we must become aware of "implicit biases and help children navigate cultural codes, norms, and expectations." It is our responsibility to teach about racism and other -isms as they arise (NAEYC 2020). Regardless of whether we identify as AANHPI early education professionals, it is important to learn more and understand the experiences of others so we can better serve and educate all children.

When I think back to the moment in the sandbox with Molly, I realize that it was incredibly important to be an ethnic match to her as she experienced the disappointment of not finding her Chinese birth mom. Molly was able to open up and ask me questions about why I thought her Chinese birth mother was not able to take care of her. While I am sure a non-Asian educator would have also been able to respond with love and care, I wonder if Molly would have opened up in the same way.

Years later, as an adoptive parent to a Chinese child myself, I have an even deeper understanding of the significance of that sandbox interaction. As Molly grieved the loss of her Chinese birth mother, her biethnic Chinese preschool teacher was there to hold her and comfort her. My hope is that in the future, there are more AANHPI educators to be seen, heard, and understood, not just for AANHPI children but for everyone.

CHAPTER 25

Homeless Shelters to Congress

My Unexpected Journey in Early Childhood Advocacy

SANDY BABA

Every morning as a teenager getting ready for school in my grandparents' flat in Hong Kong, I'd pass the same old lady at the newspaper stall downstairs. She had already been sorting papers since 5 a.m.; by 3 p.m. her son would replace them with the evening editions. That was the rhythm of information in Hong Kong: lightning fast, always updated, never late.

Life itself moved at that same warp speed. Efficiency, accountability, and delivering on your word weren't just admired; they were the bare minimum expected of everyone. That cultural DNA was woven into everything: family, school, business, even the way the MTR (the local railway service) ran on the dot. I was raised breathing that air until I moved to the United States in high school.

When I began my career in American early education and policy, I carried that same reflex: Identify problems harming children and their families, fix them immediately and completely, or you have failed them. It turned out to be a reflex that often left me bruised in a system that moves at an entirely different tempo.

"You speak too directly," a colleague told me during my car ride back from one of my first policy meetings in a Bay Area county in my early advocacy days. It was 2006 when the country had heated discussions on how to close the decade-old achievement gaps despite decades of reform efforts since the Civil Rights Movement (Barton & Coley 2006; Education Trust 2006; Haycock 2006; National Center for Education Statistics 2006; Orfield & Lee 2006). Fresh with passion and new to the California early childhood education policy landscape, I bluntly questioned why we couldn't implement universal preschool immediately, pointing to successful models already working in other countries. The room had grown quiet, and I started to feel uncomfortable as I had just pointed out the elephant: advocates and program directors exchanging glances. That night, I replayed the moment repeatedly in my head, thinking about what I could have said or done differently to build consensus. I eventually realized that I may have violated an unwritten rule of professional advocacy of building relationships and making compromises to achieve change. This and many other early lessons shaped how I would navigate policy spaces in the decades that followed.

That is when I also realized that successfully adapting to America, which I now call home, wasn't about abandoning my native values but rather finding an integration of both or more perspectives.

I learned to draw strength from the complementary nature of these seemingly different value systems, creating a leadership approach that bridges worlds rather than choosing between them.

I came to understand that in the current American political context, unlike some parliamentary systems, almost nothing significant gets passed unless both sides are willing to compromise. Mastering that art of principled compromise, not compromise of principles, became a key part of how I operate.

The Professional Journey: From Practitioner to Advocate

In 2000, while directing a state-funded homeless child care center in the heart of Silicon Valley in California, I experienced firsthand how our youngest children from the lowest socioeconomic status suffered. "The curriculum needs to be specialized," I thought to myself. "I need to help boost the children's social and emotional competence to face the adverse effects of homelessness, and I need the teachers to also stay emotionally strong for them." Eventually, I developed a modified anti-bias curriculum based on Louise Derman-Sparks's work. I adjusted the curriculum to be flexible and adaptive because the children typically spent only a short time with us before moving on once their families found more permanent housing.

I remember meeting with the teachers weekly to work together on understanding our bias and applying that perspective in developing the anti-bias curriculum for our center's children. It was not easy work, but now, looking back, I appreciate the transformative field experience. It set a solid foundation for my advocacy work, teaching me that effective change requires responding to immediate needs and addressing systemic barriers. No textbook would provide me with the experience of working directly with my staff, families, and their children, and this is the type of experience that instills in me an unwavering commitment to education equity that continues to fuel my advocacy efforts today.

Coming from a culture where keeping your word and delivering results quickly were nonnegotiable, I used to believe that the moment you identify a problem harming children, you fix it, immediately and completely. After over two decades working in this field, I've learned that policy often moves at the pace of bureaucracy, not the pace of childhood. Those critical developmental windows open and close on a biological clock we don't control (National Research Council and Institute of Medicine 2000).

So, when I talk about "professional patience," I don't mean passively waiting or accepting endless delays. I mean the disciplined refusal to give up, the stubborn commitment to keep pushing, negotiating, and chipping away even when the system feels designed to exhaust you. It means staying at the table year after year, holding people and the system accountable, and making sure promises made to children don't get forgotten just because the legislative calendar is slow. Childhood won't wait, so neither can we.

The Real Struggles: Personal Experience Informing Policy Views

I remember standing in my living-room kitchen one early morning in 2011, packing lunches for my two older elementary-aged kids while nursing my 7-month-old before heading to work. These mental calculations ran through my head: 70 work hours that week, submitting an RFP for funding to support the community and worrying that the budget formulas wouldn't get approved, working with consultants to prepare for an early childhood education coaching project launch, attending a partnership meeting later in the afternoon, and over $3,000 in child care and after-school care expenses that month. We couldn't afford our mortgage if I didn't work and stayed home. If I worked less, we couldn't afford quality care. The scale of life doesn't weigh evenly; the struggles are real, not theoretical policy problems but daily lived realities that shape children's development and families' well-being in profound and lasting cultural ways.

My kitchen table struggles weren't mine alone; they were happening at thousands of tables across America. The policies leaving my family stretched thin were breaking others completely. With each morning rush and monthly budget crunch, my impatience grew. I couldn't help but think: If this is hard for me with my privileges, how impossible must it be for families with even fewer resources? My own experience gave me an aha moment that made policy discussions feel less theoretical and far more urgent.

Cross-Cultural Leadership as a Strength

"In Singapore, education comes near national defense in budget priorities," I heard on an international news broadcast while researching global educational systems. This financial commitment reflects the country's belief that human capital drives national success. While Singapore allocates approximately 17 percent of government expenditure to defense (Stockholm International Peace Research Institute 2024) and 10 percent to education (World Bank 2025), the United States is a different story. America dedicates less than 4 percent of federal outlays to education (Pew Research Center 2025), falling well below UNESCO's international benchmark of 15 percent of public funding for education (Education Data Initiative 2025). This disparity stayed with me, prompting the question "In America, what comes first?" I had no simple answers.

This constant exploration of different collective cultures—one that prizes urgency, decisive action, and keeping your word, and another that, even in the world's most innovative nation, often moves at the deliberate pace of consensus, process, veto points, and institutional risk-aversion—shapes my approach to leadership.

Having navigated these cultural differences, I have learned to bridge these gaps when working with diverse communities. When meeting with immigrant families struggling with early education or family services systems, I provide the narrative of American education or family services systems through cultural frameworks that resonate with their experiences. Similarly, when presenting to policymakers, I transform rich family narratives into the data points and actionable recommendations they require to move forward.

This isn't code-switching for me, it's simply how I naturally communicate after years of living between cultural worlds. The intersectionality of my identity, as an Asian American woman, parent, immigrant, educator, researcher, multilingual speaker, and policy advocate, informs every aspect of my work, allowing me to see challenges and opportunities through multiple lenses with no filters needed, recognizing that families, too, navigate complex identities that shape their educational experiences and needs.

During an early childhood community research forum, an AANHPI parent approached me after I had presented on preschool access. "You understand," the parent said. That moment and many others solidified why representation matters in education leadership. I have seen firsthand the look, the joy, and the tears parents and educators have shared with me because they've felt seen and heard. My experience with my multiple intersecting identities serves as a cultural bridge builder that allows families to see themselves in systems that often feel foreign and intimidating.

The conflict I experienced between cultural expectations is now a professional strength. I don't see contradictions as problems but as opportunities for deeper understanding. When Western educational approaches emphasize individual achievement while Eastern philosophies prioritize collective harmony, I don't choose sides. I integrate perspectives, creating more beautiful musical notes we can all dance in.

In my work in Santa Clara County, California, this harmonization came to life through our arts enrichment initiative. Like a composer blending diverse instruments to create a richer symphony, we incorporated arts experiences that were culturally and developmentally relevant to the children and families we served. We worked with local artists and authors to bring in culturally diverse children's storybooks, enhancing our countywide literacy initiative while honoring the varied cultural roots families had established in the valley. Thinking back on those moments brings smiles, not just of nostalgia but of recognition that cultural integration creates more meaningful learning experiences that last for all children.

Families as Leaders and Partners

"Family represents the foundation of self, and a unity of acceptance, unconditional sacrifices, joy, support and love built on a continuum of resilience and journey in humility from past, current and future generations" (Baba 2025). Education at its best carries these same values, supporting the whole child within their family context and honoring their cultural identity while preparing them for a global future. Families are children's first and most influential teachers. They bring wisdom that cannot be replicated in any curriculum guide. This perspective isn't just philosophical, it's practical.

We witness transformation when schools treat families' cultural knowledge and lived experiences as essential curriculum components. I've seen classrooms come alive when immigrant parents share traditional stories, working-class families explain their trades, and elders teach cultural arts and customs that textbooks never mention.

By inviting families into leadership and policy work, we are enriching the entire educational ecosystem. When a parent testifies about child care struggles or describes their child's developmental gains, policymakers connect with the issue in ways that statistics never could because these are real. These authentic voices remind everyone that education policy isn't abstract; it's about real children and their families with names and faces, living and breathing in diverse communities.

Collective Power: Building Communities of Support

A decade ago, when my executive director nominated me for a senior leadership role, a major funder looked me in the eye and said, "It's not your time." Translation: An Asian woman's time apparently hadn't come yet, and in too many rooms, still hasn't. My mentor's response became my armor: "You are always bigger than they are." Those words pulled me back up every time the unspoken rules tried to keep me small. Because the hardest part of advocating for children and families isn't the policy fight; it's the quiet, persistent belief in some circles that women, especially Asian women, can bring the data, do the work, and serve the community but somehow aren't "leadership material." In early childhood and education organizations, too few Asian American women have positions at the executive levels (Kunreuther & Thomas-Breitfeld 2020). AANHPI educators and leaders remain among the most underrepresented groups in early childhood and the broader non-profit sector, comprising roughly 5 percent or less of the ECE workforce when Asian, Native Hawaiian/Pacific Islander, and multiracial workers are counted together (Paschall et al. 2020), and far fewer in executive or funder seats, where AAPI non-profit leaders make up only about 2 percent of CEOs and board chairs (McKinsey & Company, as cited in *Forum Magazine*, 2023). Every time I step forward anyway, I do it for every little girl who is watching, so that one day no one will ever again have to be told, "It's not your time."

During my leadership journey, I have been blessed to have met many warriors in this work who stand fearlessly with tact to help make the unheard heard. Their work is never about themselves; it's always about the people and the communities they serve. I have witnessed how some of these warriors and my mentors get wounded along the way, facing burnout, backlash, or institutional resistance. Through resilience and collective support with their allies, they rise again. These advocates understand that transformation isn't linear but cyclical, requiring periods of retreat and renewal with allies alongside bold actions. Their persistence despite setbacks has been my greatest inspiration, especially when my advocacy battery bank runs low with the red alarm signal on.

Being an advocate takes courage and a willingness to uplift others and mentor those coming after you. This creates a responsibility to open doors and create pathways, especially for other AANHPI professionals who may not see themselves represented in leadership positions. The most effective advocacy becomes a cycle of empowerment, where those who find their voice help others discover theirs.

NAEYC AANHPI Interest Forum

The NAEYC AANHPI Interest Forum was created with this same idea back in 2008. We established the AANHPI Interest Forum because the early childhood education practitioners needed to be seen and heard while navigating the early childhood education policy advocacy landscape. A core goal of the NAEYC AANHPI Interest Forum was to provide a blueprint and maps to our AANHPI early childhood education workforce so they can safely navigate the systems with culturally relevant and research-based tools. It was built in response to the growing importance and relevance of the need to support the AANHPI early childhood education workforce, young children, and their families locally and nationally. The AANHPI Interest Forum was built to be led by volunteer community leaders to fulfill its visions and goals. In 2008, we built the AANHPI Interest Forum from the ground up, starting with crafting the mission statement, goals, and activities approved and adopted by the advisory members and the NAEYC Governing Board.

This revolutionary interest forum is the first of its kind in the history of the United States' field of early childhood education. Our forum was originally named the "Asian Interest Forum," and we changed our name following President Biden's action in May 2021. When he signed Executive Order 14031, establishing the White House Initiative on AANHPI (Biden 2021), we saw an opportunity to better reflect our community's full diversity. The name change represents our ongoing commitment to coalition building that embraces and includes Native Hawaiians and Pacific Islanders as essential members of our collective. While we acknowledge our distinct cultural identities and experiences, we stand united in our support for one another. This change honors the spirit of solidarity that makes our community stronger together.

In the first year of the pandemic alone (2020 to 2021), anti-Asian hate crimes in major US cities surged by as much as 339 percent, and the Stop AAPI Hate coalition documented nearly 11,000 incidents nationwide (Stop AAPI Hate 2022). Our AANHPI communities, elders walking to the market, women on the subway, and small-business owners keeping their shops open suddenly became targets in a way most of us had never experienced in our lifetimes. The AANHPI Interest Forum took a stance and developed original anti-hate resources for our early childhood education community to combat the hate crimes in the different communities. We developed shelter-in-place resources for our educators and broader community while they stayed at home with their young children. Our work is ongoing and important. In 2022, we received our first congressional support and had Congresswoman Grace Meng open our annual business meeting, signifying the recognition for our existence.

Since the forum's establishment, we have been engaging with NAEYC members, early childhood education practitioners, and policymakers to offer guidance and develop original resources to support the workforce's day-to-day work with the children and families in their communities. For example, your holding of this publication reflects one of our collective works at the forum. We do not always get invited, but we are not shy to invite ourselves to important causes.

In 2018, the AANHPI Interest Forum joined forces with NAEYC's Black Caucus; Diversity and Education Adult Interest Forum; Latino Interest Forum; and Tribal and Indigenous Interest Forum to initiate the People of Color Caucus, also the first of its kind in the early childhood field with a commitment to the learning trajectories of young children as well as a knowledgeable, culturally informed early childhood education profession.

We lose countless evenings, weekends, and precious hours with our families, but every sacrifice feels worth it when we see what these spaces create. We don't yet have an impact study with statistical gains for our interest forums and caucuses. What we do have is something louder: the stories, the tears, the hugs, the joy, the whispered "I thought I was alone" that turns into "We've got you." These aren't just meetings. They are the rare places where exhausted educators and advocates can finally speak our full truth, recharge our battered spirits, lift up one another's causes, and remember why we still fight. More than anything, they are where we weave our individual sparks into one steady, living light, the kind that keeps all of us going when the work feels impossible.

That light is our evidence. And it burns brighter every year.

Reflections on Progress and the Path Forward

During my 25-plus-years journey in early childhood education, I have evolved from an impatient rookie to a grateful servant who has been shaped by every child, family, and colleague I've encountered. I am proud of my personal and professional growth and dedication. However, I wonder if our field is truly moving forward or just walking in circles. I have seen the same early childhood programs or initiatives reappear every few years with fresh, attractive signs or slogans being slapped on, which makes me question how far we have really come. Are we merely recycling yesterday's ideas while naming them tomorrow's solutions?

Twenty-five years in this work have taught me that real change demands two things at once: the long-view patience to stay in the fight after every loss, and the burning impatience that refuses to let another cohort of children slip through the cracks we already know how to close. That tension is never comfortable; comfort was never the deal. The sleepless nights; the endless mental rehearsals of Plans B, C, and D; the quiet toll on our mental health—none of it is small. Some weeks the advocacy road feels lined with broken glass. My own children are the ones who keep me walking it. They are my daily, living reminder of what it actually means to raise AANHPI kids in this country—their joys, their questions, the injustices they already question at ages most people still think are "too young to notice." When the road cuts deep, I look at them and remember: This isn't abstract. It's their future I'm carrying.

So we persist—impatiently, stubbornly, together—because the next generation is already here, and they're waiting on us.

On the hardest days, I think back to the moment in the winter of 2025, when the Board of the Council for Professional Recognition, the 50-year-old organization that has awarded more than one million Child Development Associate® (CDA®) credentials since 1975, setting the national standard for early educator excellence (Council for Professional Recognition 2024), stood up and announced they had elected me as vice president.

I was speechless. Tears rolled down my face. Because the colleagues, mentors, and fellow board members who have watched me walk this glass-strewn road for decades looked at me and said, without hesitation, "It is your time."

That moment didn't erase the broken glass. It just proved the road is still worth walking.

The path forward isn't about East versus West, or tradition versus innovation, it's about creating systems flexible enough to honor multiple needs. As we work toward more equitable early education policies, I hope future generations of the workforce, children, and families won't have to choose between worlds but will be supported in confidently navigating and exploring them all. For those whose paths haven't yet crossed with mine, or if you work alongside people who don't look like or share your background, I encourage you to approach these relationships with curiosity, listen deeply, observe thoughtfully, and ask genuine questions. This work demands patience, humility, and a willingness to confront difficult truths about inequity. It's not about cultural competency checkboxes; it's about fundamentally reshaping how we approach difference and power in education and family services settings.

The younger version of me who observed Hong Kong's rapid rhythms could not have imagined becoming an advocate who builds bridges between cultural worlds. The Hong Kong streets taught me to move quickly; American advocacy taught me when to slow down. Together, these lessons have shaped a leadership approach that honors multiple pathways to the same destination: a world where our workforce, children, and families all thrive.

CHAPTER 26

The Roller Coaster of Identity

Belonging, Loss, Reclamation

NINDERJIT GILL

> "I am no longer accepting the things I cannot change. I am changing the things I cannot accept." – Angela Davis

My name is Ninderjit Gill (**ਮੇਰਾ ਨਾਮ ਨਿੰਦਰਜੀਤ ਹੈ**). To help others pronounce my name, I often have to spell it phonetically: Nin-der-jeet. My name is meaningful to me, my family, and is part of my cultural upbringing. Yet it has been a name that I lost and reclaimed over time. I am a proud Southeast Asian Indian who identifies as Asian American and Indo-Canadian. I am the daughter of Malkiat Singh and Gain Kaur; sister of Sarbjit Kaur, Gurdavar Singh, and Harmon Singh; mother of Arjun and Aneel Singh Gill; and a first cousin to many who are like my siblings.

Professionally, I am tenured faculty at North Seattle College in the early childhood program, and I also served as the executive director of the Washington Association for the Education of Young Children (WAEYC), a state affiliate of NAEYC. In these roles, and in other paid and volunteer positions, I have become a strong advocate for early childhood, particularly when it comes to equitable language access to education, professional development, anti-bias and anti-racist training, and policy changes that center those whose voices are often silenced. We cannot create equitable systems if we continue to have the same people at the same table doing things the same way.

Navigating Cultures and Identities

I was the first in my family to be born in Canada, and thus the first citizen. I grew up in Vancouver, British Columbia, where there were a lot of Punjabi Sikhs from Punjab, India. I learned and developed my identities in my multigenerational extended family. Growing up, I felt like I had three moms and three dads because my dad's two brothers and my aunts lived with us. I also felt like I didn't just have three siblings but eight siblings that included my first cousins. People who lived on our block were the same religion and ethnicity as my family—we were all alike. It was wonderful and beautiful. Everyone spoke the same language, ate the same food, and went to the same parties. We'd go outside and play together and feel like we belonged. That was our normal to just show up as ourselves.

My family immigrated from Punjab, which is a farming province in northern India and borders Pakistan. My culture has always been a part of who I have been and how I show up. As we moved further away from more of our community, I think for my family as first-generation immigrants having children growing up in a foreign country, they fought even harder to instill traditional cultural values and beliefs. I definitely grew up in a traditional household where elders, family, and our community were very important. When we would come home, my uncle would tell us we could only speak Punjabi. We weren't allowed to watch anything but the news, Hockey Night in Canada, or Bollywood movies.

When we moved to a smaller town, Burnaby, which wasn't too far from East Vancouver, I noticed there were fewer Indian families in our neighborhood. As kids, we would walk to the elementary school together, and we stayed together. We started to become more visible and were different. We didn't have the same sense of belonging in the school or neighborhood like we did in our East Vancouver cul-de-sac. We moved again when I was 9 to a farming town about an hour away, Pitt Meadows. There were even fewer Indian families. The other Indian families were Punjabi Sikh and looked like us, but they all had English names. They'd been in the farming community for a long time, so they were much more like goras. Anyone who was Brown but fit into the White culture, we would call them "gora." It was very clear that we were different and were the minorities. I can't speak for any of my other siblings, but all I wanted to do was to just fit in. I wanted to be like the goras. My uncle Charn gave me my name, Ninderjit. He felt that it was different from the traditional Punjabi name of Narinder. I never really thought about the power my name holds when I was younger since everyone around me had similar names like me, like Sarbjit, Kamaljit, Simarjit! But the only thing I could change that I felt would make me feel less different or not stand out was my name. The challenges came when we had a substitute teacher, and with every one of them, I would have to sit, wait, and watch them as they reached my name on the attendance list. They would take a long, dramatic pause and tap their fingers on the list where my name was. I knew they were trying to pronounce it. I can't blame them for trying. And every time, it would sound like nin-der-shit instead of nin-der-jeet. And everyone would look at me and laugh or smile. It was attention I didn't want and made me feel even more different. I wanted to have the name Nancy or Nicole, the same name as one of my friends then. I just wanted to be like them as well. I just wanted to belong. I shortened my name to Ninder. Shortening it made it easier for teachers to say and avoided any extra attention on me when they attempted, and often failed, to say my full name. But when I shortened my name, no one asked why or cared about why I wanted to shorten my name.

Roller Coaster of Loss and Belonging

Settling into Pitt Meadows and going to school there after the family bought the blueberry farm, every day I knew I was different. I tried to hide my identity and fit in like the goras, but it was hard because I couldn't hide the color of my skin. I couldn't hide my name. I couldn't hide the fact that my parents picked me up and dropped me off at school. I couldn't wear makeup. I couldn't cut my hair because in Sikh culture, we should not cut our hair. I'd wear shorts underneath my pants because my parents didn't want me wearing shorts to school. Even when it was hot, I would wear pants to school, and then when I got to school, I'd go into the bathroom and take off my pants and wear my shorts around school. Then, when my dad picked us up, I'd put my pants back on.

At the same time while I was trying to fit in, I felt at a loss. The more I hid parts of my identity and culture, the more lost I felt. During the school year, I worked so hard to be like everyone else and hide my culture and traditions. Then there were the summers on the blueberry farm. They were great. All our extended family would come and work on the farm with us. There was always someone around, and there was constant connection to family and community. We would speak Punjabi and eat our same food. I belonged without trying, like when we were children.

Each year of high school felt like a roller coaster of belonging and loss. After high school, I went to Simon Fraser University in Canada, and there, again, so many people looked like me. I joined the Indian Student Association, which hosted Indian parties. It felt like coming back to where I was when I was younger. My identity was celebrated. We celebrated our community as a community. In this space, I could embrace my identities, and I loved being different.

Embracing and celebrating my identity was short-lived. When I got married, I moved to Seattle, Washington. I again felt the same sense of loss. My husband's family were Punjabi Sikh as well, but they were more immersed in American culture, and there was a smaller Punjabi Sikh community. Now, looking back, I have seen how I did not practice with my own children what my family taught me growing up: Speak our language, honor our family traditions. I wonder if my own children will look back at their lives and see it as a roller coaster of loss and belonging. They've experienced a loss of culture. We didn't recognize what was happening when my children were young. We spoke English, not Punjabi, at home. We didn't take them to the gurdwara (temple) as much as we should have. We celebrated American holidays. We didn't feed them the same type of foods that we grew up with. We wanted them to fit in and be like their friends. We did not have a huge Indian community for them to be part of except for their father's side of the family. Will they feel that they lost a big part of their connection to their cultural heritage? Fortunately, they do feel a sense of Indian belonging whenever our extended family gathers.

Power of Language

Language is never just about words. It holds memory, culture, belonging, and power. Growing up as a Punjabi Sikh where everyone spoke English, speaking Punjabi at home should have been a connection to my family; but outside our walls, it was a marker of difference, one I wanted to highlight. I realize that language is more than a tool for communication; it is a container of identity, a bridge between generations, and a way to honor where we come from. I've come to understand that advocating for language justice, ensuring that people can learn, teach, and lead in their home, and heart languages is a necessary part of reclaiming not just my own story but ensuring others don't have to silence theirs.

While Punjabi is my first language, I speak English well because I was born in Canada and educated in public schools and required to learn English the minute I started kindergarten. Because of my English fluency, I have been able to navigate spaces successfully and with confidence. For example, when teachers asked me to translate for my parents or other Indian students at a young age, it was an empowering experience. I felt the power of being able to perfect the language with no accent. I now reflect about my own experiences in being able to speak English well and my dad's own experiences as an example of linguistic bias. If my dad had spoken English well, I wonder if he could have been the mayor of the small farming town we lived in. I wonder if my mom had learned English, or even learned to speak with confidence in her home language, she could have done so much more, possibly run her own business. She was already managing a household of eight, including extended family—in-laws, nieces, and nephews.

Because of these wonderings and my own experiences navigating two cultures, in many of my professional roles, I have pushed up against systems and policies that hold tightly to one right way of doing things. One area specifically is where classes or professional learning was only offered in English. By owning my own power and thinking about my experiences with my family, I have shifted these rigid systems to expand their offerings in multiple languages. To disrupt these normative, robotic ways of thinking, sometimes it's as simple as asking the question: How can we include more languages in the offerings? At other times, it's about being a relentless advocate, showing up and speaking up on every occasion about the inequity of presuming English as the standard language. Sometimes, as a leader, I think of making it happen even if no one else is on board. When planning conferences to ensure that early childhood professionals have opportunities to learn in their home and heart languages and are able to coconstruct the professional learning that is happening, I often think of my mother. If these opportunities had been available to her, would she have been in the roles I have been in? It is with her in my heart that I advocate for language justice with early child care and education.

Language justice, for me, is not just about translation. It is about belonging, restoring dignity. As an Asian American woman who grew up interpreting for her parents and seeing the doors that they could get through because of language, I know the exhaustion and invisibility that comes when children and families are expected to navigate a system without support. I've seen the embarrassment in my mother's eyes when she didn't have the words in English, and no one made space or advocated for her to share in the words she did have. That's why language justice is a core part of my leadership not as an "add-on" but as a necessary act of equity. When we offer interpretation and transcreation, when we invite educators to lead professional development in Somali, Spanish, Mandarin, or Arabic, we are not just expanding access; we are dismantling the lie that only one way of speaking counts as professional, credible, or valuable. We are saying that you matter here. Your ways of knowing, teaching, and leading belong at the center, not the margins. This is what justice in early childhood education must look like.

Reclaiming

I only began to fully embrace my identity when I started graduate school and began learning about racial identity development, multicultural education, and did critical self-reflection about my early experiences, doing the work internally. I remember one video project assignment that made me think deeper. The assignment involved a video project of what happened when my family started making money, a lot of money. The farm became about 10 additional properties. This required my family to spend more time with businesspeople, White folks, and their companies. Having more money meant they had to immerse themselves in that culture of Whiteness. After this project, I realized when our family started making money on the farm, we lost some of our connection to our community and traditions that we once held so tightly. That realization became a turning point. My own story, my family's story, was one of both survival and loss. Reclaiming my identity has meant honoring that complexity rather than hiding it.

I continued this journey of reclamation through reflection; it became both a mirror and a map. I have reflected on and learned from my mistakes. I can name my experiences. Critical self-reflection is being able to look in the mirror and see myself, to be able to look back, and to hold it and honor it, and to cherish what I see. As a faculty member at a local college, I use a lot of critical self-reflection with my college students to support them in unpacking their identities. In my growth, I also have learned to navigate the joys and challenges of being bicultural. I have realized the importance of leaning into community, particularly finding people who look like me and who have had similar experiences. It feels like with each act of reflection, I am reconnected to the pieces of my identity that I once pushed away, reminding me that community is not just where we come from but what we choose to nurture.

That desire for visibility has grown stronger with time, evolving from silence to self-celebration. I worked so hard to be invisible as a child, but as an adult now, I'm not hiding my culture anymore. I want to be more visible. I'd love to be able to walk into spaces wearing my Indian clothes. But I also think that's a lot of work. I'd love to be able to just start a presentation or class speaking Punjabi. But I wonder, will I lose my audience if I do that? I want to be hypervisible, and I think that is rightfully a place that has been earned. This longing to be seen is not about performance but about restoration. It is reclaiming the voice and presence my younger self learned to quiet in order to belong.

I see my advocacy work in early learning policy as an extension of my reclaiming. In the 2025 legislative session, House Bill 1648 went through the House unanimously. It was a bill that I believe would be the beginning of deregulating early learning and sought to remove education and training requirements for an experienced-based pathway. In my roles, I created opportunities for folks to be in the room with legislators and invited folks to share their stories as educators, students, advocates researchers, and leaders of the field that this bill required revisions that clarified its position about supporting new and seasoned early learning professionals to lead anti-bias, anti-racist curriculum within environments that honored their identities. In a small way, in collaboration with others, we created a movement, and that in and of itself is success. In these moments, reclaiming my identity also means reclaiming power and being able to use my voice and lived experience to ensure that others, especially women and educators of color, do not have to shrink to be heard.

I guess the most personal act of reclamation has been returning to the name my family gave me. It wasn't until these last few years that I have reclaimed my name and am not giving others the right to comfort by shortening my name to Ninder. Yes, I am still the last one called on for introductions. Yes, people ask me how to pronounce my name. And yes, many still pronounce my name incorrectly. When I tell my cousins that I now go by "Ninderjit," they think it's super funny. Then some of them, upon reflection, say, "Yeah, I get it." Being so uncomfortable with who I was for so long has helped me become super comfortable with my identity now, and to be able to just show up as my authentic and unapologetic self.

In Olympia for a Senate hearing in 2025.

Leadership

I never wanted to be a leader growing up. I was very insecure. I'd rather stay in the shadows and just do things in the background. I still have a little bit of that. I don't want to be upfront. But I realize now you don't need to know everything, and you can't know everything to be a leader. We need humility. Being a program director, college faculty, and executive director really moved me into how I support other people to see their power, the ability to impact and influence young minds and future generations.

Being bicultural, Asian American, Asian Canadian, I have personal experience of what it feels like to be different and excluded. When children and staff come into schools and classrooms who have a very different culture at home and in the communities they are coming from, early childhood programs should ensure that they feel like they belong. Educators must consider what they might be doing that causes harm and make folks feel like they don't belong. There are both sides of the issue that require critical reflection toward personal and professional growth.

In my leadership roles, I also emphasize the power of language in not only being able to communicate but also the feelings, history, and experiences that language carries. For young children, when their home language is not valued, there is a loss of culture, loss of stories, loss of traditions, and loss of relationships because they may not be able to communicate with someone close to them. It's important to center and honor the home languages of all children, families, and staff. Ensure that every child's cultural and language capital is valued. Find ways to represent every family. When writing policies, leaders should consider what translations of the content may be needed to allow all families to access the information.

There are so many ways to be a leader, and for me, while I am more comfortable being at the forefront of something, I find that I still am often in the background, creating the conditions that allow for changes to happen. I am the coach, the mentor, the whisperer, the coordinator, the connector, the friend who lifts people up so they step forward and take the actions toward our collective "why." Being a leader is relational; it's about getting to the core of who someone is and supporting them to realize their strengths and passions in service of the larger organization's goals. It is also about honoring the person, their unique talents, and their assets, and particularly for folks of color, their community wisdom drawn from their ancestors. I like to believe I am the leader that I wish I had, and I know that my mom would have been a leader if she had the opportunities that I had. In my own journey from belonging, to loss, to reclamation, I have come a long way from the girl who changed her clothes at school and shortened her name, to one that feels tremendous pride as an Indo-Canadian American woman of color who sits at the decision-making table and makes room for others to sit and belong at those tables too.

CHAPTER 27

A Journey to Be Seen and Heard

A Story of Identity, Resilience, and Reclaiming Belonging

SIM LOH

Roots: A Place Where Every Culture Belongs

I was born and raised in Malaysia—a country woven from threads of diversity. It is a place where difference is embraced; where celebrations of all kinds light up our neighborhoods; where hearing three or four languages in a single conversation isn't remarkable, it's simply life.

Malaysia's identity is complex and beautiful. The Malays, Chinese, Indians, and Indigenous Bumiputera communities coexist, not without tension but with intention. Our independence as a nation was achieved not by one group but through the unity of many. That history—the struggle for freedom, the tragedy of the May 13th racial riots, and the healing that followed—taught generations of us that living together meant truly seeing one another. It wasn't just coexistence. It was cooperation, compromise, and care.

Our education system is a great example. There are two types of public elementary school: National Schools (SK) that use Bahasa Malaysia as the primary language of instruction, while National-type Schools (SJK), also known as vernacular schools, are further divided into SJK(C) for Mandarin and SJK(T) for Tamil. Both systems are public and follow the national curriculum, but their medium of instruction and cultural focus differ significantly. This is to ensure the language of each ethnicity group is preserved. That said, families can enroll in any of these schools regardless of their ethnic background.

Holidays of all ethnic groups and religions are celebrated by all. Our Muslim classmates fasted during Ramadan, and we respected that, avoiding food and drink around them during the school day. My family celebrated Chinese Lunar New Year, but we also visited Malay friends for Hari Raya and joined Indian neighbors for Deepavali. Even the food told stories of shared identity. A plate of nasi lemak (coconut rice) might be followed with Chinese desserts like thousand layer cake. Language itself became a blend: "You want makan sini (*dine in* in Bahasa) or dabao (*take out* in Cantonese)?"—a question that rolled off our tongues without a second thought, mixing English, Bahasa, and Chinese in a single breath. I grew up believing that this was how the world worked. That cultural pride and mutual respect could live side by side. That identity wasn't something you had to choose or hide. It just was.

When I came to the United States, I thought I was ready. I thought my multicultural upbringing had prepared me for anything. I was wrong.

Arrival: When Belonging Slips Away

I still remember my first weeks in America. The wide streets of New York City, the historic charm of Philadelphia, the college campus that looked just like the shows I watched growing up—scenes from *Gossip Girl*, *NCIS*, *Criminal Minds*. I was thrilled. This was the beginning of a new chapter. But very quickly, the excitement faded into something heavier.

I didn't expect to feel so foreign. I didn't expect the way people looked at me when I spoke. Or the way they responded—confused, dismissive, sometimes even mocking. I still hear the pizza vendor's voice: "What? Say that again?"—again and again and again, until I spelled my order out letter by letter, cheeks burning. I remember my professor stumbling over my middle name, "Yi," sighing, and eventually giving up. "I'll just call you by your first name," he said. A classmate rolled her eyes whenever she couldn't understand me. Another whispered "whatever" and turned away. Assumptions are made about me and my ability because of my accent.

In lecture halls and group projects, I became small. I started sitting in the back, avoiding eye contact. My accent became a target, a symbol of my otherness. So, I tried to erase it.

Every night, I played episodes of American TV shows, pausing and repeating each line until my tongue could shape the words the way theirs did. I studied their rhythm, their laughter, their ease—trying to master what I thought was the "American accent." I dropped my middle name. I softened the lilt in my voice. I even gave myself an English name—*Alexis*.

I learned the stereotypes before the world could throw them at me. So, I behaved perfectly, cautiously, carefully—determined not to feed into them. I wanted to represent my people well.

More than anything, I wanted to blend in. To be accepted. To be *American enough*. At that moment, that meant being "normal"—invisible, even.

But no matter what I did, no matter how hard I tried, something always gave me away.

And that ache—that sense of invisibility paired with hypervisibility—started to hollow me out. At first, it was just discomfort. Then, it became physical—the panic attacks, the palpitations, the acid reflux. I couldn't sit in crowded classrooms. I couldn't walk across campus without feeling the urge to disappear. I stopped raising my hand. I stopped believing I had anything worth saying.

My academic performance plummeted. My confidence crumbled. I spent most of my time hidden in quiet corners of the library. If I had to leave the house, I made myself as invisible as possible.

For over three years I lived like this—numb, silent, alone. My mantra became *If you don't let it bother you, it won't hurt you.*

I whispered it when a man on the bus shouted, "Go back to your country."

I whispered it when classmates talked over me or laughed at the way I spoke.

I whispered it until the words lost meaning.

But even as I repeated it, I knew it wasn't true. The hurt always found a way in.

I never told anyone—not my mother, not my friends, not my family back home. In my mind, I was *the lucky one*—the one who made it to America. My mother had worked hard so I could have a better life. How could I tell her that I was drowning in it? And besides, I was the one in college—the one who was supposed to know better, to handle it, to thrive. At least, that's what I kept being reminded of.

I carried it all quietly, I convinced myself that no one would understand. The truth is, even I didn't understand. I didn't know there were layers to this—to identity, to belonging, to loss. All I knew was that somewhere along the way, I had begun to lose myself.

To be clear, not everyone was unkind or did so intentionally. There were warm, patient, and caring people. But the moments that made me feel othered—the stress of uncertainty, the constant wondering whether the next person I spoke to would accept me for who I am—they began to overshadow everything else. They clouded my ability to see kindness, to receive it, to feel that I truly belonged.

A Spark: The First Time I Felt Seen

Then came the turning point.

It was during the final year of college, in a capstone class with my professor. One day, during office hours, she asked about my background. I told her everything—my journey, the struggles, everything. When I finished, she paused, then said, softly but firmly, "Do you know the word resilient? That's what you are. You are resilient."

I didn't expect those words to stay with me, but they did. They wrapped around me like a warm blanket. For the first time in years, I felt seen—not just for what I had survived but for who I was. Someone strong. Someone whole.

That moment cracked something open, split the darkness that clouded me. It let some light in.

I didn't transform overnight, but slowly I started to reclaim parts of myself. I allowed my accent to resurface. I stood my ground and made sure I was understood, no matter how many times I had to repeat myself. I stopped trying to be invisible. My mantra changed too. Now it was *Just a little more. Push yourself just a little more.*

By the time I graduated, I had found something even deeper than survival. I had found purpose. It all stemmed from that one conversation.

A Calling: From Translator to Advocate

After graduation, I stepped into the world of early childhood education—a field that, at first, I simply thought of as a job. I started as a part-time substitute teacher at a NAEYC-accredited Keystone STAR 4 program in Philadelphia, Pennsylvania. Within 10 months, I transitioned into a family partnership coordinator role, working closely with families to ensure equitable access to information and support.

That's when everything changed.

I learned that the program had been founded as a collaboration to support the children of parents working in the unionized garment industry near Philadelphia's Chinatown—and that, over the years, word had spread through the community about its language access and sources support for families—something clicked. More than half of the enrolled children were first- or second-generation immigrants from East or Southeast Asia. Suddenly, I found myself face-to-face with families who looked like me. Who sounded like me. Who were living the same confusion, fear, and longing that I once did. They came to me with questions that echoed the ones I once whispered to myself:

"Teacher, my child's name is Louis, but we call him Wen-Jie at home. Is that okay?"
"We want our child to speak only English—will that help him do better in school?"
"Someone yelled at Grandpa on the bus. We don't know why. They were mean."
"School starts in the fall and not January?"
"I don't know where to get a lunch bag. I don't go beyond Chinatown."

I recognized the fear in their eyes. The exhaustion. The desire to do right by their children, even when the systems around them felt foreign and unforgiving. I remembered how it felt to be silenced, to shrink, to change yourself to fit a mold you didn't even choose.

So, I decided, these families would not walk that road alone.

What started as helping with translations became something bigger. I was no longer just a bridge between home and school. I was an advocate. A guide. A listener. A voice. I worked to make sure their concerns were heard, that their cultural values were respected, that they had the tools to participate fully in their child's education, particularly beyond the program. I made sure they knew *You belong here.*

This wasn't just about language. It was about identity, ensuring that families—particularly those from the AANHPI community and immigrant community—were not erased in spaces where they had every right to be seen.

That was the moment I realized this was not just work. This was a mission.

Empowerment: Shifting the Narrative

In 2019, I was asked by my director at the time to help recruit and support families for a listening session hosted by the US Department of Health and Human Services. It was part of a 10-city tour gathering input on how to improve child care access for working families. One of the stops was in Philadelphia.

We helped bring in 15 families from our program—parents who rarely, if ever, had a chance to speak directly to policymakers. Many of them were from AANHPI or immigrant backgrounds, and at first, they were hesitant. "I don't know what to say," some whispered. "We're just a small group."

But something powerful happened in that room. As they began to speak, with language access support, they realized they weren't alone. Their concerns—about child care affordability, early intervention, quality education—were shared across races, backgrounds, and zip codes.

By the end of the session, they weren't just speaking—they were leading.

Watching them find their voice stirred something deep within me. I realized that my role wasn't just to speak *for* the community. It was to create space so they could speak *for themselves*. To support them in reclaiming the power they didn't know they had.

From that moment on, I shifted how I showed up in this work. I joined community tables and advocacy groups—not to be the only AANHPI voice in the room but to make sure I held the door open for others. I served on the Immigrant and Limited English Proficiency Subcommittee for the 2020 Census, collaborated with others in civic engagement efforts through the AAPI Coulter Table, and sat on the Multilingual Advisory Council for the School District of Philadelphia. I participated in the Racial Equity Early Childhood Provider Council and joined coalitions focused on health, access, and policy for children and families across southeastern Pennsylvania.

I started to ask questions.

When I noticed that data about Asian communities was missing from studies, I couldn't just accept it as a footnote or an oversight. I asked why. When I was told it was because of a "small sample size," I asked how that sample was being reached. Who was asked to participate? How were they approached? Were surveys translated? Were trusted community leaders engaged? Or were the same systems that have historically overlooked us continuing to do so—this time under the guise of data collection?

Because when our communities aren't invited into the process—when families are left out because no one spoke their language or earned their trust—the data isn't just incomplete. It's inaccurate. It tells a story that erases us.

Every meeting, every panel, every committee now became more than just a professional obligation; it became an opportunity to hold the door open wider. Who is missing from this room? Whose stories aren't being told? Whose voices have yet to be heard?

Asking isn't just about gathering answers; it's about refusing to let silence or absence go unquestioned. It's about making sure that being seen doesn't stop at visibility—but extends to understanding, representation, and respect for our full, complex humanity. This is more than just shifting the narrative; it's about reshaping the systems that sustain it. It's about building a system rooted in inclusion and equity, where every child, every family, and every educator can see themselves not on the margins but at the center of the story. It's about creating an equitable system that serves and benefits everyone, leaving no one unseen or unheard.

Reclamation: Honoring My Roots, Celebrating My Culture

With every step I took as an advocate, I also reclaimed more of myself. I stopped hiding my identity. I stopped softening my story. I began to share—proudly—that I am a first-generation Chinese Malaysian immigrant. That I once felt invisible. That I now work every day to ensure others feel seen.

I shared my culture with my colleagues, my students, and my community. I brought in stories, traditions, and languages that weren't in the curriculum. I encouraged families to speak their home languages proudly. I collaborated with coworkers to create professional development opportunities that spotlight immigrants and English as a Second Language (ESL) families' experiences. I brought that same intentionality home. My husband, who is Caucasian and grew up in central Pennsylvania, speaks only English, but he embraces my heritage wholeheartedly, and I embrace his. At our wedding, we blended our traditions: a Catholic ceremony, a Chinese tea ceremony to honor our elders, and a rehearsal dinner in Chinatown. Our guests received gift boxes with double happiness symbols, and our families witnessed a celebration that honored *both* of us.

His family now celebrates Lunar New Year with us. Our niece and nephew saw a lion dance for the first time this year. These moments—small and joyful—are also revolutionary. They represent a future where our children don't have to choose between cultures, where they can belong fully to all of who they are. A future where they not only take pride in their own heritage but grow up curious and open to others—where celebration and understanding flow in both directions, and cultural belonging is never conditional.

Intersectionality: Still Underseen but No Longer Alone

There are days I still feel invisible.

Even as I sit on advisory councils or participate in statewide coalitions, I'm often one of the few—sometimes the only—AANHPI person at the table. We are the fastest-growing racial group in the United States, yet in many of these decision-making spaces, we are still missing. Or worse, we are present but misunderstood.

This invisibility has layers.

Despite being the fastest-growing racial group, our voices are scarce in leadership. Our experiences are rarely centered in policy. In many K-12 systems, our histories are not taught. In research, our data is often lumped into the "Other" category. And even when we are included, we are often overgeneralized—lumped together under the AANHPI umbrella as if we are one singular, monolithic group, but we are not.

We are Chinese, Korean, and Japanese families who have lived in the United States for multiple generations; Malaysian, Taiwanese, South Asians from India, Pakistan, and Bangladesh navigating migration in pursue of educational and economic opportunities; Vietnamese, Cambodian, and Laotian families who arrived as refugees fleeing war; Filipino and Filipino American communities with rich diasporic histories; Pacific Islanders like Chamorro and Samoan families; and countless multiracial, mixed-heritage, and first-generation families finding their way in a new country. When our diversity is flattened into a single category, disparities are hidden, pain is masked, and stories go untold—not because we lack resilience but because the systems were never designed with us in mind. These gaps affect how our children are seen, how families are served, and how policies are shaped. When we are not at the table, decisions are made *about* us, without us. And when we are only invited as token voices, the responsibility becomes heavy. You feel like you must represent an entire continent. You fear making mistakes. You fear confirming biases.

In hindsight, I see that the people who struggled to hear my accent, who could not see beyond my differences, who made assumptions about me in college—their reactions were not personal. They are a reflection of the systems we live in, but I'm not alone anymore.

Today, I'm surrounded by a growing network of AANHPI early educators, community organizers, parents, allies, and advocates who are showing up with courage and clarity. Younger generations are more vocal than ever. They are unafraid to challenge systems, ask difficult questions, and declare, "We belong."

And when I look back at my journey—from a student desperate to fit in, to an educator who speaks proudly in rooms filled with policymakers—I know that progress is possible. Because I've lived it.

My Hope: That We Choose to See Each Other

There are still days when I look in the mirror and see the girl who tried to hide her accent. Who dropped her middle name. Who told herself, "If it doesn't bother you, it won't hurt you."

But more often now, I see someone else.

I see a woman who reclaimed her voice—and uses it to uplift others. I see a first-generation immigrant who no longer strives to fit in but, instead, stands firmly in who she is. I see a bridge—between cultures, between systems, between generations. I see a leader, a partner, and an advocate. I see someone who is proud of her roots and who wants every child to feel the same.

My hope for the field of early education and care is that we become more curious, more courageous; that we ask better questions, especially of ourselves:

- Who are we not seeing?
- Whose voice is missing?
- What assumptions are we making?
- How can we honor the fullness of every child's identity, not just in theory but in practice?

I hope we remember that belonging isn't something children should have to earn; it's something we must guarantee. I hope that the next generation of AANHPI educators won't have to choose between authenticity and acceptance; that they can walk into any room, speak in any accent, carry any name—and still be seen as leaders.

Because visibility isn't just about being looked at; it's about being understood. When we are understood, we can begin to heal. When we are heard, we can begin to hope. When we are believed in, we can begin to lead.

So Many More Voices . . .

> **Being Asian American means feeling like you're supposed to be the model minority. Often being the majority but still feeling like the minority.**

Carter Chang,

Chinese-Korean American university student in Seattle, Washington

CHAPTER 28

My Ancestors' Wildest Dreams

A Legacy Project

JACKIE THU HU'O'NG WONG

My refugee story begins in Vietnam, during the fall of Saigon in 1975. My family did not come to the United States by choice; they were forced to flee for their lives and feared being persecuted or killed if they had stayed. Amidst the end of a civil war, our journey was about survival. My parents left behind everything they knew—our home, our family, and the life they had built to begin anew. The trauma of being displaced, having to leave everything behind, and living in uncertainty has shaped my worldview in ways I could not fully understand at the time.

As a child of refugees, I vividly remember feeling different in those early years in America. Even though we came to the United States seeking safety, we often felt like outsiders, unsure of where we fit in. The church sponsored us, and many families like ours. The support networks that helped us settle were a lifeline, but even as we received aid, my parents had an immense sense of pride. They did not want to take a "handout," but the reality of our situation forced them to accept help in order to rebuild our lives and provide opportunities for their children. I grew up watching them try to hold on tightly to their dignity, knowing they had come to this country out of necessity. They weren't here to take advantage—they were here to survive and for us to thrive, much like the elders did before them and the ancestors did centuries before them. In our culture is a deep-rooted history that shapes us, whether or not we are aware of its path or its origin.

Those early experiences have stayed with me, driving me in ways I did not completely comprehend. As a kid, I remember playing with a school friend and discovering that she did not have some of the toys I had. Without thinking, I rushed home after school and packed up some of mine to give to her. It was a simple act, but it reflected a deeper instinct: a spirit of giving, of sharing, and of helping others who were struggling. Growing up, I saw my parents hold on tightly to everything they had, not out of greed but because they had known what it was like to have nothing and to lose everything. They had fled their lives in Vietnam, carrying only what they could on their backs, and, even now, they hold on to things, wanting to make sure they never have to live with that feeling of scarcity again.

Empathy became my guiding force in life. But as a child, I did not always understand why I felt the way I did. I was not just giving because I was nice; I was giving because I understood, on a deep level, what it felt like to be without. I understood the struggle. It was not just about material things; it was about feeling secure and feeling safe, and that sense of security became a basic need for me. The desire to help others came from the spirit of survival that was instilled in me as a refugee, and the understanding that when others are struggling, it was in our blood to help. It was the lessons of our elders that taught us that we do not live as individuals, but we live to build community in honor of our heritage.

Growing up, my parents had a very clear idea of what was considered a secure career—doctor, lawyer, accountant. For them, these professions represented stability, safety, and success. They came from a place of fear and trauma. They wanted the best for me and my siblings, and their idea of "the best" was rooted in their idea of security. However, I did not follow the path they envisioned, and when I made the decision not to go pre-med, I knew I was diverting from the dream that they had hoped I would follow. I felt the weight of that decision, especially because so much of my future was to be the model for my generation. My parents, though supportive in every way they could, did not understand and could not articulate the fear they had when I took a different path. I was thrust into the world of self-reliance—something that was both daunting and empowering. I realized that my success wouldn't come from following the conventional path but from defining my own purpose, and that was in social work.

Education and Career

As I moved through my education and obtained my master's in social work, I knew I wanted to be involved in social work and policy, specifically related to children and families. My journey into the early childhood policy space was shaped by both my personal experiences and the decisions I made along the way. I chose to attend a graduate school at Sacramento State, knowing that the proximity to the capitol would give me access to where decisions were made. Politics, I realized, is all about relationships and observing the power dynamics at play. It became clear to me that while social work was important, I could have a greater impact if I shifted to policy, where I could help create systems that supported the most marginalized families and communities.

I got my start in the California State Legislature, working for one of the two Asian America members at the time, Mike Honda, a champion for AANHPI representation, and deeply committed to increasing our visibility in policy discussions, particularly with the upcoming wave of term limits. My new boss, who had spent time in a Japanese internment camp, understood the importance of representation, and that experience was something I carried with me as I navigated my role as his aide. However, I often found myself to be the only AANHPI person in a space where decisions were being made—decisions that would impact the very communities I cared about, including my own. It was a reminder that power politics often doesn't represent the humanity of those most affected by the policies being made. At times, it was disheartening, but it also motivated me to push harder. I realized that to create better public policy, we had to make space for diverse voices and perspectives, especially those from the communities who are often left out of the conversation. The passion I have for advancing policies that put children and families first, that uplift the voices

Me in the middle with (in order) my father, mother, younger sister Jane, middle sister Juiie, and brother Phu on my graduation day from the University of California, Berkeley with a Bachelor of Arts in psychology and social welfare.

of those who have been historically silenced, and that create real change for the communities who need it most was strengthened by the sense of duty I inherited from my time in the California State Legislature.

While policymaking can be exciting and not for the faint of heart, after doing it for a few years, I missed the grassroots, community practice. My social work degree allowed me to return to Oakland to work with families and children in the school system. It was here that I saw the direct impact of policymaking, and things came full circle for me. Working with and for marginalized communities brought me back to the days of sharing my toys with my friends; a great sense of community building with the children and families I served; and a drive to do more. From here, I moved into roles with the California Department of Education, the National Center for Youth Law, and eventually back to the California State Senate to continue my work on family-centered policies and programs. It was during this time that I was first elected as a trustee to the Washington Unified School District and continued to serve those around me to ensure families in my district have a voice when it comes to the education of their children. Two years later, I took on a role with the End Child Poverty California campaign as a leading advocate for policies to fight for children and families experiencing poverty. Over the next several years, we had major policy and budget wins for children and families statewide. As I was experiencing great success in my career and I had found my voice as an advocate, I could not help but feel a deep sense of gratitude to my parents and ancestors who came before me for their sacrifice. Had it not been for them, I may not have ever had the opportunity to realize the power in me to help others.

Stronger Starts

As the executive director of First 5 California, I've had the privilege of leading an organization that is focused on the well-being of our youngest children, ages 0 to 5, who are still at a critical stage of brain development. When I look at the future of California's children, I see not just the potential to thrive but also the responsibility we have to ensure that they grow up in an environment where they can feel safe, loved, and supported, especially when life presents difficult challenges. That is why I am proud, as the first executive director of Color at First 5 California, to have spearheaded the Stronger Starts campaign, which aims to give parents the tools they need to help their children through tough times and prevent the long-term impact of toxic stress. Stress, in general, is a natural response to life's challenges—it is something we all experience. For instance, getting stuck in traffic, or rushing to make a meeting, or even a child's fear of going to the doctor or sitting in the dentist's chair—that is what we typically consider stress. It is the kind of stress we can usually handle, bounce back from, and move on, but toxic stress is a different story. Toxic stress comes from prolonged exposure to traumatic experiences, especially when a child is without a buffer, or someone to help them manage and process what is happening in their life. Without intervention, toxic stress does not just go away; it builds up and begins to affect the child's development, their emotional health, and even their physical health. These outcomes are largely the result of Adverse Childhood Experiences (ACEs), which are traumatic events children may experience either at home or outside the home that can cause the onset of toxic stress response. These events can be emotionally or physically harmful, and without the right support, they can leave a lasting imprint on a child's life. When children experience toxic stress over an extended period, their bodies stay in a constant state of heightened alertness. They're always in survival mode, unable to calm down and find peace. This prolonged stress response can have far-reaching consequences, both short-term and long-term, including health issues like hypertension, diabetes, asthma, and conditions like anxiety and depression, and can lead to developmental delays. Research also shows that toxic stress can even play a role in a child's future financial stability and overall life outcomes.

The Stronger Starts campaign is personal for me as someone who has experienced ACEs and toxic stress largely due to the trauma of my childhood. I wanted to ensure my trauma did not pass to my children and that the cycle stopped with me. Having awareness and getting help when needed is the most important thing one can do for their children and themselves. By helping parents recognize the signs of toxic stress and by supporting them with strategies to intervene early, we can break the cycle before it has a chance to take root. It is my belief that every child deserves a strong start in life, and that starts with giving families the knowledge and resources they need to protect and nurture their children, no matter what challenges they may face. Through the Stronger Starts campaign, we are working to make that vision a reality for families across California.

Reflections

When I returned to Vietnam with my family recently, I was reminded of how my relatives lived and helped one another over the decades. It was a sharp contrast to the individualism I sometimes feel here in the United States, and it reminded me of what community truly means. My family in Vietnam is a constant source of strength, and I am proud to know that our names are written in the books of our ancestors to remind others of the journey we are all on. I understood more deeply the choices my parents made when they decided to adopt American values and their choice to embrace this new country while honoring their roots sometimes created tension. There are moments when American ideals of success and individualism can feel at odds with the communal values that are so deeply embedded in me from my Vietnamese heritage. However, no matter where I am or where I go, I know it is my birthright to shine and succeed, and it is my responsibility to bring others with me, to make sure that as I climb, I must lift and help others rise too. That is the legacy I carry—one of resilience, empathy, and the drive to support my community, our community, and to live out the dreams of my ancestors. As I am my ancestors' legacy project, the work that I do to advance our voice in public policy is my legacy project for others. We all are our ancestors' wildest dreams realized.

CHAPTER 29

Like the Koa Tree

Leading with Purpose and Resilience

THERESA F. LOCK

In my birth place, Kēōkea, on the island of Maui in Hawaiʻi, is the majestic acacia koa, commonly known as the koa tree. Baker et al. (2009) suggest that this native tree, which can be found at elevations ranging from sea level to above 6,000 feet, thrives in dry volcanic soil with roots that support the tree through harsh storms and difficult conditions. As the tree grows, it adapts to the environment, shaping its growth patterns to maximize light and resources. In addition, the forest supports a diverse ecosystem by creating a habitat for native plants and birds. Historically and today, the koa tree has economic, ecological, and cultural value while the koa wood is treasured for its utility, durability, and beauty, often crafted into canoes, instruments, and heirloom furniture.

The koa tree symbolizes my five-decade-long leadership story in early childhood education. Although being a leader is often connected with a formal role or position, I also adopt the definition of leadership in early childhood education "as a process of influencing change to achieve a positive outcome to improve early care and education" (Douglass 2017, 29). I have witnessed how cultivating this type of distributive leadership empowers early educators to be on a journey of continuous learning and improvement, evolving with changing circumstances in order to provide high-quality early childhood education so children and families and communities will flourish.

Through this chapter, I will focus on three aspects of the koa tree to represent my early childhood education leadership story. The first aspect is the root system, which is broken down into two parts: the taproot, which represents the origins of my social identities, and the root system that is nurtured by personal values which have guided my sense of purpose. The second aspect, the leaf-like structures, branches, and trunk of the koa tree, represents examples of adapting and thriving through opportunities and difficult conditions in my early childhood education career. Finally, the third aspect of this story is how the koa forest establishes a vibrant, diverse ecosystem, which highlights creating a collaborative, inclusive, supportive system for early childhood education professionals.

Start with the Roots of My Social Identities

Koa trees can grow in rugged volcanic soil, often in areas where other plants struggle to take root. To grow, a koa tree has one main taproot, which is a root that goes deep into the soil to anchor the tree and help the tree access water and nutrients (Baker et al. 2009). The taproot of the koa tree reminds me of my social identities, such as my cultural, ethnic, gender, and class identities.

I am a third-generation Hawai'i-born Chinese American middle-class woman. My husband and I have three adult children, who are married, and six grandchildren. In 1890, my paternal great-grandparents were poor farmers from Guangdong, China, who traveled by ship with their baby daughter to the Hawaiian Islands. Despite the dangerous trek to a foreign land, their vision for a better life and education for their child and future children helped them persevere. After their arrival, they worked as sugar plantation contract laborers for three years in Kohala on the island of Hawai'i. When their contracts ended, my great-grandparents leased agricultural land on the island of Maui, in the community of Kēōkea, where other Chinese plantation laborers settled, farmed, and raised their families.

My great-grandparents had eight children, and their sixth child was my grandfather, who was born in 1903. From a young age, my grandfather worked on the family farm and at the small family grocery store that his father started. After completing grammar school, my grandfather took over managing the family store. In 1921, he married my grandmother, who was also Chinese first-generation Hawai'i born. My grandmother became the storekeeper, while my grandfather began a small trucking business. My grandparents raised four daughters and one son, my father. In 1950, my father married my Chinese first-generation Hawai'i-born mother, who was from Honolulu, O'ahu. Following cultural customs for a firstborn son, my parents lived with my grandparents in a home that was adjacent to the family general store. This is the home that my four siblings and I grew up in. In 1959, when I was 6 years old, my grandfather died and our parents took over the trucking and construction company while our grandmother continued as the storekeeper. My siblings and I grew up helping our grandmother and parents in our family businesses.

While growing up in rural Kēōkea, our large extended family connected through our Chinese roots with first and second biracial cousins being part-Spanish, part-Caucasian, part-Hawaiian, part-Portuguese, and part-Japanese. We communicated in Pidgin English, a creole language in Hawai'i, which is a mixture of English, Hawaiian, Chinese, Portuguese, and other local languages. Furthermore, in between running the store, our grandmother would practice her ukulele, craft Hawaiian feather lei hat bands, and make Hawaiian "hula" (dance) implements for my sisters and me.

Spreading Root System—Personal Values

In addition to the taproot, the koa tree also has a shallow, spreading root system that extends outward from the base of the tree. This extensive root system supports the tree and helps it absorb nutrients more effectively in Hawai'i's environment (Baker et al. 2009). This spreading root system represents four personal values that have guided and nourished me as a leader. They are my Christian faith, lifelong learning, interpersonal relationships, and social justice.

My Christian faith was planted by the prayers of my Catholic family members when I came into the world as a premature newborn in 1953. Our family doctor searched for and borrowed an incubator from another small rural hospital over 46 miles away. Because of this fragile beginning, one of my aunt's named me after Saint Theresa (considered the patron of the ill in the Catholic religion). Because of complications with asthma, as a young child I found strength and comfort in talking and listening to God. As I look back over my life, I am deeply grateful for God's powerful unwavering love, helping me face my weaknesses and overcome setbacks, and giving me strength to carry out my calling and purpose with gratitude and intention.

Lifelong learning or ongoing, voluntary pursuit of learning helped me to be open and curious about new opportunities and perspectives of others. As a child, I loved borrowing and reading books from the public library bookmobile, which stopped on a regular basis in front of our family home. Throughout my kindergarten to 12th grade experience, I loved the challenges I faced at school, and I strived to do well. I especially valued my teachers who promoted a caring learning community. My grandmother and parents encouraged me to obtain a college degree after high school, so I attended the University of Hawaiʻi at Mānoa, which was located on another island. After graduating with my bachelor's degree, I obtained my master's degree. In 2017, after my children were grown up with children of their own and my mother was 92 years old, I finished my doctoral degree. My love for learning and teaching was evident as I spent about two decades as a faculty member in the University of Hawaiʻi system, first as a community college instructor and now as a university instructor.

Interpersonal relationships based on trust and reciprocity were values that I practiced as the second eldest among my siblings and kept improving through the years. My typical responsibilities were caring for my siblings, organizing how we did our chores, and resolving conflicts. From 4th through 12th grade, I was a member, and later a junior leader, for a local 4-H club. The 4-"H" stood for Head, Heart, Hands, and Health. Through 4-H, I learned practical skills like sewing, baking, gardening, and service to others, and public speaking and leadership skills through state- and island-wide competitions, camps, fairs, and conferences. While at the University of Hawaiʻi at Mānoa (UHM) for my bachelor's degree, I worked as a staff assistant in a resident hall, which helped me hone my skills as a mentor, organizer of activities and events, and mediator between college students. After I decided to major in human development, I began assisting my professors with leading small group class discussions and participating in clinical experiences with several human service agencies. My first job after I graduated was working for a state-funded multicultural center that focused on recovering stories from different ethnic and cultural groups to tell the historical stories about Hawaiʻi's diverse population.

A focus on social justice, which was rooted in my Christian faith, took on greater importance as a graduate student in human development at Pacific Oaks College in Pasadena, California, in 1976. I discovered that Pacific Oaks, which was grounded in progressive education and developmental theories, was started by a Quaker community who envisioned teaching their children how to be peacemakers. After an immersive year working in the college's Children's Center, under the guidance of an excellent master teacher, I knew this was my calling. I was intrigued by how teachers used the daily serve-and-return interactions to teach young children about identity, diversity, and justice through a play-based curriculum. During my first year living in Los Angeles, I also experienced what it meant to be a "visible" minority. While interacting with Hispanic, Black, and Asian parents, I often heard them ask questions such as, "How do I bring up my child in this society?," "What must I give up that I have been taught in my culture?" These questions led me to work closely with Louise Derman-Sparks, who had begun to conduct research on anti-racist and anti-bias education. Furthermore, my master's research project was on the transmission of cultural values among Asian American mothers of young children in Los Angeles. This study examined factors that influence ethnic identity, parents as transmitters of culture, and how they coped with racism, including one mother's parents who were raised in the Japanese internment camps during World War II.

Like a koa tree with roots growing in hard volcanic soil, my leadership roots were grounded and nourished by my social identities and my personal values of faith in God, lifelong learning, interpersonal relationships, and social justice.

Thriving in Difficult Conditions—Adapting and Growing

As the young koa tree matures, the true leaves with many tiny leaflets are replaced by phyllodes. According to Baker et al, (2009), these phyllodes, which are modified stems that are flat and sickle shaped, serve as the main photosynthetic organs, which enable the koa tree to adapt to the dry conditions and intensive sun. As the koa tree grows, the branches and leaves create new patterns to maximize light and resources. Here, I describe how I thrived in difficult conditions by adapting and growing through lessons I learned along the way. These lessons taught me new insights and gave me courage to take on more progressive and broader responsibilities in early childhood education.

After completing my master's degree, I became a member of NAEYC and attended my first NAEYC Conference in 1978 in New York City. At this conference, I was part of a workshop panel presentation led by Louise Derman-Sparks on anti-racist and anti-bias education. Furthermore, at this conference, I found a table sign with the words "Looking for a job to teach young children in Washington, DC?" and spoke to the friendly woman sitting behind the table. I explained that I had just moved to DC and was searching for an early childhood educator position. Within a week, I was notified to apply for a lead teacher position in a Head Start program. I did and was hired to work in a program located a few blocks away from my home. On the first day of my new job, I observed that I was the only Asian American teacher in a Head Start program with predominantly African American children, families, and staff.

My African American teacher assistant had been working in this program for a number of years. This was evident as she not only knew the children and families in our classroom but had easy rapport with many of the children and some of the families in the other classrooms. While she was confident and expressive with the children and families, I found she seemed standoffish with me, even after I made several attempts to share who I was and ask her more about herself. After this went on for about a week, I began to worry that I may have offended her in some way. One day while the children were napping, I asked about her background as an African American woman. She then shared that where she grew up, she was warned about interacting with people outside of her African American neighborhood and community. Therefore, she had only worked with African American colleagues, young children, and their families. I appreciated her openness and shared that in Hawaiʻi, I had limited interactions with African Americans, but that changed when I lived in Los Angeles. I shared that working in Washington, DC, in a Head Start program where I was the only Asian American was new for me. When I asked if she could help me learn more about the African American families and children in our Head Start community, the lines of communication dramatically improved, and we grew closer as a team. On our last day before the program closed for the summer, she said something to me that I have never forgotten. She smiled and said, "You're not bad for not being Black."

After this first year with this citywide Head Start program, my supervisor asked me to be a lead teacher and director for a new site in another neighborhood in DC, and I accepted this challenge. Over the course of a few months, I had to order furniture, equipment, and materials, and hire and orient staff. What was most gratifying was hiring experienced and well-trained African American early educators and staff who had previously worked with young children and families in DC. We quickly bonded as a team and worked hard to open up our new site, coordinate the comprehensive services, and build partnerships with community agencies. As we began to enroll families and their preschool-age children into our program, we learned that the majority of the families were primarily recent Black and Hispanic immigrants, many who did not speak English, who worked as domestic staff in the embassies along the city's Embassy Row.

My staff and I were dedicated to providing a quality comprehensive early childhood program for these young children and their low-income families. To help children and families transition into our Head Start program, my two lead teachers and I brushed up on our limited Spanish phrases, conducting home visits with each child and family prior to our opening day. During these home visits, families graciously welcomed us with smiles and food while their children, who initially were shy, quickly warmed up to our presence and were excited to show us their favorite toys. The success of these home visits was evident, as each child adjusted smoothly in our program, and families trusted that they could leave their children in our hands. Through the year, this new Head Start program was a joyful learning community where children, families, and staff thrived.

Before the next new school year started, the organization received funding to extend this site from a half-day school-year program to a full-day full-year program. To help increase staffing, the agency had signed an agreement to hire new teacher aides through a federally funded workforce agency. After I found out that the two teacher aides assigned to my site had no training and minimal experience in working with young children and families, my supervisor said I would need to train them. Before they started working with children, I established a training program, which included a dress code. Yet, on the first day, one of the women came to school wearing high-heeled shoes, so I spoke to her privately, and the next day she came to work with more appropriate shoes.

There were several more serious incidents of unethical and unprofessional behavior by the two aides. When this happened, even though I documented the incidents and communicated my concerns with my supervisor, there was very little or no follow-up. I often had to resolve it on my own while also adding more to our own site policies. Because I did not receive the timely support I needed, these incidents began to negatively impact staff morale, relationships, and stress levels of my team and me. Finally, when my physical and emotional health began to decline, I felt I had little choice and had to resign from the program. It was difficult to leave the children, families, and staff who I genuinely cared about.

This major setback early in my professional career taught me many lessons. One lesson was to hire staff with relevant experience and education and provide ongoing professional development. The second lesson was about the importance of being a reflective and responsive supervisor that listened and trusted my staff. The third lesson was how stress impacts the mental health and wellness of educators.

Throughout my career in early childhood education, I continued to grow and adapt, as I led a statewide early childhood education program for Native Hawaiian children and worked at county, state, and national levels on early childhood public policy. This was also the case when I was appointed the state early childhood coordinator for Hawai'i's Office of the Governor in 2011 and a year later hired as the Governor's Director of the Executive Office on Early Learning. At the heart of advancing equity in early childhood systems, I sometimes had to facilitate the power imbalances between political leaders and community advocates. Fortunately, I learned from seasoned mentors how to create structures and practices that shift power toward shared decision-making and incorporating authentic community voices. For example, I convened a listening session with a group of passionate and knowledgeable early childhood education advocates, who opposed an early childhood education workforce development strategy being proposed by the governor. At the start of the listening session, I began by naming the diverse roles, interests, and positional authority in the room. Then I used community agreements to emphasize shared purpose and mutual respect. Furthermore, I used a relevant data story which highlighted how early childhood education advocates were valuable experts, then I asked the early childhood education advocates to give honest feedback and alternative solutions to what the governor proposed. These strategies helped to improve relationships and work towards collaborative solutions.

As I look back, first to 1978, when my African American assistant teacher said, "You're not bad for not being Black," then to the following year, when I faced a setback under an unresponsive supervisor and organization, and finally to three decades later, when I was sitting at the governor's table facilitating a heated conversation, I learned the importance of deeply listening before jumping in too quickly with a solution to improve relationships, practices, programs, and systems.

Early Childhood Education Ecosystem

Research supported by Baker et al. (2009) explains that the koa forest is a community of organisms, an ecosystem, that interact with one another in a living system. The koa forest is an ecosystem that is needed in Hawai'i's watersheds because it helps to capture atmospheric water and pollutants while providing wind protection and erosion control. In addition, the koa forest supports the pollination of other native plant species and provides a habitat for native birds and animals.

This forest ecosystem is like Bronfenbrenner's ecological systems theory which explains how a child's development and early learning is at the center of this system and influenced by the world around them (Bronfenbrenner 1979). Similarly, if we place the early childhood education workforce at the center of the system, we can begin to identify the different entities that impact the early childhood education workforce.

One of these entities is higher education. In 2021, I became the director of the Hawai'i Early Childhood Educator Excellence and Equity Early Childhood Education Project (ECE3 Project) through the UHM College of Education after receiving a grant award from the Early Educator Investment Collaborative (EEIC) for their "Transforming Lead Teacher Preparation Programs Through a Multi-Partner Innovation Grant." This three-year grant was designed in response to two landmark reports published by The National Academies Press. They were the 2015 *Transforming the Workforce for Children Birth Through Age 8: A Unifying Foundation*, and the 2018 *Transforming the Financing of Early*

Care and Education. This unique opportunity aided eight higher education grantees with their system partners to transform their preparation programs for early educators, break down systemic barriers to higher education primarily for women of color, and increase financial assistance and compensation for students studying to be early educators. In September 2024, the EEIC released a report entitled *Moving Beyond the Pilot* by School Readiness Consulting (2024), which features the eight higher education grantees sharing lessons learned and their implications for the broader field.

Through the ECE3 Project, my team and I facilitated the development of a student-focused, competency-based bachelor's degree in early childhood care and education (ECCE) serving children from birth through third grade. We incorporated a collaborative process between a four-year university and a two-year community college early childhood education faculty. First, early childhood education faculty worked on aligning all early childhood education courses with the 2020 *Professional Standards and Competencies for Early Childhood Educators* held by NAEYC (NAEYC 2020). Next, they met to develop a curriculum map to identify overlaps and gaps in courses offered to students pursuing an associate degree in early childhood education and began recommending what could be included in a new bachelor's degree in early childhood care and education. This competency-based framework also enabled early childhood education higher education faculty to work with early learning service providers to develop Credit for Prior Learning and a registered apprenticeship program.

Knowing the importance of building local capacity to address the shortage of qualified EC educators in Hawaiʻi, the ECE Project commissioned the RAND Corporation to study the landscape of EC educator wages, benefits, working conditions, recruitment, and turnover issues. The target population of this study was the ECE workforce employed in our state's Department of Human Services (DHS) licensed child care centers and regulated family child care homes. The study's findings were published in a final report by Karoly et al. (2022) entitled "Early Childhood Educators in Hawaiʻi: Addressing Compensation, Working Conditions, and Professional Advancement." This report included policy and financing options and a high-level road map on how to advance these options statewide.

Shortly after the release of this report, I convened the Hawaiʻi Careers with Young Children (HCYC), a collaborative that started in the 1990s to focus on a well-prepared, well-supported, and well-compensated early care and education workforce. Through HCYC, a Compensation Design Team, with members representing a variety of agencies, was formed to develop a more detailed and prioritized action plan for Hawaiʻi based on RAND's high-level road map. Furthermore, the Compensation Design Team members and our allies, like the Hawaiʻi Association for the Education of Young Children (HIAEYC), Hawaiʻi Children's Action Network (HCAN), and the Early Childhood Action Strategy Hawaiʻi, worked closely to coordinate our advocacy efforts for state investments for several state legislative measures, including an improved workforce registry, funding for facilities, wage supplements, cost modeling, salary scale, and an apprenticeship grant program.

In 2023, with support from HIAEYC, HCYC, and funding from a local philanthropic organization, the ECE Project launched the Hawaiʻi Advancing the Early Childhood Education Profession Initiative to build support for how Hawaiʻi is acting on the recommendations in the *Power to the Profession Unifying Framework* (2020). This *Unifying Framework* is a road map to advance a unified, diverse, equitable, and effective early childhood education profession. Toward this commitment, the ECE3 Project established a task force for this initiative composed of HIAEYC members who worked directly with young children or supported those who worked directly with young children. This reinforced how the early childhood education ecosystem consists of "innovative, entrepreneurial, and skilled early educator leaders to drive transformative change—from the classrooms and home-based programs to communities and beyond" (Douglass 2017, xiv).

In 2025, the ECE3 Project engaged with the University of Massachusetts, Boston's Early Education Leaders Institute to deliver their Leading for Change in Early Care and Education (LFC) 40-hour entrepreneurial leadership development program to two cohorts of early educators, family child care providers, program administrators, and other early childhood education professionals in Hawaiʻi. This program enabled early educators to gain a deeper understanding of themselves as leaders and change agents or cocreators of change and explored how they can improve their professional practice when working collaboratively with others to serve young children and families. The culminating event was an Early Educators Leadership Forum, where LFC members presented their change projects and received feedback from supportive colleagues and stakeholders.

A Native Hawaiian Sense of Place and Sense of Purpose

I am not Native Hawaiian, but I am honored to call Hawaiʻi my home. As a faculty member, I am in full support of the University of Hawaiʻi System's strategic plan for 2023 to 2029, which includes how we are striving to "model what it means to be an Indigenous-serving and Indigenous-centered institution: Native Hawaiians thrive, traditional Hawaiian values and knowledge are embraced, and UH scholarship and service advance all Native Hawaiians and Hawaiʻi" (2025). This means embracing a Native Hawaiian sense of place, a deeply rooted concept that reflects the interconnected relationship between people, the land, the ocean, and the spiritual and genealogical ties that bind them. This requires attention to the lived experiences of Native Hawaiian people, or Kānaka Maoli, especially regarding the complex issues of Native Hawaiian rights to their ancestral lands and their struggles for national liberation from US colonialism. This includes examining multicultural forms of settler colonialism that might "conceptualize liberation in ways that are accountable to Native aims for decolonization" (Saranillio 2013, 217).

Furthermore, the UHM College of Education's vision is

> *"A Sense of Purpose. A Sense of Place. Preparing knowledgeable, effective, and caring educational leaders to contribute to a just, diverse, and democratic society."* . . . Our vision guides the direction and work of the college in and beyond lāhui Hawaiʻi and is informed by tenets of aloha ʻāina, aʻo, mālama, ʻike Hawaiʻi, and pono, creating our sense of purpose and sense of place." (2026)

This vision offers hope for the next generation of early childhood education pedagogical and policy leaders in Hawaiʻi who will continue to advance a high-quality, diverse early childhood education ecosystem for young children with a Native Hawaiian sense of purpose and a sense of place.

In closing, I am honored to be in the company of many bold, purposeful, and resilient early childhood education leaders. Like a forest of koa trees, we are collectively shaping our growth patterns to maximize light and resources while cultivating our own leadership mindsets and leadership mindsets in others for continuous quality improvement in early childhood education.

A Closing Thought ...

So Many More Voices . . .

I am Siengkham.

My name means bright gold.

Lamet woman is my birthright.

American is who I had to become.

Lamet-American is who I am.

Straddling and navigating how to be and live as both,

but finding comfort in the hyphen in between.

Lamet are the forgotten ones.

Embarrassed by always being the unknown,

yet angered by the world's ignorance.

Our language lost,

our people's culture and traditions dying.

The seeds of my ancestors were planted in a land I no longer know,

but their spirits and strength are in me,

reminding me how strong, resilient, and flexible our roots are.

Across oceans and land, over mountain tops and bright stars,

the strength of the wind from Laos softly whispers to me,

"Sieng, daughter of farmers and warriors, birthed in a bamboo shack from a woman of strength and courage, raised in the culture and traditions of your ancestors . . . be proud. Be Lamet. They will know who we are because you will teach them."

Siengkham Douangdala
Advocate and community builder for immigrants and refugees in
Seattle, Washington
11/24/2025

Index

Page numbers followed by *b*, and *f* indicate boxes/shaded areas, and figures, respectively.

A

B

C

D

E